云图英语

时文速递

云图分级阅读研究院 编著

基础篇 NO.1

北京理工大学出版社
BEIJING INSTITUTE OF TECHNOLOGY PRESS

版权专有　侵权必究

图书在版编目（CIP）数据

云图英语时文速递·基础篇 / 云图分级阅读研究院编著. —北京：北京理工大学出版社，2021.6（2021.7 重印）
ISBN 978 - 7 - 5682 - 9916 - 9

Ⅰ. ①云… Ⅱ. ①云… Ⅲ. ①英语—阅读教学—初中—教学参考资料 Ⅳ. ① G634.413

中国版本图书馆 CIP 数据核字（2021）第 112044 号

出版发行	/ 北京理工大学出版社有限责任公司
社　　址	/ 北京市海淀区中关村南大街 5 号
邮　　编	/ 100081
电　　话	/ （010）68914775（总编室）
	（010）82562903（教材售后服务热线）
	（010）68944723（其他图书服务热线）
网　　址	/ http://www.bitpress.com.cn
经　　销	/ 全国各地新华书店
印　　刷	/ 三河市良远印务有限公司
开　　本	/ 889 毫米 × 1194 毫米　1/16
印　　张	/ 11
字　　数	/ 317 千字
版　　次	/ 2021 年 6 月第 1 版　2021 年 7 月第 2 次印刷
定　　价	/ 36.80 元

责任编辑 / 时京京
文案编辑 / 时京京
责任校对 / 刘亚男
责任印制 / 李志强

图书出现印装质量问题，请拨打售后服务热线，本社负责调换

云图教育中心编委会

一线审读名师

蒋莉（中小学中级教师）

刘星（中小学中级教师）

编审人员（按姓氏音序排列）

陈　珊　陈潭潭　陈　云　侯　琳　马巧儿

苏丽君　肖　骏　张紫娟　赵依含

美术设计（按姓氏音序排列）

褚　琼　孙振刚　唐畔畔

ENGLISH READING

作者的话

英语阅读理解题在中考英语中的分数占比一向很高，因此，各校师生常试图通过加大训练量来提高阅读能力，获得高分。将阅读理解能力不足简单地归结为做题不够，只重视解题技巧而忽视了非语言信息对阅读理解能力的影响，这些都导致学生在传统题海中疲于应对，尤其使学生在面对新话题、热点事件和跨文化交际等文章时感到力不从心。

时文阅读作为一种非常有意义的新型阅读模式，不仅可以帮助学生增加阅读量、扩展阅读范围，还能引导学生关注国内外社会热点，关注人类命运和地球家园，促进学生形成跨文化交际的意识，培养学生跨文化交际的能力，从而进一步拓宽学生的国际视野。现在，越来越多的英语教师选择将英语时文引进课堂教学，让学生接触原汁原味的英文，在培养学生语言能力的同时，还为学生营造一种本土英语的教学氛围，加深学生对英语知识、外国文化和风土人情的理解，帮助学生在跨文化交际中克服由于文化背景、交际习惯和思维模式的差异导致的阅读障碍。因此，初中阶段渗透时文阅读具有重要意义。

为了满足广大师生的需求与期望，《云图英语时文速递》在一线名师的共同努力下应运而生。作者精选时文材料，准确把握难易度。全册书共分为基础篇、强化篇和冲刺篇3册，每册设置了14周的阅读内容，每周包括6篇阅读理解题和1篇中国传统文化赏析趣闻，符合学生一学期的学习要求。全册书主要包括以下显著特点：

1. 选材新颖，体裁多样

作者从权威网站、杂志广泛选取不同国家实时热点文章，涵盖人物传记、明星娱乐、体育运动、文化风俗、新闻速递等十几个主题，并根据中学生的英语水平加以创造性改编。其内容丰富，趣味性强，在国内各类考试中从未使用过，是学生了解国内外热点信息、提升英语阅读能力的不二之选。记叙文、说明文、议论文等不同体裁的文章，能让学生着眼于整篇文章的思路结构，在潜移默化中习得各种体裁文本的阅读策略。

2. 题目设置科学，准确把握难易度

本书以新课标为依据，题目设置紧密契合中考要求。题型丰富，既有传统的阅读理解题，也有符合各地区不同需求的完形填空和任务型阅读等题型。因此，本书适用于人教版、仁爱版、外研版、北师大版等多版本初中教材使用者，能满足各地区学生中考阅读的需求。

难度的把控是同类书共同的难点。作者在编写本书时，充分考虑并准确把握词汇的丰富度、用语的精准度、句型结构的多样性以及时文的篇幅和词汇量等。全书难度符合新课标五级目标要求，并适合初中三个年级学生的认知水平，对学校平时的测验命题也有一定的借鉴性。

3. 把握中考动向，增设中国传统文化赏析趣闻

教育部考试中心英语学科命题专家表示："引导学生在通过外语了解世界的同时，注重传承和发扬中华民族优秀文明成果，用外语讲好中国故事，增强文化自信。"近年来，中考命题愈加突出价值引领，寓教于考，强调了对中华民族优秀传统文化的考查。《云图英语时文速递》在每周的6篇时文后，都增加了1篇中国传统文化赏析趣闻，以此帮助学生用英语讲述中国优秀传统文化，促进中华文化的传承与传播。

4. 四大板块设计，帮助学生吃透阅读

文前小标签给出了词数、难度和建议用时等信息，方便读者进行自我评估。

"答案解析"梳理思路，解答清晰。

"词汇碎片"积累核心词汇。

"重难句讲解"梳理句式，沉淀语法。

作者期望通过最新的热点和最优质的题文设计，为学生打开探寻国内外热点讯息的一个小小窗口；作者期望能帮助家长和老师一起把握中考动态，为学生提供训练素材；作者期望能让学生在做题的过程中，有效提高阅读能力，并逐渐了解国内外社会动态发展趋势，打开国际视野，把握时代脉搏。

ENGLISH READING

Contents 目录

Week One　新闻速递

- 001　**Monday**　　　　[完形填空]　Elizabeth Ann: An Endangered Ferret Is Cloned
- 002　**Tuesday**　　　 [阅读理解 A]　AI Development in China
- 003　**Wednesday**　　[阅读理解 B]　Report: 85% of Users Paid by Scanning QR Codes in 2020
- 004　**Thursday**　　　[阅读理解 C]　Technologies Make Learning Easier
- 005　**Friday**　　　　 [任务型阅读 D]　Computer Chip Shortage Hurts Car Makers
- 006　**Saturday**　　　[短文填空]　China's Tianwen-1 Reaches Mars
- 007　**Sunday**　　　　[拓展阅读]　Technology Helps People to Protect the Rock Paintings

Week Two　人物传记

- 008　**Monday**　　　　[完形填空]　The Tireless Cartoonist
- 009　**Tuesday**　　　 [阅读理解 A]　Winter Sports Medalists
- 010　**Wednesday**　　[阅读理解 B]　A Miao Woman's Hopes and Dreams in Embroidery
- 011　**Thursday**　　　[阅读理解 C]　Education Choices of Wang Ziyi
- 012　**Friday**　　　　 [任务型阅读 D]　Old Porcelain Ware Collector Yu Xueyun
- 013　**Saturday**　　　[短文填空]　World in a Camera
- 014　**Sunday**　　　　[拓展阅读]　Longjing, an Imperial Tea

Week Three　生活成长、人际交往

- 015　**Monday**　　　　[完形填空]　Why Students Turn Off Their Cameras in Online Classes

016	**Tuesday**	[阅读理解 A]	Toys with Creativity
017	**Wednesday**	[阅读理解 B]	Special Education in China
018	**Thursday**	[阅读理解 C]	Arts at MIT
019	**Friday**	[任务型阅读 D]	A 15-Year-Old Poet Champion
020	**Saturday**	[短文填空]	Tips for Better Communication in English at Work
021	**Sunday**	[拓展阅读]	Chime-Bells

Week Four　兴趣爱好、学校教育

022	**Monday**	[完形填空]	Surf, Swim, Sing: Finding Joy in Lifelong Learning
023	**Tuesday**	[阅读理解 A]	3 Products for Teaching
024	**Wednesday**	[阅读理解 B]	The Best Title Wanted
025	**Thursday**	[阅读理解 C]	An Experience of a Math Professor
026	**Friday**	[任务型阅读 D]	Schools Face More Failing Grades During Pandemic
027	**Saturday**	[短文填空]	Passion for Trains Connects Two Railway Workers in Guizhou
028	**Sunday**	[拓展阅读]	Firecrackers on New Year's Day

Week Five　明星娱乐

029	**Monday**	[完形填空]	CCTV Lights Up Lantern Festival with Gala
030	**Tuesday**	[阅读理解 A]	Hao Lei: Practicing Buddhism and Reading Help Me Grow as an Actress
031	**Wednesday**	[阅读理解 B]	The Best Title Wanted
032	**Thursday**	[阅读理解 C]	Jay Chou Returns to Cinema with His Fascination for Racing Cars
033	**Friday**	[任务型阅读 D]	TV Series Follows Rock'em, Sock'em Love Story

Contents

- 034 **Saturday** [短文填空] Biggie's Mom, Voletta Wallace, Shares how Country Music and Reggae Influenced His Rap Career
- 035 **Sunday** [拓展阅读] Temple of Heaven Built from 22,000 Matchsticks

Week Six 饮食购物、疾病健康

- 036 **Monday** [完形填空] The Hidden Cost of COVID-19
- 037 **Tuesday** [阅读理解 A] COVID-19 Exposes Hearing Problems
- 038 **Wednesday** [阅读理解 B] The Best Title Wanted
- 039 **Thursday** [阅读理解 C] Foods, Tastes Change Because of the Coronavirus Crisis
- 040 **Friday** [任务型阅读 D] How Different Places Start the Day
- 041 **Saturday** [短文填空] Ways to Reduce Reluctance to Take COVID Vaccines
- 042 **Sunday** [拓展阅读] Chinese-Western Breakfast Sets Are Popular Among Locals

Week Seven 体育运动

- 043 **Monday** [完形填空] Swimmers Enjoy Cool Jumps
- 044 **Tuesday** [阅读理解 A] Man Climbs Skyscraper in Wheelchair
- 045 **Wednesday** [阅读理解 B] The Best Title Wanted
- 046 **Thursday** [阅读理解 C] Breaking the Tradition
- 047 **Friday** [任务型阅读 D] Should People Be Allowed to Walk Around?
- 048 **Saturday** [短文填空] No National Anthem at Sports Events
- 049 **Sunday** [拓展阅读] Lantern Festival: A Romantic Celebration in China

Week Eight　自然社会、社会现象

- 050　**Monday**　　　[完形填空]　　You're Stroking Your Cat Totally Wrong
- 051　**Tuesday**　　　[阅读理解 A]　The 1970s Black Utopian City Became a Modern Ghost Town
- 052　**Wednesday**　[阅读理解 B]　Climate-Caused Disasters Killed 475,000 People over 20 Years
- 053　**Thursday**　　[阅读理解 C]　The Best Title Wanted
- 054　**Friday**　　　[任务型阅读 D]　Backpacks for Snowy Owl
- 055　**Saturday**　　[短文填空]　　Clever Dogs Learn like Children
- 056　**Sunday**　　　[拓展阅读]　　The Lunar New Year Begins

Week Nine　历史地理

- 057　**Monday**　　　[完形填空]　　How Black Soldiers Helped End the U.S. Civil War
- 058　**Tuesday**　　　[阅读理解 A]　The Best Title Wanted
- 059　**Wednesday**　[阅读理解 B]　The Best Title Wanted
- 060　**Thursday**　　[阅读理解 C]　National Museum Exhibition Reviews History of Chinese Costume Culture
- 061　**Friday**　　　[任务型阅读 D]　Taijiquan
- 062　**Saturday**　　[短文填空]　　Historian Aims to Shed Light on Korean War
- 063　**Sunday**　　　[拓展阅读]　　Treasure Stolen from Old Summer Palace Returns Home After 160-Year Odyssey

Week Ten　环境环保

- 064　**Monday**　　　[完形填空]　　NASA: 2020 Was One of the Hottest Years on Record

065	**Tuesday**	[阅读理解 A]	What Will Climate Change Look like near Me?
066	**Wednesday**	[阅读理解 B]	Economy Along the Yangtze River
067	**Thursday**	[阅读理解 C]	A Glacial Flood in India
068	**Friday**	[任务型阅读 D]	Three Signs for "New Arctic"
069	**Saturday**	[短文填空]	On the Front Line of Climate Change
070	**Sunday**	[拓展阅读]	Students Show Thanks with Traditional Laba Porridge

Week Eleven 旅行交通

071	**Monday**	[完形填空]	21-Year-Old Rows Across Atlantic, Sets Record
072	**Tuesday**	[阅读理解 A]	Climbing Toward the Good Life
073	**Wednesday**	[阅读理解 B]	The Best Title Wanted
074	**Thursday**	[阅读理解 C]	Digital Technologies Make Travel Safer and More Convenient
075	**Friday**	[任务型阅读 D]	Cutting Travel Time to Guangzhou
076	**Saturday**	[短文填空]	Americans Continue to Fly During the COVID-19
077	**Sunday**	[拓展阅读]	Things You May Not Know About Rain Water

Week Twelve 文化风俗、异国风情

078	**Monday**	[完形填空]	Chinese Opera Cartoon Festival Kicks Off on Thursday
079	**Tuesday**	[阅读理解 A]	How Does a Bus Driver Spend His Chinese New Year's Eve?
080	**Wednesday**	[阅读理解 B]	What Is the Thanksgiving like During the COVID-19?
081	**Thursday**	[阅读理解 C]	The Best Title Wanted

082	**Friday**	[任务型阅读 D]	Old Photos Shed New Light on Yuanmingyuan's Former Glory
083	**Saturday**	[短文填空]	Henan Beauty
084	**Sunday**	[拓展阅读]	Traditional Operas Increasingly Staged in Old Courtyards

Week Thirteen　文学艺术

085	**Monday**	[完形填空]	App Writes New Chapter in Reading
086	**Tuesday**	[阅读理解 A]	2020 Top 2 Art Exhibits in China
087	**Wednesday**	[阅读理解 B]	Wuhan Gets Back on Its Musical Feet
088	**Thursday**	[阅读理解 C]	Masters of the Zisha Pots
089	**Friday**	[任务型阅读 D]	Women's Written Language
090	**Saturday**	[短文填空]	Rice-Straw Dragon Dance
091	**Sunday**	[拓展阅读]	Little New Year

Week Fourteen　科普科技

092	**Monday**	[完形填空]	China Spending 400b Yuan on Fighting COVID-19
093	**Tuesday**	[阅读理解 A]	The Best Title Wanted
094	**Wednesday**	[阅读理解 B]	Tianwen-1 Is the 1st Chinese Spacecraft to Reach Mars
095	**Thursday**	[阅读理解 C]	China Urges Global Unity on Climate Measures
096	**Friday**	[任务型阅读 D]	Shanghai Museum Holding an Ox Art Show
097	**Saturday**	[短文填空]	Thousands of Ancient Tombs Found near Xi'an
098	**Sunday**	[拓展阅读]	The Tongliang Dragon Dance

答案解析 / 词汇碎片 / 重难句讲解

Week One 科普科技

Monday
[完形填空]

体裁：记叙文
题材：科普科技
正确率：_____/10
词数：193
难度：★★★☆☆
建议用时：10 分钟
实际用时：_____
答案页码：____099

Elizabeth Ann: An Endangered Ferret Is Cloned

Scientists have cloned (克隆) a healthy black-footed ferret by using DNA from a ferret (雪貂) that died over 30 years ago. This cloned ferret is named Elizabeth Ann.

Elizabeth Ann's story is __1__ unusual one. In the 1980s, samples (样本) from a ferret named Willa were stored in the "Frozen Zoo". Back then, no one was __2__ of creating clones.

The idea of cloning was understood, __3__ it was hard to carry out (实现) for many animals. But in 1996, a scientist cloned a sheep, called "Dolly". Since then, many other __4__ have also been cloned.

The USFWS (美国鱼类及野生动植物管理局) has been __5__ about cloning black-footed ferrets since 2013. In 2018, they __6__ tried it.

On December 10, 2020, Elizabeth Ann was born. It's the first native endangered species (濒危物种) ever cloned __7__ the U.S. Elizabeth Ann is __8__ and enjoys spending her days.

She won't ever be released (释放) into the wild, but soon, she may have some cloned brothers and __9__. And later, she will probably have babies. Sooner or later, her children will have babies with wild black-footed ferrets, and her DNA will begin to __10__.

1. A. a   B. an
   C. the   D. /
2. A. listening B. making
   C. thinking   D. looking
3. A. and   B. but
   C. or   D. also
4. A. scientists B. people
   C. animals   D. babies
5. A. writing   B. singing
   C. talking   D. playing
6. A. exactly   B. slowly
   C. finally   D. clearly
7. A. at   B. in
   C. with   D. on
8. A. sick   B. healthy
   C. sad   D. kind
9. A. children   B. sisters
   C. friends   D. families
10. A. change   B. stop
    C. leave   D. spread

Tuesday
[阅读理解 A]

AI Development in China

体裁：说明文
题材：科普科技
正确率：_____/5
词数：160
难度：★★★☆☆
建议用时：6 分钟
实际用时：_____
答案页码：100

China tops the list of countries with the most AI unicorn companies (人工智能独角兽公司) in the world, according to a report.

With 206 AI unicorn companies, China took a leading role in the number of such companies in 2019, said the report. From 2015 to 2019, Chinese AI companies raised (筹集) $40 billion, ranking second in the world and accounting for (占比) 22 percent of the total.

Statistics show that, in the middle of October, China had 1,499 smart robot companies, 2,707 drone (无人机) companies, 6,722 face recognition (识别) companies, 2,855 smart voice companies, and 6,143 smart driving companies. In 2019, Chinese government made about 276 policies to help AI develop in the country. It is expected that China's face recognition market share will account for 44.59 percent of the world's total by 2023.

About 783,000 robots are now working in Chinese factories and the outbreak (疾病发作) of the COVID-19 sped up the development of AI in the medical field, the report said.

1. The _____ of Chinese AI companies is at the top around the world.
   A. money   B. number
   C. history   D. problem
2. Which of the following is true about Chinese AI companies?
   A. They don't develop well.
   B. There are different kinds of them.
   C. There are the least smart driving companies.
   D. There are the most smart robot companies.
3. From the passage, we can know that Chinese government _____ the development of AI company.
   A. stops   B. supports
   C. controls   D. slows
4. What can we know from the last paragraph?
   A. Robots are hard-working than men.
   B. Robot is widely used in the medical field.
   C. Chinese factories only use robots.
   D. Technology helps people a lot.
5. Which of the following will the author agree with?
   A. AI has a bright future in China.
   B. The COVID-19 is a good thing for the medical field.
   C. Robots will replace (取代) human beings in the future.
   D. Chinese AI companies are the best in the world.

Wednesday
[阅读理解 B]

Report: 85% of Users Paid by Scanning QR Codes in 2020

With the development of technology, mobile payment（支付）has become popular in China, with 85 percent of users having scanned QR codes（扫描二维码）to pay in 2020, according to a report released by China UnionPay.

The survey studied Chinese consumers'（消费者）mobile payment behavior. 98 percent of users considered mobile payment as the most commonly used payment method, up 5 percentage points from a year earlier. The proportion of people who paid by scanning QR codes reached 85% in 2020, up 6 percentage points from 2019. The report said Chinese people used mobile payment three times a day on average.

People from the post-1995 generation（一代人）were the most active users of mobile payment, especially the men in this generation, who used mobile payment four times a day on average.

Making shopping easier is the first reason of choosing mobile payment, followed by habits and sales promotion（促销）. New business forms are developing quickly. About 30 percent of users said they buy daily necessities via livestreaming（直播）, which is popular among consumers.

1. According to the report, mobile payment is popular in _____.
   A. Japan   B. India
   C. America   D. China
2. The underlined word "proportion" means _____ in Chinese.
   A. 比例   B. 数量
   C. 年龄   D. 重量
3. From the Paragraph 2 we can know _____.
   A. everyone uses mobile payment in China
   B. fewer people used mobile payment in 2020
   C. scanning QR codes is an important way to pay
   D. everyone uses mobile payment three times a day
4. What can we know about the post-1995 generation?
   A. They dislike using mobile payment.
   B. Men use mobile payment more than women do.
   C. Women use mobile payment four times a day.
   D. Men are less active users than women.
5. Which of the following is true according to the last two paragraphs?
   A. Livestreaming is popular only among young people.
   B. There are different reasons for the popularity of mobile payment.
   C. People can only buy daily necessities via livestreaming.
   D. New business forms are developing quickly because of livestreaming.

Thursday
[阅读理解 C]

体裁：说明文
题材：科普科技
正确率：_____ /5
词数：195
难度：★★★☆☆
建议用时：6分钟
实际用时：_____
答案页码：101

Technologies Make Learning Easier

Collating（校对）the mistakes of her school tests used to be a nightmare（噩梦）for Yimeng, a 15-year-old student from Beijing, and several of her friends, because it needed a lot of time and efforts to find the right answers to the problems. This exercise is often seen as a useful way for self-improvement（自我提高）.

Yimeng has to find answers to 5 to 20 mistakes for each of her seven subjects, which means another hour of studies after her daily homework. "Since I am in the last year of junior high school, every minute of sleep is important to me, not to mention the <u>shortage</u> of an hour," she said.

But hope is coming for Yimeng and her friends in the form of an intelligent（智能的）question answering device（装置）. It was developed by a Chinese online education company. If a student takes a picture of the mistakes with the mobile phone, the device will show the question and the answer based on the image.

The product（产品）is helpful for millions of Chinese students. Such products are becoming increasingly popular with students in China, thanks to their use of advanced technologies to solve the problems of students.

1. It took Yimeng a lot of _____ to find answers to the mistakes of school tests.
   A. money   B. time
   C. ideas   D. fun
2. Which of the following is NOT true according to Paragraph 2?
   A. Yimeng has many subjects.
   B. Yimeng is a junior high school student.
   C. Yimeng doesn't like doing homework.
   D. Yimeng thinks a good sleep is important.
3. The underlined word "shortage" means _____ in Chinese.
   A. 缺乏   B. 增加
   C. 保持   D. 争取
4. From Paragraphs 3 and 4 we can know _____.
   A. the device is easy to use
   B. the device is helpful for every student
   C. the device uses no technology
   D. the device is only popular in China
5. What does the passage mainly discuss?
   A. The students in China.
   B. The sleep time of Chinese students.
   C. The use of technology in learning.
   D. The daily homework of Chinese students.

Friday
[任务型阅读 D]

Computer Chip Shortage Hurts Car Makers

Car makers have to make fewer cars because they can't get enough computer parts (零件).

Tiny computers, called microprocessors (微处理器), are very important in modern cars. __1__. They have been used to control many different parts of a car. Modern cars may have as many as 150 chips. __2__ from how the fuel (燃料) goes into the engine (引擎), to the way the car brakes, as well as controlling many other systems.

__3__, so they can't produce all the cars they planned to make. Last year, many car makers had to close their factories because of the COVID-19. __4__, they stopped buying chips from the chip makers. That forced the chip makers to stop making so many chips for cars. __5__.

So when car makers start making lots of cars again, there aren't enough chips.

阅读短文，从下列选项中选出能填入文中空白处的最佳选项。

A. They began selling lots of chips to other kinds of companies
B. These microprocessors are commonly known as "chips"
C. But now car makers don't have enough chips
D. Chips control many things
E. Since they weren't making cars

Saturday
[短文填空]

China's Tianwen-1 Reaches Mars

On Wednesday, China's Tianwen-1 reached Mars and began orbiting (沿轨道运行) the planet. Though China has had (1)_____ successes in space recently, this is the first time it has succeeded in sending a mission (飞行任务) to Mars.

Tianwen-1 won't (2)_____ orbit Mars. Instead, after orbiting for a few (3)_____, the Tianwen-1 will try to send a rover (火星车) to the land of the planet. The Tianwen-1's rover is nearly the (4)_____ of a golf cart and is solar-powered (太阳能的).

Landing on Mars is something many (5)_____ have tried and failed at. Only the U.S. has managed to land several times. (6)_____ even the U.S. has had one landing mission fail.

China (7)_____ to send the rover to the Martian surface (火星表面) in May or June. China's space agency (机构) has chosen a (8)_____ area called Utopia Planitia for landing the rover. This is the same area where NASA (9)_____ its Viking 2 lander in 1976.

If the Tianwen-1 rover lands successfully, it will look (10)_____ water underground, as well as for any signs (迹象) of life from long ago.

体裁：记叙文
题材：科普科技
正确率：_____/10
词数：179
难度：★★★★☆
建议用时：11 分钟
实际用时：_____
答案页码：　102

阅读短文，从方框中选择合适的单词并用其正确形式填空，使短文通顺，意思完整。

simple
land
size
several
and
wide
plan
for
month
country

Sunday
[拓展阅读]

Technology Helps People to Protect the Rock Paintings

| 体裁：说明文 | 题材：传统文化 | 词数：153 |
| 难度：★★★☆☆ | 建议用时：6分钟 | 实际用时：_____ |

Northwest China's Ningxia Hui Autonomous（自治的）Region has used digital（数字的）technology to protect ancient cliff carvings（雕刻）and paintings（绘画）.

Workers have scanned（扫描）more than 2,000 immovable（无法移动的）rock carvings and paintings at Helan Mountain. The digitalization of the Helan Mountain cliff carvings and paintings started in 2019.

Rock carvings appeared before the invention of writing systems. More than 20,000 cliff carvings and paintings have been discovered at Helan Mountain by now.

The works show the lives of the people who lived 3,000 to 10,000 years ago. There are images of animals, humans, plants, planets, fingerprints and so on.

The protection of rock paintings and carvings is very important. Now there is no effective（有效的）, natural scientific and technological way to stop their disappearance（消失）. It is said that by the end of this century, a quarter of the world's rock paintings will disappear.

Technology has won time for the protection of the rock paintings.

Week Two 人物传记

Monday [完形填空]

The Tireless Cartoonist

体裁：记叙文
题材：人物传记
正确率：_____ /10
词数：188
难度：★★★☆☆
建议用时：10 分钟
实际用时：_____
答案页码：103

Famous cartoonist Tsai Chih-chung is better known as C. C. Tsai in the West. He is 73 years old this year, but he has no plans to slow down or __1__ a more "normal"（正常的）life.

Born in 1948 in Taiwan, Tsai has been creating comic books that have been __2__ around the world since 1984. His works have been translated（翻译）into 26 __3__ languages.

The artist keeps a special schedule（时间表）. He goes to bed at 5 pm and wakes at 1 am. Then, he __4__ till around 2 pm. "When you are really focused（专心的）, __5__ is quiet. You are the only thing in the world. Time seems to slow down. This is __6__ I like getting up in the middle of the __7__," says Tsai.

"I can create a book in no more than five days," he says. "__8__ cartoonists don't work like writers. They have to __9__ one word after another."

__10__ he is old, Tsai says that he still works hard. In fact, his goal is to create 500 new books in five years.

1. A. think   B. feel
   C. give   D. live
2. A. interesting B. popular
   C. wonderful   D. important
3. A. different B. kind
   C. difficult D. same
4. A. works   B. sits
   C. exercises D. studies
5. A. nothing   B. everything
   C. anything   D. something
6. A. what   B. which
   C. why   D. who
7. A. morning   B. afternoon
   C. night   D. day
8. A. We   B. They
   C. You   D. Those
9. A. imagine   B. write
   C. guess   D. speak
10. A. And   B. But
    C. Because   D. Although

Tuesday
[阅读理解 A]

Winter Sports Medalists

Wu Dajing • Born in 1994 • Good at: skating • Medal: gold • In 2018, he won the first gold medal in a men's individual (个人的) ice sport for China at the Olympics (奥运会).
Liu Jiayu • Born in 1992 • Good at: snowboard • Medal: silver • She won a silver medal in the women's snowboard halfpipe (半管滑道) during the 2018 Winter Olympic Games.
Yu Shumei • Born in 1975 • Good at: biathlon • Medals: 2 gold, 1 silver, 2 bronze • In 1996, she took part in 5 events (项目) and won 2 gold, 1 silver and 2 bronze medals. She became China's first biathlon world champion in Norway on March 18, 2001.
Gu Ailing • Born in 2003 • Good at: skiing • Medals: 2 gold • She won the first gold medal for China at the extreme (极限的) sports event on 29 January 2021. Later, she won the second gold medal on 30 January 2021. She was born in America and now is competing (比赛) for China.

体裁：——
题材：人物传记
正确率：_____/4
词数：171
难度：★★★☆☆
建议用时：5 分钟
实际用时：_____
答案页码：103

1. According to the chart, _____ won the most medals.
   A. Wu Dajing B. Liu Jiayu
   C. Yu Shumei D. Gu Ailing
2. Both Wu Dajing and Liu Jiayu _____.
   A. are good at skating
   B. are good at snowboard
   C. won gold medals in 2018
   D. took part in the Olympics
3. Both Wu Dajing and Gu Ailing _____.
   A. won a gold medal in 2021
   B. won 2 gold medals for China
   C. won the first gold medal in an event for China
   D. won a gold medal in the skating event
4. Which is not true about Gu Ailing?
   A. She was born in America.
   B. She is competing for China.
   C. She is the youngest one of the four medalists.
   D. She won 2 gold medals on 30 January 2021.

Wednesday
[阅读理解 B]

A Miao Woman's Hopes and Dreams in Embroidery

体裁：记叙文
题材：人物传记
正确率：_____ /4
词数：156
难度：★★★☆☆
建议用时：5 分钟
实际用时：_____
答案页码：104

Married at age 16, Chen Xiulan has lived a quiet life in the mountains of Hainan Province (省). She has worked on the field for most of her life, like other women in her village. But now she is the owner of a Miao embroidery (刺绣) studio (工作室).

"When I was 12, I took a small piece of cloth and learned embroidery after class. I made my first scarf at 16, and still keep it with me," Chen said.

At 28, she put a cloth bag on her back, and rode out into the mountains on a motorcycle, going village by village to sell her embroidery works. That has continued for almost 20 years.

Without enough education in her youth, Chen said that it's hard for her to sell her works online because she has never learned to use a computer. She hopes the younger generation (一代人) will carry the tradition of embroidery forward.

1. Chen made her first scarf at the age of _____.
   A. 12   B. 16
   C. 18   D. 20
2. How did Chen sell her embroidery works?
   A. By riding a bicycle.
   B. By riding a motorcycle.
   C. By walking from village to village.
   D. By taking a bus.
3. Chen couldn't sell her embroidery works online because _____.
   A. she loved riding her motorcycle
   B. she didn't want to sell them online
   C. she didn't know how to use a computer
   D. she wanted the younger generation to do it.
4. The main purpose of this passage is to tell us _____.
   A. to hold on to our dreams
   B. how to do embroidery to make money
   C. that we should learn to use a computer
   D. that Miao people are living a good life

Thursday
[阅读理解 C]

Education Choices of Wang Ziyi

Wang Ziyi still remembers the day when she first picked up her golf club—it was May 2, 2004. She was only 6 years old at the time. Wang is a Beijing native (本地人). She competed for the Chinese national golf team before. She was the youngest champion of China LPGA Tour (中国女子职业高尔夫球巡回赛)—at the age of 16, she won the 2014 China LPGA Xiamen <u>Challenge</u>.

In June 2016, Wang became a student-athlete (学生运动员) at Stanford University (斯坦福大学). She planned to become a professional (职业的) golfer after finishing her studies at Stanford. Yet, last year, the 21-year-old girl decided to give up that childhood dream and study politics (政治学) at Oxford (牛津大学). She realized that she had a deeper interest and passion (热情) for politics than for sport.

"My friends and coaches (教练) feel sorry for me because I gave up the golf career after years of hard work. But I think I've learned a lot from practicing golf," she says. "In golf, I'm always facing loss, and it helps me to face difficulties."

体裁：记叙文
题材：人物传记
正确率：_____/4
词数：187
难度：★★★★☆
建议用时：6 分钟
实际用时：_____
答案页码：105

---

1. During her childhood, Wang Ziyi's dream was to be a _____.
   A. student-athlete
   B. professional golfer
   C. champion
   D. coach

2. The underlined word "Challenge" in Paragraph 1 probably means _____ in Chinese.
   A. 奖杯　　　　B. 荣誉
   C. 运动队　　　D. 挑战（赛）

3. Why did Wang Ziyi decide to study politics?
   A. Because she was more interested in politics.
   B. Because she wanted to try something new.
   C. Because she didn't like golf anymore.
   D. Because she thought that golf was too hard for her.

4. Which is not true about Wang Ziyi?
   A. She is good at playing golf.
   B. She loves politics more than sport.
   C. She has studied politics for many years.
   D. She has learned to face loss from golf.

Friday
[任务型阅读 D]

Old Porcelain Ware Collector Yu Xueyun

体裁：记叙文
题材：人物传记
正确率：_____ /4
词数：181
难度：★★★★☆
建议用时：5分钟
实际用时：_____
答案页码：105

    Yu Xueyun is a collector (收藏家) of old porcelain (瓷器) pieces. He lives in a village in Sanming, Fujian Province. Until December, he has donated (捐赠) more than 1,500 pieces to public museums. He hopes that the art can be better protected (保护).

    Yu remembered that he first had the idea of collecting porcelain pieces at the age of 12. He found a small dish on his way home from school. The dish had two butterflies painted on it. From then on, he began to be interested in old porcelain in the soil around his village in Jiangle County.

    In the past 30 years, Yu, 50, spent about 30 million yuan ($4.6 million) in porcelain ware (器皿). He began to collect the old items as a boy but later he put all his money into protecting and researching them.

    The older of his two daughters said her father put all the money in porcelain. At first, she couldn't understand (理解) why her father used up his money in such a hobby. But as she grew up, she said she learned a lot from her father.

阅读短文，回答下面 1~4 小题。

1. When did Yu start to have the idea of collecting old porcelain pieces?
_____
_____

2. How much money did he spend in porcelain ware in the past 30 years?
_____
_____

3. How did his older daughter think about his hobby?
_____
_____

4. Will you spend all your money on your hobby? Why or why not?
_____
_____
_____

Saturday
[短文填空]

World in a Camera

Over the past 10 years, the 42-year-old Qi Juanjuan, has traveled to 84 countries on five continents (洲).

In 2012, Qi (1)_____ to Cuba (古巴). There was (2)_____ Internet except in big hotels. The buildings in Havana (哈瓦那) were mostly old. "There were (3)_____ of people dancing and playing musical instruments in the streets at night. I stayed in a small house and the owner had a (4)_____. I asked him why he bought a computer with no connection (连接) to the Internet. He told me that the connection would happen some day," says Qi.

"One of the most meaningful things about traveling is that you can (5)_____ the world with a fresh perspective (视角)."

When Qi arrives in a city for the (6)_____ time, he usually visits two locations to start his exploration (探索)—food markets and parks. (7)_____ taking photos, videos and writing diaries to record his trips, Qi also likes (8)_____ when he arrives in a foreign place. "Running in a city, which I have not visited before, allows me to see something new and soak in (沉浸于) its sights, sounds and smells."

体裁：记叙文
题材：人物传记
正确率：____/8
词数：193
难度：★★★★☆
建议用时：9分钟
实际用时：_____
答案页码：106

阅读短文，在短文空缺处填入适当的单词，使短文通顺，意思完整。

(1)_____
(2)_____
(3)_____
(4)_____
(5)_____
(6)_____
(7)_____
(8)_____

Sunday
[拓展阅读]

Longjing, an Imperial Tea

体裁：说明文　　题材：传统文化　　词数：187
难度：★★★☆☆　　建议用时：6分钟　　实际用时：_____

　　Longjing is a famous tea in China and it has a long history, too. Drinking Longjing tea is good for people's health, and it tastes sweet. So, people all around the world love drinking it. The tea leaves are sourced（来源）from Longjing Village in Hangzhou, Zhejiang Province（省）.

　　During the Qing Dynasty（朝代）(1644-1911), the Kangxi Emperor（皇帝）(1654-1722) decreed（颁布法令）Longjing tea a gong cha or "imperial tea." But he wasn't the only emperor loving the drink. His grandson, the Qianlong Emperor (1711-1799), also came to love the drink.

　　According to a tale（传说）, Qianlong was on a visit to Hangzhou. Suddenly, he was told that his mother was ill. He was picking tea leaves at the time. He picked them into his sleeve and set out for Beijing right away. When he arrived by his mother's bedside, she noticed a fragrance（芳香）coming from his clothing. Qianlong remembered the leaves and made a cup of tea for her. Miraculously（奇迹般地）, she recovered after drinking it. The emperor was so glad that he ordered Longjing tea to be gifted to his mother every year.

Week Three 生活成长、人际交往

Monday
[完形填空]

体裁：议论文
题材：生活成长
正确率：_____ /10
词数：181
难度：★★★★☆
建议用时：12 分钟
实际用时：_____
答案页码：108

Why Students Turn Off Their Cameras in Online Classes

Two Cornell University (康奈尔大学) teachers have found that most students don't like to show their faces on video during online classes because they are worried about how they look.

Their study __1__ found that self-consciousness (自我意识) was the key. One student in the study said, "Everyone else __2__ their cameras and I would feel __3__ if I turned mine on." __4__ student said he would be able to focus (集中) more during online classes __5__ he kept his video camera off.

According to their survey, they suggest that teachers should __6__ their students to use cameras, __7__ shouldn't force them. Most of the time, encouragement worked with students and they noticed that students would be very thankful if it was not required.

Another important advice is to __8__ to the students, so students will better understand __9__ teachers are asking for these things. For those who do not use their cameras—either because they are unable or unwilling (不情愿的)—the teachers could suggest them to speak __10__ the microphone (麦克风) to take part in the discussion.

1. A. results   B. ways
   C. reasons   D. purposes
2. A. took off   B. got off
   C. turned off   D. cut off
3. A. boring   B. angry
   C. difficult   D. nervous
4. A. One   B. Another
   C. Other   D. Which
5. A. unless   B. if
   C. although   D. even
6. A. make   B. encourage
   C. cause   D. control
7. A. but   B. and
   C. so   D. or
8. A. agree   B. answer
   C. choose   D. explain
9. A. where   B. when
   C. what   D. why
10. A. in   B. on
    C. to   D. with

Tuesday
[阅读理解 A]

Toys with Creativity

体裁：记叙文
题材：生活成长
正确率：_____/4
词数：186
难度：★★☆☆☆
建议用时：5 分钟
实际用时：_____
答案页码：108

　　In the past three years, a 32-year-old father Zhang made a lot of fun toys from waste cardboard (纸板) for his daughter. His toy-making videos are very popular on the Internet and many people say that it is a creative and friendly way to spend quality time with children.

　　"When other children ask their parents to buy them a toy, my daughter always asks me to make one," Mr. Zhang says. In Zhang's eyes, everything can have a hard cardboard copy (复制品) and some classic video games like *Need for Speed* (《极品飞车》) and *Tetris* (《俄罗斯方块》) can also be played in the real world. His daughter prefers these cardboard toys to video games. Although they are a little different from the digital (数码的) version, Mr. Zhang's toys are very popular. This father says, "As people are becoming more obsessed with (沉迷于) digital products, there are <u>negative</u> effects (影响) brought by technology, like difficulty in concentration (专注)."

　　He hopes that his video can provide a creative solution for parents, especially fathers, on how to enjoy a quality time with their children and encourage them to use screens less.

1. Mr. Zhang used _____ to make toys for his daughter.
   A. wood   B. paper
   C. cardboard   D. box
2. Which of the following is true according to the passage?
   A. Zhang's daughter asks him to buy toys for her.
   B. Zhang's daughter likes video games better.
   C. Zhang thinks it is impossible to make a cardboard copy for everything.
   D. Video games can also be played in the real world in Zhang's eyes.
3. The underlined word "negative" means _____ in Chinese.
   A. 良好的   B. 有用的
   C. 负面的   D. 伤心的
4. Parents could learn _____ from this passage.
   A. a new way to get along with their children
   B. how to make the most use of cardboard
   C. to use more screens with their children
   D. to make interesting toys for their children

Wednesday
[阅读理解 B]

Special Education in China

China has made great progress in special education in the past ten years and the number of students going to school grew quickly especially over the last three years. But when compared with the development of education for healthy kids, the gap (差距) actually is still large.

According to a report from the Ministry of Education, 795,000 students with special needs received school lessons in 2019. Of them, 49 percent studied at common schools, 21.5 percent studied from home, 0.48 percent studied at a single class of common schools, and the rest with serious disabilities (残疾) went to special schools.

Children with special needs also have the right to be educated in common schools. If a school is not able to accept them, then it's the school that should be sorry, not the parents. Special schools are necessary because common schools still have not enough resources (资源) and abilities to offer students with special needs a quality learning experience. And if this problem can be solved, special education will go further (进一步地) towards the right direction.

1. China's _____ is much better than before.
   A. common education
   B. special education
   C. learning environment
   D. teaching environment

2. According to the passage, we can know that in 2019 _____ students with serious disabilities studied at special schools.
   A. 29.02%   B. 49%
   C. 21.5%   D. 0.48%

3. Why are special schools necessary for students with special needs?
   A. Because special schools are more popular among parents.
   B. Because common schools refuse to accept students with special needs.
   C. Because common schools can't provide a good learning experience.
   D. Because common schools have enough teachers and classes.

4. According to the last paragraph, we can infer that the author may tell us _____ next.
   A. the reason why special schools are necessary
   B. the reason why students go to common schools
   C. how to help common schools provide better learning experience
   D. how to help students with disabilities successfully go to schools

Thursday
[阅读理解 C]

Arts at MIT

The Maihaugen Gallery The Maihaugen Gallery is a library that stores historical documents, photographs, rare (罕见的) books, maps, art works and so on.	Open: 10:00 am–4:00 pm from Monday to Thursday Address: close to the Institute Archives (14N–118)
List Visual (视觉的) Arts Center It is a creative laboratory that provides students and artists with a space to do artistic experiment and collects lots of sculptures by artists such as Henry Moore, Anish Kapoor, Cai Guoqiang and Alexander Calder.	Open: 12:00 pm–6:00 pm from Tuesday to Sunday 12:00 pm–8:00 pm on Thursday Address: Building E15, Atrium Level 20 Ames Street Ticket: Free admission
The MIT Museum The MIT Museum has just over 1,000,000 works in its collections, and welcomes you to enjoy all kinds of architecture and design collections.	Open: 10:00 am–5:00 pm Address: Building N51, 265 Massachusetts Avenue Ticket: $10 for adults $5 for youth under 18 Free for children under 5
Hart Nautical (航海的) Gallery This gallery has forty of the Museum's finest full ship models. You can know more about one thousand years of shipping.	Open: 10:00 am–5:00 pm Address: Cambridge Building 5, 55 Massachusetts Avenue Ticket: Free admission

体裁：——
题材：生活成长
正确率：＿＿/4
词数：182
难度：★★★☆☆
建议用时：5 分钟
实际用时：＿＿
答案页码：110

1. If students want to know more about photography, they can go to ＿＿＿＿.
   A. The Maihaugen Gallery
   B. List Visual Arts Center
   C. The MIT Museum
   D. Hart Nautical Gallery
2. Where can students see the exhibition about ships?
   A. Beside the Institute Archives.
   B. Atrium Level 20 Ames Street.
   C. 55 Massachusetts Avenue.
   D. 265 Massachusetts Avenue.
3. Students can go to ＿＿＿＿ at 7:00 pm on Thursday.
   A. The Maihaugen Gallery
   B. List Visual Arts Center
   C. The MIT Museum
   D. Hart Nautical Gallery
4. A mother with her 12-year-old child should pay ＿＿＿＿ for the MIT Museum.
   A. $0   B. $5
   C. $10   D. $15

Friday
[任务型阅读 D]

A 15-Year-Old Poet Champion

体裁：记叙文
题材：生活成长
正确率：_____/5
词数：172
难度：★★★★☆
建议用时：7 分钟
实际用时：_____
答案页码：110

At 12 years of age, Solli Raphael became the youngest winner of the Australian Poetry Slam (满贯) held at the Sydney Opera House after he performed *Australian Air*. It was a poem related to political (政治的) wisdom, environmental consciousness (意识) and the importance of social consciousness. He then became famous after his winning performance was watched online over four million (百万) times in 24 hours.

Now 15 years old, Solli is a famous young poet and speaker around the world. He speaks at meetings, schools and universities. Solli's first book *Limelight*, was published in 2018 and has received praises for its abilities to encourage more students to create poetry. What's more, Solli is an environmental activist (活动家) and humanitarian (人道主义者) who works closely as an ambassador (大使) for four charities (慈善机构) and organizations.

Solli enjoys writing powerful (有力量的) and warm poems for changes in some areas. He feels that these changes are important for social equality (社会平等), the environment and animal protection. <u>This active teenager grows with the global youth movement (运动) and shows successful possibilities for young persons.</u>

阅读短文，回答下面 1~5 小题。

1. How old was Solli Raphael when he became the youngest winner of the Australian Poetry Slam?
_____
_____

2. What's the poem *Australian Air* about?
_____
_____

3. Why did Solli's first book receive praises?
_____
_____

4. What features do Solli's poems have?
_____
_____

5. 请翻译文中画线的句子。
_____
_____

Saturday
[短文填空]

Tips for Better Communication in English at Work

When we are learning (1)_____ new language, carrying on a conversation can be difficult. So today, here are four (2)_____ for you to better listen and carry on conversations.

Predict（预测）. The first tip (3)_____ to predict what you will hear. Maybe your customers sometimes say they have (4)_____ with placing an order（下单）. You can think about the ways they usually ask about this problem. What words do they often use in that kind of conversation? For example, customers may often use the word "order".

Focus（专注）. The second tip is to prepare a list of those words and try to listen to them (5)_____ a customer begins talking with you. The next time when you are listening to a customer, paying (6)_____ to the key words will help you understand their question.

Ask. Next, think (7)_____ what you can say to the customer to let them know you need a little help to understand them.

Finally, you can put all these actions and thoughts together. You are not sure of the product the customer wants. But you do note the words "order" or (8)_____ key words, so you can ask a question to get the customer's request.

体裁：说明文
题材：人际交往
正确率：_____/8
词数：200
难度：★★★★☆
建议用时：9分钟
实际用时：_____
答案页码：111

阅读短文，在短文空缺处填入适当的单词，使短文通顺，意思完整。

(1) _____
(2) _____
(3) _____
(4) _____
(5) _____
(6) _____
(7) _____
(8) _____

Sunday
[拓展阅读]

Chime-Bells

体裁：说明文　　题材：传统文化　　词数：136
难度：★★★★☆　　建议用时：7分钟　　实际用时：_____

Chime-bells（编钟）, or Bianzhong, was one of the most important instruments in ancient China. Chime-bells is made up of bells in different sizes according to the order of the pitch（音高）. The bells are played by mallets（木槌）and create seven musical sounds, much like the piano.

In the early Shang Dynasty, there has been Chime-bells which was made up of three pieces of bells. This instrument was used in royal（皇家的）performances and it was unpopular among the ordinary families.

The most famous Chime-bells is the one which was found in the tomb（墓地）of the Marquis（侯爵）Yi of the Zeng state in the Warring States period in Hubei Province. This set of bells with five octaves（八度音阶）has the largest number and scale, and it was well preserved（保存）. It's one of the cultural wonders in the Chinese history.

Monday
[完形填空]

体裁：记叙文
题材：兴趣爱好
正确率：_____/15
词数：190
难度：★★★★☆
建议用时：16 分钟
实际用时：_____
答案页码：112

Surf, Swim, Sing: Finding Joy in Lifelong Learning

In the new year, people resolve（决定）to improve themselves: Stop being so mean（刻薄的）, eat more vegetables, learn the piano!

__1__ Tom Vanderbilt didn't wait for a new year to improve himself. After __2__ his daughter learn to play chess, he __3__ to join her. Then Vanderbilt __4__ his own study, learning to sing, surf, swim, juggle（玩杂耍）and draw.

What he wanted were the __5__ he could relax into and slowly develop in his life. To learn how to sing, he found a(an) __6__ teacher. "You should open your mind and think of it as a __7__ experience," __8__ teacher told him.

He found that the __9__ to learning new things was shifting（转移）the focus off yourself. __10__ surfing, he learned to look at the coast, not his feet or __11__. When he started juggling, he found that jugglers didn't look at the balls; they watched the apex（顶点）where __12__ are thrown.

He didn't __13__ any prizes or break new ground—nor was that the intention（意图）. And doing these things made him __14__. Perhaps he would encourage you to __15__ 2021 finding delight（快乐）in developing new or forgotten skills.

1. A. So   B. Or
   C. But   D. Because
2. A. controlling B. watching
   C. discussing   D. hearing
3. A. decided   B. refused
   C. forgot   D. needed
4. A. started out B. started on
   C. started over D. started for
5. A. activities   B. exercises
   C. skills   D. ways
6. A. head   B. piano
   C. art   D. voice
7. A. sorry   B. proud
   C. harmful   D. happy
8. A. the   B. /
   C. a   D. an
9. A. key   B. reason
   C. example   D. fun
10. A. From   B. With
    C. After   D. Before
11. A. guard   B. board
    C. coach   D. ground
12. A. hats   B. shoes
    C. balls   D. bottles
13. A. want   B. catch
    C. search   D. win
14. A. happy   B. sad
    C. angry   D. nervous
15. A. succeed   B. enjoy
    C. spend   D. waste

Tuesday
[阅读理解 A]

3 Products for Teaching

Teachers, are you looking for some fun, practical (实践的，实际的) activities for your English classes? We've got 3 fantastic products to make your life as a teacher so much easier!

---

1. The Pack
Fun, dynamic (充满活力的) ready-to-go lessons in 5 levels.
With these classes, your students will use lots of useful languages and practise all the important skills: speaking, listening, reading and writing.
Provide audio (音频) and video files (文件).
Over 20 lessons per level.

---

2. Business Skills
Give your students the Business English they need and prepare them for the world of business with these fantastic lesson ideas.
Practical ideas for lessons on e-mail, negotiation (谈判), meetings, presentations (展示), socialising (交际)…

---

3. Games Pack
Our Games Pack comes with some great ideas to motivate (激发) your students and provides a new way of learning language. Four levels and hundreds of fantastic games and activities help your students learn quickly and easily!

You can telephone your order 24 hours a day. The number is 88886666.

体裁：——
题材：学校教育
正确率：____/5
词数：157
难度：★★☆☆☆
建议用时：5 分钟
实际用时：____
答案页码：113

---

1. What may students learn from The Pack?
① How to talk about some subjects in English.
② How to watch people who are speaking.
③ How to send an email to a business woman.
④ How to understand what they have heard.
A. ①②   B. ②③
C. ①④   D. ②④

2. How many lessons are there in The Pack?
A. Less than 20 lessons.
B. More than 100 lessons.
C. 5 lessons in total.
D. 20 lessons in total.

3. Which of the following is correct?
A. Business Skills offer useful ideas.
B. Business Skills provide 5 lessons.
C. Games Pack has a hundred activities.
D. Games Pack has video files per level.

4. Where is the passage most probably from?
A. A movie poster.   B. A notebook.
C. A textbook.   D. A magazine.

5. The text is useful for _____.
A. businessmen   B. students
C. teachers   D. parents

Wednesday
[阅读理解 B]

The Best Title Wanted

Zhao Bin is a food deliveryman (送货员) in Wuhan. He and other local deliverymen worked day and night with no time off and often forgot about meals during the days when the coronavirus (冠状病毒) was raging (肆虐).

"It was the busiest time I had ever seen as a food deliveryman," Zhao said. "It's so tiring, but I feel what I did was valued."

Zhao Bin has noticed that customers now show more respect (尊重) and understanding toward food delivery workers. "After the pandemic, customers will send us a message to let us know it's fine if we're running late," Zhao said.

Zhao loves taking pictures of people in this city since he has spent most of his time on the street as a food deliveryman. He said he took up taking pictures as a hobby after working as a museum security (安全) guard.

He believes no matter how heavy the daily workload is, people still need dreams and hobbies. One of his wishes during the pandemic was to get a photo of people hugging on the street, he said.

And now, the dream has come true. "The city that I love is back," he said.

体裁：记叙文
题材：兴趣爱好
正确率：_____/5
词数：204
难度：★★★☆☆
建议用时：6 分钟
实际用时：_____
答案页码：113

1. We can learn from the passage that _____.
   A. Zhao Bin often stayed up during the pandemic
   B. Zhao Bin thought what he had done was of worth
   C. Zhao Bin would send messages to customers on rainy days
   D. Zhao Bin explained the reason of being late

2. What is Zhao Bin's hobby?
   A. Taking photos.
   B. Watching people.
   C. Drawing pictures.
   D. Walking on the street.

3. The underlined word "workload" may mean _____ in Chinese.
   A. 工作时间   B. 工作压力
   C. 工作难度   D. 工作负荷

4. Which is the correct order according to the passage?
   ① Zhao Bin made sure the safety of the museum.
   ② Coronavirus was spreading very quickly.
   ③ The city in which Zhao Bin lives—Wuhan came back to life again.
   A. ①③②   B. ①②③
   C. ②③①   D. ②①③

5. What is the best title for the passage?
   A. A Food Deliveryman Loving Taking Photos
   B. A Food Deliveryman Working Hard in Wuhan
   C. A Food Deliveryman's Spare Time After Work
   D. A Food Deliveryman's Dream to Be a Photographer

Thursday
[阅读理解 C]

An Experience of a Math Professor

A university professor in Singapore gave a two-hour online lecture but didn't realize he was on mute (无声的). Professor Wang, a math teacher, didn't know that throughout his online presentation (展示), the microphone (麦克风) on his computer was off. This meant that none of the students attending his online class heard what he was talking about. His lecture started well but then it stopped moving. The video came back but the microphone was off and Professor Wang did not notice. One of his students said it might have been because the professor was using an iPad, not a common computer.

Students tried many times to remind (提醒) Professor Wang during the lesson but could not get through to him. They waved their arms and even tried calling him on his personal phone. After realizing what had happened, Professor Wang was surprised and nervous. He was sorry for wasting two hours of his students' time. He has offered to redo the lecture at a different time so his students do not miss that class. One of his students posted on social media (社交媒体) about the professor's experience. She wrote, "I took a class under him before and he taught well. I feel bad for him."

体裁：记叙文
题材：学校教育
正确率：____/5
词数：207
难度：★★★☆☆
建议用时：6分钟
实际用时：_____
答案页码：114

1. Which of the following is true?
   A. Professor Wang turned off his online courses.
   B. Professor Wang didn't like to move during his class.
   C. Professor Wang found everything was going well.
   D. Professor Wang gave a math class for 2 hours.
2. What happened in Professor Wang's class?
   A. None of the students attended his online class.
   B. Very few students listened carefully in his class.
   C. There was no sound in the video of his lecture.
   D. He used a common computer to give lessons.
3. What did students do to remind the professor?
   A. By shouting into their microphones.
   B. By calling professor on his telephone.
   C. By sending messages on social media.
   D. By trying to send him lots of emails.
4. The underlined word "redo" most probably means _____ in Chinese.
   A. 重做 B. 反复
   C. 调整 D. 更新
5. What might one of professor's students think of this two-hour online class?
   A. Surprised. B. Upset.
   C. Nervous. D. Excited.

Friday
[任务型阅读 D]

Schools Face More Failing Grades During Pandemic

School districts (地区) across the United States have reported the number of students failing classes has risen many times higher than usual numbers.

___1___ Students learning from home often miss homework—or school completely. And teachers who do not see their students in person have fewer ways to notice who is falling behind.

___2___ At a school in the Salem-Keizer Public School district, hundreds of students at first had grade scores of 0.0 percent. ___3___

In New Mexico, more than 40 percent of middle and high school students were failing at least one class as of late October. In Houston, Texas, 42 percent of students received at least one F in the first grading period of the year.

___4___ Other schools are changing their grading policies and giving students more time to complete homework.

___5___ They have been urged (敦促) to find different ways of teaching.

体裁：议论文
题材：学校教育
正确率：____/5
词数：194
难度：★★★☆☆
建议用时：6分钟
实际用时：____
答案页码：114

阅读短文，从下列选项中选出能填入文中空白处的最佳选项。

A. This showed that students simply were not taking part in school at all.
B. Now, teachers have been asked to give less homework.
C. The increase in failing grades has been seen in districts of all sizes around the country.
D. Educators see a number of reasons for the change.
E. Many schools have tried hard to return to in-person learning.

Saturday
[短文填空]

Passion for Trains Connects Two Railway Workers in Guizhou

体裁：记叙文
题材：兴趣爱好
正确率：_____/10
词数：164
难度：★★☆☆☆
建议用时：10 分钟
实际用时：_____
答案页码：115

Two young men are lucky enough to work with something they love—trains—in Guiyang of Southwest China's Guizhou Province.

Zhang Yuqi and Liu Yuqi, who have no (1)_____ relationship, are connected by their (2)_____ hobby—collecting model trains. And they have been called "high-speed train (3)_____" by other people. As their parents were employed（雇用）in the train industry, they (4)_____ up with the beautiful sound of train whistles（汽笛声）and now work for the Guiyang North Railway Station.

At the (5)_____, Liu Yuqi worked as an intern（实习生）in Zhang Yuqi's team. They learned job skills together. After getting to (6)_____ each other better, they found that they both liked collecting model trains in their (7)_____ time.

Now both of (8)_____ carefully check and repair trains to ensure the safe operation（运行）of bullet trains（动车）at work and share their (9)_____ of model train collections (10)_____ work. Currently, these two have collected more than 200 model trains.

阅读短文，从方框中选择合适的单词并用其正确形式填空，使短文通顺，意思完整。

spare
know
grow
they
blood
experience
after
share
begin
brother

Sunday
[拓展阅读]

Firecrackers on New Year's Day

体裁：记叙文　　题材：传统文化　　词数：176
难度：★★★★☆　建议用时：7 分钟　实际用时：_____

　　The first day of the first lunar（农历的）month is the first day of the year, of the season and of the twelve months. In *Stories of Spring and Autumn*, it is called Duan Yue, the beginning of the month. On that day, people get up at cockcrow（鸡叫；黎明）. They light firecrackers（爆竹）in the yard to drive away the *shan sao*, the legendary ghosts that haunt（出没）the mountains.

　　According to *The Book of Fairies and Ghosts*, a strange creature lives in the western mountains. It is single-legged and a little over a foot tall. By nature, it is unafraid of human beings. If offended（冒犯）, it will hurt the offender with fever. It is called the shan sao. To scare it, people burn bamboo which bursts（爆破）with a popping sound. In *The Book of Yuan Huang*, this creature is called "the shan chao ghost".

　　People believe that the practice of burning bamboo originated from the lighting of torches（火把）in the royal（皇家的）palace. So it is thought that the nobles（贵族）and ordinary people should not adopt this royal practice.

Week Five 明星娱乐

Monday
[完形填空]

体裁：记叙文
题材：明星娱乐
正确率：_____/15
词数：157
难度：★★★★☆
建议用时：16 分钟
实际用时：_____
答案页码：117

CCTV Lights Up Lantern Festival with Gala

CCTV __1__ the annual（一年一度的）Lantern Festival gala at 8 pm on Feb 26.

Many programs, such as singing, dancing and traditional Chinese operas, were staged and performed by both old and __2__ Chinese artists, including singer Hu Songhua, actress Tian Hua, and singer-actors Wang Yibo and Yi Yangqianxi.

The gala was very popular __3__ the audience（观众）. Articles with the __4__ about Lantern Festival have been viewed more than 1.1 billion __5__, with over 5 million comments（评论）__6__ the Internet.

The Lantern Festival marks the __7__ of Spring Festival. It's on February 26 __8__ year. As one of the most __9__ traditional Chinese festivals, audience usually enjoy the gala and __10__ yuanxiao. Yuanxiao is made __11__ rice and filled with different fillings, __12__ sugar, chocolate and sesame（芝麻）. The round __13__ of the yuanxiao stands for family togetherness. The Chinese people believe eating yuanxiao __14__ happiness and good luck to __15__ family in the new year.

1. A. celebrated B. held
   C. suggested D. started
2. A. young B. perfect
   C. little D. brave
3. A. over B. around
   C. with D. for
4. A. name B. topic
   C. unit D. list
5. A. pieces B. watches
   C. times D. signs
6. A. on B. under
   C. through D. in
7. A. beginning B. end
   C. start D. break
8. A. that B. these
   C. this D. those
9. A. boring B. beautiful
   C. safe D. important
10. A. clean B. eat
    C. draw D. watch
11. A. to B. from
    C. of D. by
12. A. for example B. as well as
    C. as long as D. such as
13. A. shape B. size
    C. length D. color
14. A. puts B. takes
    C. brings D. buys
15. A. they B. theirs
    C. them D. their

Tuesday
[阅读理解 A]

Hao Lei: Practicing Buddhism and Reading Help Me Grow as an Actress

> 体裁：记叙文
> 题材：明星娱乐
> 正确率：＿＿＿/5
> 词数：190
> 难度：★★★☆☆
> 建议用时：6分钟
> 实际用时：＿＿＿
> 答案页码：118

Hao Lei is one of the most famous actresses in Chinese art films. Since she acted in *Seventeen no Cry* in 1997, Hao has been active on the stage and big screen for over 20 years.

She was invited to attend (出席) a masterclass, where veteran (经验丰富的人) actors and directors shared their experiences in filmmaking on Friday in Sanya, China's Hainan Province. The event was part of the third Hainan Island International Film Festival.

Hao said that the best way to learn acting is reading books in an interview with CGTN. "Today's young people don't like reading. Instead, they often ask questions like, 'how should I learn acting?' or 'where should I learn acting?' Well, it is quite easy, just read books!"

During the interview, Hao also told CGTN that years of practicing Buddhism (佛教) has helped her a lot.

"Learning Buddhism helps me become open-minded and tolerant (宽容的). When I was working on a role, I didn't have a perfect understanding. But now Buddhism helps me look upon work and life from a higher <u>perspective</u>," she said.

1. What does Hao Lei do?
   A. She is a doctor.
   B. She is a teacher.
   C. She is an actress.
   D. She is a director.
2. According to the second paragraph, who attended the masterclass?
   A. Young actors and directors.
   B. Experienced actors.
   C. Experienced directors.
   D. Both B and C.
3. What did Hao Lei think is the best way to learn acting?
   A. Practicing Buddhism.
   B. Reading books.
   C. Writing articles.
   D. Both A and B.
4. The underlined word "perspective" most probably means ＿＿＿.
   A. 希望　　B. 风景
   C. 角度　　D. 思维
5. Which of the following is true?
   A. Hao Lei acted in *Eighteen no Cry* in 1997.
   B. Hao Lei told CCTV the best way to learn acting is reading books.
   C. According to Hao Lei, today's young people like reading.
   D. Hao Lei thinks practicing Buddhism is helpful for her.

Wednesday
[阅读理解 B]

The Best Title Wanted

China's box office revenue (收益) in February reached 11.2 billion yuan ($1.73 billion) as of 3:40 pm on Wednesday, according to data from app Maoyan. It is a record-high number in terms of box office revenue for a single month in China, and also for a single month in a single market in the whole world.

Main contributors (贡献者) to the revenue include time-travel comedy (喜剧) *Hi, Mom*, which has pocketed 4.34 billion yuan, followed by action comedy *Detective Chinatown 3*, which has earned (赚得) 4.13 billion yuan, and fantasy thriller *A Writer's Odyssey*, taking in more than 780 million yuan. Other works, like animation (动画片) *Boonie Bears: The Wild Life*, *New Gods: Nezha Reborn* and comedy drama *Endgame*, have also each earned more than 300 million yuan in revenue.

This year, the total box office revenue for the seven-day Spring Festival holiday over Feb 11-17 stood at 7.8 billion yuan. Moreover, the revenue in 2021 was over 10 billion yuan on Feb 16, 230 days earlier than 2020, in which the revenue reached this number on Oct 3.

体裁：记叙文
题材：明星娱乐
正确率：_____ /5
词数：178
难度：★★★☆☆
建议用时：6分钟
实际用时：_____
答案页码：118

---

1. According to the passage, which film made the greatest contribution to the revenue in February?
   A. *A Writer's Odyssey*.
   B. *Hi, Mom*.
   C. *Boonie Bears: The Wild Life*.
   D. *New Gods: Nezha Reborn*.
2. *Endgame* has got _____.
   A. less than 300 million yuan
   B. more than 30 million yuan
   C. more than 300 million yuan
   D. less than 780 million yuan
3. According to the last paragraph, the revenue in Feb 2021 is _____ the revenue in Feb 2020.
   A. as much as   B. more than
   C. less than   D. the same as
4. According to the passage, which of the following is not true?
   A. China's box office revenue reached a record-high number in Feb.
   B. *Boonie Bears: The Wild Life* is an animation.
   C. *New Gods: Nezha Reborn* has got more than 780 million.
   D. This year, the total box office revenue for the seven-day Spring Festival holiday is quite high.
5. What's the best title for the passage?
   A. China's Box Office Revenue Reached a Record-High Number in Feb
   B. The Total Box Office Revenue for the Seven-Day Spring Festival Holiday
   C. *A Writer's Odyssey* Has Got over 300 Million Yuan in Revenue
   D. Main Contributors to the Box Office Revenue

Thursday
[阅读理解 C]

Jay Chou Returns to Cinema with His Fascination for Racing Cars

Jay Chou's latest film will be shown across the theaters in China on Friday. It's his first time to act with his wife, Hannah Quinlivan.

The film's English title is *Nezha*. Interestingly, the film itself has nothing to do with the ancient figure Nezha. Centering on three young racers, the story sets in contemporary (当代的) China and follows their growth in facing up to difficulties and pursuing (追求) honor on the tracks.

Directed by Chen Yi-xian, the film also stars Tsao Yu-ning, Van Fan, and Alan Kuo. Chou and pop idol Wang Junkai also show up in the film.

It's reported that with a budget (预算) up to more than 400 million yuan ($61.8 million), the film used some expensive racing cars for the action scenes, accounting for about 80 percent of the whole content.

As a big fan of car racing, Chou starred in famous director Andrew Lau's popular street racing film, *Initial D*, which was Hong Kong's 2005 box office champion (冠军).

体裁：记叙文
题材：明星娱乐
正确率：_____/5
词数：174
难度：★★★★☆
建议用时：7 分钟
实际用时：_____
答案页码：119

---

1. The English title of Jay Chou's latest film is _____.
   A. *Racers*   B. *Nezha*
   C. *Initial D*   D. *Racing*
2. The underlined phrase "has nothing to do with" most probably means _____.
   A. 与……无关
   B. 不妨碍……
   C. 对……没有影响
   D. 对……不重要
3. How many young racers does the film center on?
   A. Three.   B. Four.
   C. Five.   D. Six.
4. According to the passage, who is the director of the film *Nezha*?
   A. Tsao Yu-ning.
   B. Jay Chou.
   C. Alan Kuo.
   D. Chen Yi-xian.
5. What can we know from the passage?
   A. The three young racers in the film pursue honor easily.
   B. It costs much money to make the film *Nezha*.
   C. Jay Chou didn't act in *Initial D*.
   D. There is a role named Nezha in the film.

Friday
[任务型阅读 D]

TV Series Follows Rock'em, Sock'em Love Story

Liu Ning: Hi, Mike. Do you know the TV series *Dt. Appledog's Time* running on online platform（平台）iQiyi?

Mike: __1__ It's adapted（改编）from an online novel. My idol Hu Yitian plays the leading role in it.

Liu Ning: __2__

Mike: It depicts（描述）the pursuit of dreams and the love story of Wu Bai and Ai Qing, two robot fighting competitors（对手）. And it's said that professional companies in the robot fighting industry were invited to build the competition venue（场地）, design competition rules and guide the actors and actresses on how to operate in the competitions.

Liu Ning: Wow! __3__ I can't wait to watch it. __4__

Mike: Fang Ying.

Liu Ning: __5__

Mike: According to her, "Wu and Ai's relationship development is closely related to their career（职业）. We want to show both the beautiful love and their desire to pursue their dreams in the series."

体裁：——
题材：明星娱乐
正确率：____ /5
词数：182
难度：★★★☆☆
建议用时：6 分钟
实际用时：____
答案页码：120

阅读对话，从每题A、B、C、D四个选项中，选出一个最佳答案完成对话。

1. A. Yes, of course.
   B. No, I did.
   C. Yes, it is.
   D. No, they aren't.
2. A. When will the TV series be shown?
   B. Who will act in the TV series?
   C. How was the TV series made?
   D. What is the TV series about?
3. A. I feel so bad!
   B. It sounds interesting!
   C. It looks so nice!
   D. It tastes so delicious!
4. A. What can we learn from the TV series?
   B. How do you think the TV?
   C. Who is the general producer of the TV series?
   D. Where can we watch the TV series?
5. A. What did she say about the TV series?
   B. How about her?
   C. How much money did she spend making the series?
   D. Where did she make the TV series?

Saturday
[短文填空]

Biggie's Mom, Voletta Wallace, Shares how Country Music and Reggae Influenced His Rap Career

"When Biggie was a little boy and was growing up, I always had the radio on and tuned in to the country music station," Ms. Wallace says.

Fans learn more about the two's shared love of country music (1)_____ Ms. Wallace's memories (回忆). And she believes the genre (类型) played a role in shaping her son's love of storytelling.

"When Biggie was (2)_____, he was fascinated (迷住) by my brothers Dave and Lou because they are musicians. I remember Lou trying to teach him how to (3)_____ guitar while Dave would be the singer. When they were together, they were always playing their reggae (雷盖) music."

"When Biggie was young, he was (4)_____. He would get mad if his friends told anyone he knew how to rap," says Butler, Biggie's longtime friend. "We grew up together, so it was hard to look at him and view him like the rappers of our (5)_____."

阅读短文，从方框中选择合适的单词填空，使短文通顺，意思完整。

time
through
play
shy
little

Sunday
[拓展阅读]

Temple of Heaven Built from 22,000 Matchsticks

> 体裁：记叙文　　题材：传统文化　　词数：186
> 难度：★★★★☆　建议用时：7分钟　实际用时：_____

　　Ahmed Hassan is 63 years old. He liked the design（设计）and architecture（建筑风格）of China's Temple of Heaven very much, so he decided to build a model of it with matchsticks.

　　In his free time, Hassan spent more than two months working on the Temple of Heaven. Finally, he used about 22,000 matchsticks to finish the whole model. Just as the original（原来的）building is completely wooden with no nails（钉子）, he used only matchsticks, white glue and a cutter blade（刀片）to build the model of the temple. The model is about 50 centimeters（厘米）high, 1 meter long and 1 meter wide.

　　"The only thing missing now is writing the name of the temple in Chinese. I am still practicing writing the Chinese letters so that they would look proper on the sign of the temple model," Hassan points out, adding that the Chinese letters are very difficult for him to write.

　　He says building a matchstick model of the Temple of Heaven wasn't an easy job, because it was his first time to carry out a model of a landmark（地标）from Asia.

Week Six 饮食购物、疾病健康

Monday
[完形填空]

体裁：记叙文
题材：疾病健康
正确率：_____ /10
词数：155
难度：★★★☆☆
建议用时：10 分钟
实际用时：_____
答案页码：122

The Hidden Cost of COVID-19

It has been a year since Zhang Xiangyang, a doctor in Wuhan, Hubei Province, tested positive (阳性的) for COVID-19. She returned to work after becoming well, __1__ Zhang has found that "back to normal psychologically (心理上地)" is not __2__.

"People kept a distance (距离) when __3__ to me. I understood their worries, but these made me uncomfortable," she says. __4__ telling anyone, Zhang pretended (假装) that __5__ was OK and kept herself __6__ with her patients.

Zhang later telephoned a psychologist about the case, and when the psychologist asked __7__ she felt, she burst into tears. "Having been through all the fears and difficulties since the beginning, it was the first __8__ I felt that someone cared about me," Zhang says.

According to the Healthy China 2030 plan, China will __9__ to better people's health psychologically, as the country aims to __10__ the number of treatments of depression (抑郁症) by 80 percent by 2030.

1. A. but B. before C. and D. when
2. A. hard B. easy C. cool D. nervous
3. A. laughing B. smiling C. talking D. closing
4. A. For B. By C. On D. Without
5. A. anything B. everything C. something D. nothing
6. A. sad B. happy C. busy D. mad
7. A. how B. when C. why D. where
8. A. thing B. experience C. feeling D. time
9. A. make B. let C. try D. offer
10. A. draw B. increase C. back D. pull

Tuesday
[阅读理解 A]

COVID-19 Exposes Hearing Problems

The WHO says one in ten people is to suffer（遭受）from hearing loss（丧失）by 2050.

But in the United States, around 20 percent of America's adult is already experiencing some level of hearing loss and the coronavirus pandemic（新冠疫情）has made the problem much harder.

Masks take away visual cues（视觉线索）and change and soften（弱化）the speech signal（信号）.

We might use mouth movements and body language to understand what somebody is saying or help us fill in the blanks when we miss some information.

About 20 percent of American adults aged from 20 to 69 have some trouble with hearing and almost 28.8 million could benefit from the use of hearing aids（助听器）.

There are some signs of hearing loss. First, turn up the sound of the television, radio, or stereo and others say that it is too loud. Second, have difficulty in understanding people speaking to you and ask people to repeat themselves. Third, cannot hear the door bell. Fourth, people tell you that you speak too loudly.

体裁：说明文
题材：疾病健康
正确率：_____/5
词数：173
难度：★★★☆☆
建议用时：6分钟
实际用时：_____
答案页码：122

阅读短文，判断正（A）误（B）。

1. There will be 10% of the population having hearing problems by 2050.
2. About half of American people are suffering from hearing loss.
3. About 20% of American adults aged from 20 to 59 have to use hearing aids.
4. People usually turn up the TV when they have hearing problems.
5. When you cannot hear the door bell, it is not a big problem.

Wednesday
[阅读理解 B]

The Best Title Wanted

That is the question people are asking as governments race to vaccinate (给……接种疫苗) people around the world to stop the spread of COVID-19.

Herd immunity (群体免疫) is when a large number of people in a community will either have recovered from infection (感染) or been vaccinated. Herd immunity does not mean everyone is protected from the virus (病毒). It means that the coronavirus can no longer spread easily, helping to protect those who are at risk.

Once people are sick or receive the vaccine, they start to develop antibodies (抗体). Experts think the number of people with antibodies needs to reach 70 percent or more for herd immunity. However, the virus is always changing and developing into new kinds.

Does herd immunity need to be global? Yes, it is important to reach herd immunity around the world. But some parts of the world will struggle with the coronavirus longer than in others.

体裁：说明文
题材：疾病健康
正确率：_____ /5
词数：147
难度：★★★☆☆
建议用时：6分钟
实际用时：_____
答案页码：123

---

1. What does herd immunity mean?
   A. Few people have been vaccinated.
   B. Many people have been vaccinated.
   C. All the people have recovered or been vaccinated.
   D. A lot of people have recovered or been vaccinated.

2. People have antibodies when they _____.
   A. are sick
   B. receive the vaccine
   C. reach herd immunity
   D. fall ill or are vaccinated

3. In Paragraph 3, the number of people who have antibodies should reach at least _____ for herd immunity.
   A. 50%   B. 70%
   C. 90%   D. 100%

4. What can we infer from the passage?
   A. Herd immunity will not be global.
   B. Herd immunity will soon be global.
   C. Herd immunity might soon be reached in some countries.
   D. Herd immunity will never be reached in the whole world.

5. What is the best title of this passage?
   A. Herd Immunity
   B. What Is Herd Immunity?
   C. Herd Immunity Is Possible
   D. How Will We Know when We Reach Herd Immunity?

Thursday
[阅读理解 C]

Foods, Tastes Change Because of the Coronavirus Crisis

The coronavirus (冠状病毒) has influenced almost every part of daily human life—including what we eat.

Nearly a year into social distancing (社交距离), many people are enjoying food long forgotten or once rejected (拒绝) for taste, feel or smell. Some have added healthy food to their diets to make the body stronger. Home cooking activity is up everywhere for restaurants and other food shops are closed. People are increasingly trying new foods in their own kitchens.

"Health became number one for many people last year," Sharova said. She added that being at home caused many people to make new foods. Thirty-year-old Alicia Harper has discovered fermented (已发酵的) foods. She is a nutritionist (营养学家) in New York City. She did not like the strong tastes and smells of fermented foods at first.

Some experts think that changes in the way we eat also come from having more time to think about how food comes to our tables. In hard times like this, diners are looking for authentic (真正的), homemade food.

1. The coronavirus has influenced the way we _____ in this passage.
   A. dress   B. eat
   C. drink   D. live
2. Before the coronavirus crisis, where could people enjoy food?
   A. At home.
   B. At restaurants.
   C. At food shops.
   D. All of the above.
3. What kind of food do people like to eat now?
   A. Healthy food.
   B. Fermented food.
   C. Homemade food.
   D. Food from restaurants and food shops.
4. What can we infer from this passage?
   A. People will not eat food from restaurants any more.
   B. People will always eat homemade food from now on.
   C. Fermented food will be the most popular food.
   D. People have changed some of their eating habits during the coronavirus crisis.
5. This passage is probably about a topic of _____.
   A. business life
   B. healthy lifestyle
   C. culture exchange
   D. environmental protecting

Friday
[任务型阅读 D]

How Different Places Start the Day

体裁：说明文
题材：饮食购物
正确率：_____ /5
词数：158
难度：★★★☆☆
建议用时：6 分钟
实际用时：_____
答案页码：124

When it comes to breakfast foods around the world, there are as many ways to enjoy the first meal of the day as there are to say "good morning."

On weekdays, the Swiss (瑞士人) have quick breakfasts such as the traditional oats with fruit and nuts. But on weekends, it's time for egg bread.

Japanese breakfasts are perfect food. In fact, much of what you can eat for breakfast in Japan wouldn't be out of place at any other meal of the day. A traditional Japanese dish? Fish, miso (味噌) soup, and rice are all represented.

In Germany, sausage (香肠) and other meats are the traditional German breakfast. Italians are almost too busy for breakfast. In coffee bars, guests take their espresso (意式浓咖啡) at the beginning of the day. On weekdays, breakfasts are simpler in Russia: Caviar (鱼子酱) is spread across black bread. Most importantly, a pot of black tea is a must on every breakfast table.

阅读短文，回答下面 1~5 小题。

1. How many countries are mentioned in this passage?
_____
_____

2. What are represented in a traditional Japanese dish?
_____
_____

3. What will Italians eat for breakfast when they are too busy?
_____
_____

4. Are breakfasts simpler in Russia on weekdays?
_____
_____

5. What do you usually eat for breakfast?
_____
_____

Saturday
[短文填空]

Ways to Reduce Reluctance to Take COVID Vaccines

体裁：说明文
题材：疾病健康
正确率：＿＿＿／5
词数：195
难度：★★★☆☆
建议用时：6分钟
实际用时：＿＿＿
答案页码：125

Like many people around the world, I am waiting for a COVID vaccine（疫苗）. __1__ My sister says she doesn't trust it. "I avoid all vaccines," she told me. She is not alone. It suggested that about 30 percent of Americans doubt about COVID vaccinations（接种疫苗）. __2__

First, it's not necessary to change their minds. Second, some groups, such as black people, have strong historical reasons to doubt it. Third, low levels of vaccination, especially in low-income communities, often show real problems. Offering more hours and having more people know that there is no cost are two ways to improve the number.

__3__ Fifth, overcome（克服）the human habit to procrastinate（拖延）. Sixth, for forgetful types, simple reminders（提醒）—__4__—can be useful. A 2019 study showed that daily reminders to complete drug treatment greatly increased good results. "You'd think that would be bad, but it was useful," Milkman says. So when it comes time for that second COVID vaccine dose（剂量）, she suggests, __5__

阅读短文，从下列选项中选出能填入空白处的最佳选项，选项中有一项为多余选项。

A. "Let's find a different way."
B. "Let's trouble people."
C. by text or voice message
D. But not everyone wants it.
E. Here are six key ideas to solve the problem:
F. Fourth, talk about how popular the vaccine is.

Sunday
[拓展阅读]

Chinese-Western Breakfast Sets Are Popular Among Locals

体裁：说明文　　题材：传统文化　　词数：156
难度：★★★☆☆　　建议用时：6分钟　　实际用时：_____

　　For many Chinese people, a satisfying breakfast is the one that includes either hot porridge（粥）or steamed stuffed buns（包子）. Cold sandwiches, which are usually popular with Westerners, are one of the last choices on their minds.

　　But that is not to say that Chinese people, especially those in a city like Shanghai, would avoid everything considered Western for breakfast. For example, coffee, which has become more and more popular in China, is one beverage（饮料）that many cannot do without today.

　　To meet this growing demand for breakfast sets that combine（结合）elements from the East and the West, food companies（公司）have some new styles. One example is Shanghai Qiao Coffee. Apart from its traditional food, the store also sells various types of coffee. Western food companies, too, have been offering Chinese breakfasts. Pizza Hut（必胜客）now offers hot dry noodles（热干面）, or *re gan mian*, while KFC and McDonalds have a rice set meal and a Shaanxi-style bun.

Week Seven 体育运动

Monday
[完形填空]

体裁：记叙文
题材：体育运动
正确率：_____/10
词数：195
难度：★★★☆☆
建议用时：10 分钟
实际用时：_____
答案页码：127

Swimmers Enjoy Cool Jumps

An open-air swimming pool was very popular this winter. It was usually open from May to September, __1__ this year it stayed open in the autumn and winter too.

__2__ the lockdown（封锁）on January, outdoor pools were allowed to remain open. Over Christmas and New Year, water playground had to offer extra places to meet swimmers' need.

Cold-water swimming has __3__ in popularity in the UK over the past few years. In __4__ areas, such as the river Wharfe in Yorkshire, this new trend has encouraged environmental groups to __5__ that the water is cleared of pollution and clean enough for bathers.

Some people make it a regular practice; __6__ just enjoy a cool jump __7__ Christmas Day, Boxing Day or New Year's Day. Every year around the UK, people are photographed __8__ into icy water, often in beautiful dress.

The Outdoor Swimming Society（户外游泳协会）advises people to get in the water __9__, so as not to shock the body. Likewise（同样地）, they recommend（建议）warming up gradually（逐渐地）. Paul Davies, a scientist who studies the __10__, said the forecast indicates "the likelihood of the cold weather continuing through January".

1. A. but   B. and
   C. or   D. for
2. A. After   B. Since
   C. Before   D. When
3. A. fallen   B. grown
   C. invented   D. minded
4. A. these   B. those
   C. some   D. all
5. A. make up   B. make sure
   C. make from   D. make out
6. A. other   B. another
   C. the other   D. others
7. A. in   B. on
   C. at   D. during
8. A. looking   B. climbing
   C. jumping   D. moving
9. A. happily   B. quickly
   C. suddenly   D. slowly
10. A. weather   B. water
    C. pool   D. river

Tuesday
[阅读理解 A]

Man Climbs Skyscraper in Wheelchair

体裁：记叙文
题材：体育运动
正确率：_____/5
词数：204
难度：★★★☆☆
建议用时：6 分钟
实际用时：_____
答案页码：128

Last Saturday, Lai Chi-wai used a rope system (系统) to pull himself up over 250 meters along the side of a skyscraper (摩天大楼). Mr. Lai, who can't move his legs, was tied into his wheelchair as he climbed.

Before 2011, Mr. Lai was a world-famous rock climber. But ten years ago, Mr. Lai got injured in a car accident. Since then, he has needed to use a wheelchair to get around. But Mr. Lai couldn't stop his love for climbing. He found a way to tie his wheelchair to a rope system to climb again.

That day, the weather was good in the morning. But by early afternoon, strong winds had come up. After 7.5 hours of climbing, the wind was stronger than ever. Still, Mr. Lai went on to pull himself up. Finally, after reaching a height of about 250 meters, the wind became too strong, and Mr. Lai had to give up.

But he set a new record. He also raised over $700,000 for a charity (慈善团体) that is working to help others who have been paralyzed (瘫痪的). "If disabled people can bring opportunity, hope and light, they don't have to be viewed as weak," said Mr. Lai.

1. Lai Chi-wai was _____ 10 years ago.
   A. a mountain climber
   B. a rock climber
   C. a racing driver
   D. a wheelchair seller
2. Why did Mr. Lai start to climb again?
   A. Because he needed to earn money.
   B. Because he wanted to raise money for the disables.
   C. Because he couldn't give up his love for climbing.
   D. Because he wanted to exercise through climbing.
3. What can we know about Mr. Lai from the passage?
   A. He felt painful after the car accident.
   B. He is a very strong person.
   C. His families strongly support his work.
   D. He felt it easy to climb along the side of the skyscraper.
4. The underlined word "they" in the last paragraph most probably refers to _____.
   A. rock climbers
   B. ordinary people
   C. charity groups
   D. the disabled
5. What message did Mr. Lai's success send?
   A. The disabled are not necessarily weak.
   B. He is good for raising money for a charity.
   C. He can climb in a way just like before.
   D. Everyone can succeed in climbing skyscraper.

Wednesday
[阅读理解 B]

The Best Title Wanted

体裁：记叙文
题材：体育运动
正确率：_____/5
词数：198
难度：★★★☆☆
建议用时：6分钟
实际用时：_____
答案页码：128

10 climbers from Nepal have successfully reached the top of K2 in this winter and set a world record.

K2 is the world's second-highest mountain. It is viewed as more difficult to climb than the world's tallest mountain. On one famous passage (通道) called "the bottleneck (瓶颈)", climbers are in danger of being hit by ice blocks. K2 was named "the Savage (荒凉的) Mountain" by US climber George Bell, who tried and failed to climb it in 1953.

This winter, 60 climbers raced to be the first to reach its top in winter. However, it looked as if the climbers would have to give up after a strong storm broke some tents and important tools.

Nepalese climber Purja formed a new team, including nine Nepalese Sherpas. Sherpas live in the Himalayan mountain range and are known for their mountaineering (登山) skills. On 16 January, they reached the top, singing the Nepalese national anthem (国歌). It was a joint record—no single person was being named the first climber to get to the summit. Purja said, "THE IMPOSSIBLE IS MADE POSSIBLE! History made for mankind, history made for Nepal!"

1. The ten climbers who succeeded in climbing the K2 are from _____.
   A. China   B. Pakistan
   C. Nepal   D. America
2. What can we know from the passage?
   A. Many climbers were hit by the huge ice blocks.
   B. The process of climbing was smooth.
   C. Purja was the first to reach the top of K2.
   D. Purja and his teammates won a great honor for their country.
3. Why did Purja choose nine Sherpas to form the new team?
   A. Because they were good at climbing.
   B. Because they were from Nepal.
   C. Because they had better climbing equipment.
   D. Because they were Purja's friends.
4. The underlined word "summit" most probably means _____ in Chinese.
   A. 终点   B. 顶峰
   C. 极限   D. 成功
5. The best title of this passage probably is _____.
   A. Climbing K2 Is Difficult
   B. Climbers Make History on K2
   C. Nepal Climbers Are Great
   D. 60 Climbers Compete on K2

Thursday
[阅读理解 C]

Breaking the Tradition

With exciting moves, fantastic music and competitors (竞争者) who use cool names, breaking (霹雳舞) is a sport like no other. Breaking was recently announced as one of the Olympics sports for the first time when the Games will be held in Paris, France, in 2024.

In breaking, dancers are known as B-girls and B-boys. The UK woman champion is 14-year-old B-Girl Terra from Wolverhampton, England. "I'm really excited that breaking will be at the Olympics. I really want to win the gold medal," B-Girl Terra said. One YouTube video of her breaking has nearly 22 million views. Terra is known for the move that she spins (旋转) on her head. "Head-spinning is not scary for me," she says. "It's really fun and I can do it for a long time."

In a breaking competition, two dancers will take turns to perform their routine (一套动作) on a stage. It is yet not known how the 2024 Olympic games will be arranged. It is likely there will be separate (单独的；分开的) men and women competitions, and possibly mixed-doubles games with both men and women.

体裁：记叙文
题材：体育运动
正确率：_____ /5
词数：188
难度：★★★☆☆
建议用时：6 分钟
实际用时：_____
答案页码：129

阅读短文，判断正（A）误（B）。

1. Breaking is different from other sports.
2. B-girl Terra has won a gold medal in Olympics.
3. Terra has 22 million followers on YouTube.
4. Two dancers compete with each other in a breaking competition.
5. It has announced that there will be separate men and women competitions.

Friday
[任务型阅读 D]

Should People Be Allowed to Walk Around?

The right to walk around is an old tradition (传统) in countries including Norway and Sweden. __1__.

In Scotland, a law allowed people to walk freely wherever they want as long as (只要) they obey the Outdoor Access Code (户外活动准则). __2__.

More than 100 actors, writers and artists recently signed a letter to Prime Minister Boris Johnson and asked him to expand (扩大) the areas where the public could walk freely.

In 2000, a law was passed, which made it legal (合法的) to walk around 8% of England's countryside. __3__. Some people say this isn't good. Others point out there are businesses that need to keep the land private.

__4__: Walking out and about in the countryside is good for people's mental and body health.

Reason why people should not be allowed to walk around: Fenced land is a livelihood (生计) for many people. __5__.

阅读短文，从下列选项中选出能填入文中空白处的最佳选项，选项中有两项为多余选项。

A. The rest 92% was owned by businesses, the Government, private estates and very rich individuals

B. Some say people have reasons to walk around freely

C. Reason why people should be allowed to walk around

D. However, in England, people were only allowed to walk freely in around 8% of the open countryside

E. This tradition allows people to walk around freely

F. Much land is opened freely to the public

G. The right to walk around would damage their businesses

Saturday
[短文填空]

No National Anthem at Sports Events

(1)_____(play) the anthem at sporting games has become an empty gesture of patriotism (爱国主义). The NBA's Dallas Mavericks (达拉斯小牛队) (2)_____(quiet) began skipping (跳过) this part. 13 games had passed before anyone (3)_____(notice).

The Mavericks had canceled the national anthem. It made them (4)_____ first team to do this. However, the National Basketball Association said later every team must play the song.

But playing the anthem shouldn't be a pregame ritual (赛前仪式) in American sports. Many people are (5)_____ (deep) uncomfortable with what the national anthem has been (6)_____(use) to harm black and brown Americans.

When people are paying attention to the forms of racial injustice (种族不平等) again, the NBA's (7)_____ (decide) to force teams into playing the national anthem just doesn't seem right. It will encourage people who insist upon an exclusive (排外的) form of patriotism. In a direct (8)_____(respond) to the Mavericks, Governor Dan Patrick announced (宣布) he would speed up an act which would require the national anthem to be played at all (9)_____(game) that receive public funding.

However, enforced (强制性的) patriotism doesn't give Americans reason for pride; it only (10)_____(stress) the country's failures.

Sunday
[拓展阅读]

Lantern Festival: A Romantic Celebration in China

体裁：说明文　　题材：传统文化　　词数：172
难度：★★☆☆☆　　建议用时：5分钟　　实际用时：_____

The Lantern Festival, a traditional Chinese festival, is celebrated on the 15th day of the first lunar (农历的) month. It falls on Friday this year.

It is a continuation (延续；继续) of celebrating the Spring Festival. The day leads to the first full moon night of the year, and is also the night when the earth returns to spring. It is also a romantic (浪漫的) festival in ancient China, which provides an opportunity for unmarried (未婚的) men and women to meet.

In ancient times, young women, especially daughters of rich and famous families, hardly stepped out their houses. But during the Lantern Festival, it was a tradition that all people, including those young women, came out for lantern shows.

Watching lanterns at night was just an opportunity for young women to find a man whose moral character and appearance (外貌) attracted them. And guessing the answers to lantern riddles gave young people a chance to chat with each other and know more about each other. For thousands of years, there have been lots of love stories originating (发生) during the Lantern Festival.

Week Eight 自然社会、社会现象

Monday
[完形填空]

体裁：说明文
题材：自然社会
正确率：_____/10
词数：176
难度：★★★★☆
建议用时：12 分钟
实际用时：_____
答案页码：132

You're Stroking Your Cat Totally Wrong

Lots of cats probably don't want to be stroked（抚摸）. They probably just bear it __1__ some benefits（好处）, like the food and attention you give them. When it comes to petting, it's best to remember that cats aren't social and __2__ touch.

If you doubt your cat only bears your petting to __3__ another bite（一口）of dinner, you're probably right. People often think cats like being stroked, __4__ research suggests that this can actually produce the most negative responses（反应）from __5__.

So, what subtle（细微的）signs of being __6__ should you look out for? When annoyed（惹恼）, cats might suddenly turn their head towards our hands. They might also simply freeze or __7__ interaction（互动）actively. __8__ they're doing this, they're going to have ears that are not pointing directly forward. A moving tail close to the ground is also usually a __9__ sign.

I have __10__ many cats being touched, and they had these very subtle signs quite often, but people usually didn't notice them.

1. A. for   B. to
   C. in   D. with
2. A. need   B. expect
   C. dislike   D. enjoy
3. A. give   B. make
   C. steal   D. get
4. A. and   B. or
   C. but   D. so
5. A. people   B. cats
   C. researchers D. animals
6. A. careful   B. excited
   C. angry   D. happy
7. A. start   B. stop
   C. accept   D. like
8. A. How   B. Why
   C. When   D. Where
9. A. negative   B. encouraging
   C. welcome   D. positive
10. A. gotten   B. imagined
    C. guessed   D. watched

Tuesday
[阅读理解 A]

The 1970s Black Utopian City Became a Modern Ghost Town

Visit Soul City, North Carolina, today, and you won't find much: an abandoned (废弃的) health-care clinic (诊所); a pool and an entertainment center with a NO ENTRY sign; a 1970s building area with streets that are broken; and an industrial (工业的) plant that has been changed into a prison.

When Floyd McKissick arrived here in 1969, he wanted to transform this old slave plantation (种植园) into a new city. McKissick wished the city would bring money and opportunity and change the leaving trend of black people. He planned that by the year 2000, it would have 24,000 jobs and a population of 50,000.

However, development stopped 10 years later, and there were just 135 jobs and 124 full-time residents. In the fourty years since, Soul City has been gradually forgotten, becoming a modern-day ghost town. Most people have never heard of it.

The history of Soul City is worth remembering. McKissick's unrealized dream encourages the fight for racial equality (种族平等) and against the many social, political and economic forces that continue to stand in the way.

体裁：记叙文
题材：社会现象
正确率：_____/5
词数：173
难度：★★★☆☆
建议用时：6 分钟
实际用时：_____
答案页码：133

---

1. The old industrial plant in the Soul City has been changed into _____.
   A. a health-care clinic
   B. a prison
   C. an entertainment center
   D. a building area

2. The underlined word "transform" in Paragraph 2 means _____ in Chinese.
   A. 转变   B. 移动
   C. 交换   D. 运输

3. McKissick wanted to _____.
   a. make a lot of money in Soul City
   b. improve black people's social status (社会地位) in Soul City
   c. bring money and opportunity to Soul City
   d. stop black people from leaving Soul City
   A. ab   B. ad
   C. bc   D. cd

4. About _____ years since its development stopped, Soul City has been gradually forgotten by people.
   A. 10   B. 40
   C. 50   D. 30

5. What can we infer from the passage?
   A. McKissick created many job opportunities in Soul City.
   B. Soul City is well-known in the US.
   C. McKissick's dream is of no influence at all.
   D. Americans should be encouraged by McKissick.

Wednesday
[阅读理解 B]

Climate-Caused Disasters Killed 475,000 People over 20 Years

Nearly a half-million people died over the past 20 years from climate disasters (气候灾难). Most of them are from the world's poorest countries.

Rich countries like the U.S. and many European countries face serious climate risk, but they usually have the ability to deal with it. Average (普通的) developed countries are also influenced, and they have to act quickly to make the influence smaller. However, developing countries suffer (遭受) most from climate disasters.

According to a 2021 report, there were about 11,000 climate disasters worldwide between 2000 and 2019. This report didn't include all the data (数据) of the U.S. These disasters <u>claimed</u> about 475,000 lives and caused a $2.5 trillion loss (亏损). In a 2020 report, the United States ranked 27th among all countries for climate disaster influences between 1999 and 2018. If the whole U.S. data had been included in the 2021 report, the losses would have been about $1 trillion higher.

It's said that such disasters warned the United States. That's because governments can be shaken by natural disasters, which often leads to greater social problems.

体裁：记叙文
题材：自然社会
正确率：_____/5
词数：186
难度：★★★☆☆
建议用时：6 分钟
实际用时：_____
答案页码：133

1. A huge number of victims (受害者) of the climate disasters are from _____.
   A. the poorest countries
   B. developing countries
   C. developed countries
   D. rich countries

2. According to the degree of climate disasters' influence, which order is correct?
   a. developing countries
   b. very wealthy countries like the U.S.
   c. average developed countries
   A. abc   B. cab
   C. bac   D. acb

3. What does the underlined word "claimed" in Paragraph 3 probably mean?
   A. 声称   B. 认领
   C. 夺走   D. 获得

4. How much money would probably be lost if the whole U.S. data had been included in the 2021 report?
   A. $2.5 trillion.   B. $1 trillion.
   C. $3.5 trillion.   D. $1.5 trillion.

5. What can we know from the last paragraph?
   A. The United States is facing social problems.
   B. Climate disasters might result in social problems.
   C. To avoid climate disasters is very important for a country.
   D. Climate disasters have caused great social problems in Europe.

Thursday
[阅读理解 C]

The Best Title Wanted

The UK Safer Internet Centre (UKSIC) did a new research. It shows that more than 70% of young people in the UK think the Government and social media companies should do more to deal with false (不真实的) information online.

Their survey found 48% were seeing false information online every day. More than one in ten said they were seeing it at least six times a day. Another study found 46% of young people had believed false information online in the past year.

During the pandemic (流行病), the Internet has become more important than ever for young people. Because of lockdowns (封锁), many students have to learn online because schools are closed.

UKSIC worked with young people to create a Young People's Charter. The charter is made up of four points: teach safer Internet use; protect us online; hold platforms to account; and let us shape the Internet.

Each of these points includes ideas for what the Government and social media companies could do to improve the Internet. <u>These</u> include making safe Internet use become part of the school curriculum (课程). The charter also says young people should know more about how the Internet is managed.

体裁：记叙文
题材：社会现象
正确率：_____ /5
词数：192
难度：★★★☆☆
建议用时：6 分钟
实际用时：_____
答案页码：134

---

1. Many young people in the UK think _____ should do more to deal with the fake (假的) information online.
   A. the Government
   B. social media companies
   C. everyone
   D. both A and B

2. Which of the following is not correct about Paragraph 2?
   A. There are too much false information online.
   B. Over half of the young people saw false information every day.
   C. Nearly half of the young people had believed false information online.
   D. False information online has great influence on young people.

3. Why was the Internet more important in 2020 than ever?
   A. Because many students had to use the Internet to study.
   B. Because there was more information on the Internet than ever.
   C. Because young people were more interested in using the Internet.
   D. Because the Internet was more interesting.

4. What does "These" in the last paragraph probably mean?
   A. Four points in the Young People's Charter.
   B. Government and social media companies' ideas.
   C. The UKSIC and young people's ideas.
   D. The Young People's Charter.

5. The best title of this passage probably is _____.
   A. The False Information Online
   B. UK Youth Want Safer Internet
   C. UKSIC Makes Internet Safer
   D. False Information Online Influences UK Youth

Friday
[任务型阅读 D]

Backpacks for Snowy Owl

In the Arctic (北极), when snowy owls (猫头鹰) fly south for the winter, people aren't sure where they go or what they do. Project Snowstorm is trying to solve these mysteries.

The program uses GPS tracking devices (全球定位系统追踪设备) to follow snowy owls. But where do you put a tiny tracker on a big bird? In a tiny backpack, of course.

First, scientists use a harmless net trap to catch a snowy owl. Then they put a tiny backpack on the bird. This backpack won't influence its ability to fly. The solar-powered tracker transmits (传送) the bird's location (位置) back to scientists.

So far, scientists have discovered many snowy owls to stay by openings (洞；缺口) in the frozen Great Lakes to hunt waterbirds such as ducks and geese.

The tracking data also shows that snowy owls in some areas are making lots of short flights (飞行). A co-founder (联合发起人) of Project Snowstorm thinks that is because the birds have to fly away from curious people in populous (人口稠密的) areas. "Humans might love snowy owls too much," he says. "If you're lucky enough to see one, give it some space."

体裁：记叙文
题材：自然社会
正确率：_____/5
词数：192
难度：★★★☆☆
建议用时：6 分钟
实际用时：_____
答案页码：135

阅读短文，回答下面 1~5 小题。

1. Why did scientists start Project Snowstorm?
_____

2. What are the three steps to track a snowy owl?
_____

3. Where do the owls stay by to hunt food?
_____

4. According to the co-founder, what is the reason for snowy owls' short travel in some areas?
_____

5. What does the co-founder suggest us to do?
_____

Saturday
[短文填空]

Clever Dogs Learn like Children

According to a recent study, the cleverest dogs (1)_____(be) able to learn the name of a new toy after only (2)_____(hear) it four times while playing with their owners.

Researchers (3)_____(choose) two clever dogs for a series of tests. For the first test, the dogs (4)_____(give) seven objects they knew the names of and one new object with a new name. When researchers used the new name, the dogs were able (5)_____(fetch) the new object. However, when more than one new item was given, the dogs often (6)_____(get) confused (困惑的). So the dogs were only able to identify (识别；辨别) the new object by (7)_____(pick) it from the ones they already had known.

However, it (8)_____(seem) only the smartest dogs could do it. The researchers tried the same experiment with 20 family dogs, and none of them can (9)_____(learn) the names.

"Such rapid (快速的) (10)_____(learn) seems to be similar to the way human children learn their vocabulary, at around two to three years of age," said one of the starters of the study.

体裁：记叙文
题材：自然社会
正确率：_____/10
词数：172
难度：★★★☆☆
建议用时：10分钟
实际用时：_____
答案页码：135

阅读短文，用括号内所给单词的适当形式填空，使短文通顺，意思完整。

(1)_____
(2)_____
(3)_____
(4)_____
(5)_____
(6)_____
(7)_____
(8)_____
(9)_____
(10)_____

Sunday
[拓展阅读]

The Lunar New Year Begins

| 体裁：说明文 | 题材：传统文化 | 词数：196 |
| 难度：★★★☆☆ | 建议用时：6分钟 | 实际用时：_____ |

This year, the Lunar New Year was on 12 February. It is celebrated by around 1.5 billion people across the world, especially in some Asian countries including China, the Republic of Korea, Thailand and Vietnam.

How is Lunar New Year celebrated?

Lunar New Year is different in different countries, but celebrations usually include familiy gatherings（聚会）. Schools and businesses close for a few days when the celebrations start. Traditional foods like dumplings and rice cakes are thought to bring happiness and wealth. Parents and grandparents give children money in red-envelopes（红包）. There are also lion dances and dragon dances（舞狮舞龙）. In China, the Lantern Festival marks the end of Chinese New Year.

How is the date for Lunar New Year decided?

In the UK, Europe and North America, we follow the Gregorian calendar（公历）, which is based（根据）on the Sun's movements（移动）. This means that every year we celebrate New Year on the same day—1 January. However, the traditional Chinese calendar is based on the Moon's movements. The date for Chinese New Year is decided through the traditional Chinese lunar calendar. It is the day when the new moon arrives in Asia between January and February.

Week Nine 历史地理

Monday
[完形填空]

体裁：记叙文
题材：历史地理
正确率：_____ /10
词数：165
难度：★★★★☆
建议用时：12 分钟
实际用时：_____
答案页码：137

How Black Soldiers Helped End the U.S. Civil War

It wasn't just a war for freedom（自由）. It was a war for the future.

Blacks who took up arms __1__ the Civil War（美国南北战争）weren't just fighting for themselves. They were fighting for their children and all __2__ came after. They were fighting __3__ tomorrow.

By 1862, President（总统）Lincoln had __4__ to form the Black Union armies. Although they had to fight just to serve, more than 200,000 black men guarded the Union on land and at __5__ by the end of the Civil War. About 40,000 black men __6__ for the war.

American Blacks' service in the Civil War would do good to them. Whether they were born free __7__ broke their own chains（枷锁）, black soldiers proved they would fight as __8__ as their white brothers.

The war was over at last. Black people __9__ this: They had not waited for someone else to save them. Civil War was over. __10__ the war for civil rights was just beginning.

1. A. at   B. during
   C. for   D. on
2. A. who   B. whom
   C. which   D. that
3. A. to   B. in
   C. on   D. for
4. A. made   B. followed
   C. allowed   D. told
5. A. land   B. the land
   C. sea   D. the sea
6. A. died   B. lived
   C. cried   D. hurt
7. A. and   B. or
   C. nor   D. if
8. A. bravely   B. happily
   C. hardly   D. sadly
9. A. said   B. began
   C. remembered D. wrote
10. A. When   B. Where
    C. Or   D. But

Tuesday
[阅读理解 A]

The Best Title Wanted

"Christmas is your Chinese New Year." I've heard this in China during holidays, whether Christmas or Chinese New Year. I found the two share commonalities (共性). Here are some interesting ones I've observed:

Good fortune	Many Chinese New Year customs, such as the red couplets (红对联) and firecrackers (鞭炮) are usually seen as a lucky start to the new year. But some Christmas traditions are also said to represent good luck, such as decorating the Christmas tree.
The color red	Red is a beloved color for Christmas and a lucky one for Chinese New Year.
Marking beginnings	While Chinese New Year signals the start of the new lunar (农历的) year, Christmas once fell on the exact date of the winter solstice (冬至), the shortest day of the year in the Northern Hemisphere (北半球), being the "rebirth" of the sun.
Going home to family	Between the holiday song *I'll Be Home for Christmas* and the Chinese saying "moneyed or not, return home for Chinese New Year", both holiday traditions show the idea of family reunions (团圆).

体裁：——
题材：历史地理
正确率：____/5
词数：182
难度：★★★☆☆
建议用时：6 分钟
实际用时：____
答案页码：137

1. The color _____ is loved by people at Christmas and Chinese New Year.
   A. red   B. white
   C. green   D. yellow
2. The underlined word "rebirth" means _____ in Chinese.
   A. 团圆   B. 生命
   C. 重生   D. 复燃
3. Which of the following things are thought lucky at Christmas or Chinese New Year?
   a. The red couplets.
   b. Firecrackers.
   c. The decorated Christmas tree.
   d. Number six.
   A. acd   B. abc
   C. bcd   D. abd
4. What can we infer from the passage?
   A. Christmas comes from Chinese New Year.
   B. Chinese New Year comes from Christmas.
   C. Christmas celebration (庆祝) is all the same with Chinese New Year.
   D. There are common points between these two cultures.
5. The best title of this passage probably is _____.
   A. The Story of Holidays
   B. Christmas and Chinese New Year
   C. Christmas is not Your Chinese New Year
   D. Different Holidays, Interesting Commonalities

Wednesday
[阅读理解 B]

The Best Title Wanted

It must have been an amazing sight, 66 million years ago, for the dinosaurs (恐龙) to look up and see a large rock getting bigger and bigger in the sky. But the fun would have stopped when the rock hit the ground. Human did not exist (存在) back then and might not have existed today if not for the extinction (灭绝) that resulted from that hit.

But a similar extinction event probably will not repeat in our future, because science can protect us from this. If the dinosaurs had had <u>telescopes</u>, they could have known the coming rock and perhaps made it miss the earth. In general, astronomy (天文学) can save lives.

How can we avoid the risks from solar system (太阳系)? If a risk is identified, we could use many skills so that it will miss the earth. But our advantage also brings a sense of responsibility for our earth. The biggest problem we face is how to live long rather than arrive at the brink of self-extinction through the technologies we use.

体裁：说明文
题材：历史地理
正确率：＿＿＿/5
词数：170
难度：★★★☆☆
建议用时：6 分钟
实际用时：＿＿＿
答案页码：138

---

1. 66 million years ago, almost all of the dinosaurs were killed because of ＿＿＿.
   A. telescopes   B. rocks
   C. technologies   D. humans

2. The underlined word "telescopes" means ＿＿＿ in Chinese.
   A. 放大镜   B. 护目镜
   C. 望远镜   D. 墨镜

3. How can human avoid being killed by a rock from the sky?
   A. Identify the rock and use technologies to hit it.
   B. Identify the rock and use technologies to miss it.
   C. Identify the rock and use technologies to catch it.
   D. Identify the rock and get ready to hide.

4. What can we infer from the passage?
   A. We can live longer than the dinosaurs.
   B. The dinosaurs wouldn't have been extinct without the rocks.
   C. Human is trying to protect the earth.
   D. Human can avoid all the risks from solar system.

5. The best title of this passage probably is ＿＿＿.
   A. Danger for Dinosaurs
   B. The History of Dinosaurs
   C. Human and the Dinosaurs
   D. The Rocks Killing the Dinosaurs

Thursday
[阅读理解 C]

National Museum Exhibition Reviews History of Chinese Costume Culture

体裁：说明文
题材：历史地理
正确率：_____/5
词数：142
难度：★★★☆☆
建议用时：6 分钟
实际用时：_____
答案页码：138

  There is a beautiful dress once worn by Kangxi Emperor (皇帝) of Qing Dynasty (清朝). Costumes and objects of dressing show technical progress and aesthetic (审美的) changes. They also stand as evidence to the cultures, social values and class of society.

  Ancient Chinese Culture: Costume and Adornment (装饰), an exhibition newly opened at the National Museum of China, shows the history of techniques, aesthetic changes, social culture and the values of the country's ancient period including centuries-old clothes, shoes, hats and sewing (缝纫) tools. Also on show are pottery and classical paintings which offer some looks into the fashions of ancient China.

  The exhibits come from the collections of various museums across the country, and date as early as the Neolithic period (新石器时代) and through the end of Qing Dynasty (1644-1911), China's last empire. The exhibition will run for a year through February 2022.

1. The history of social changes includes the change of _____ habits in this passage.
   A. dressing   B. eating
   C. drinking   D. living
2. The underlined word "evidence" means _____ in Chinese.
   A. 真相   B. 信件
   C. 证据   D. 证件
3. What kind of things does the exhibition show?
   a. Clothes.
   b. Shoes and hats.
   c. Sewing tools.
   d. Pottery and classical paintings.
   A. ac   B. abc
   C. bc   D. abcd
4. What can we infer from the last paragraph?
   A. The dressing fashion in China has a long history.
   B. The exhibition shows 2022 years of dressing history.
   C. People didn't wear clothes before the Neolithic period.
   D. All the exhibits come from the collections of the National Museum.
5. This passage is probably an introduction about _____.
   A. an exhibition
   B. ancient China
   C. Kangxi Emperor
   D. National Museum

Friday
[任务型阅读 D]

Taijiquan

Taijiquan（太极拳）is a major kind of Chinese martial art（武术）. Taijiquan means "supreme ultimate fist（至高无上的拳头）". __1__

There have been different sayings about the origin of Taijiquan. The traditional legend goes that Zhang Sanfeng of the Song Dynasty created Taijiquan, while most people agreed that the modern Taijiquan originated from Chen style Taijiquan in the Qing Dynasty. __2__ It follows the simple principle of "subduing the vigorous by the soft（以柔克刚）". __3__ It is represented by the famous symbol of the Yin and Yang which expresses the continuous flow of Qi, which interact and balance（平衡）with each other.

The most famous forms of Taijiquan practiced today are the Chen, Yang, Wu, Wu and Sun styles. __4__ Nowadays, when most people talk about Taijiquan, they are usually referring to the Yang style. __5__ And it is practiced by millions of people.

阅读短文，从下列选项中选出能填入文中空白处的最佳选项，选项中有一项为多余选项。

A. It is only famous in China.

B. It has already spread around the world.

C. Taijiquan has its philosophical（哲学的）roots in Taoism.

D. All the five styles come from Chen style Taijiquan.

E. Taoism（道教）is the oldest philosophy（哲学）of China.

F. Tai means "Supreme", Ji means "Ultimate", and Quan means "Fist".

Saturday
[短文填空]

Historian Aims to Shed Light on Korean War

Sun Yanhua has (1)_____(interview) more than 200 veterans (老兵) involved in the War to Resist US Aggression and Aid Korea (抗美援朝战争) (1950-1953) and (2)_____(record) a history that is little (3)_____(know) among the younger generation (年轻一代). She lived and (4)_____(work) in Tonghua, Jilin Province. In her spare time, she always loved interviewing people and (5)_____(write) down their stories.

The idea of tracing the history of people who participated (参加) in the war in Korea came to her as she (6)_____(be) interviewing Xu Zhenming. Last year, Sun published an album (相册) with (7)_____(photo) of 229 veterans. So far, Sun has (8)_____(collect) the stories of about 500 veterans, and published five books and photo albums.

"I want to do something meaningful, not only for each individual but also for the country," she said. "And I hope the younger generation will come to know more about that history." The year 2020 (9)_____(mark) the 70th anniversary (周年纪念日) of the war. In a span of two (10)_____(year) and nine months, 197,000 Chinese soldiers died on the Korean Peninsula.

体裁：记叙文
题材：历史地理
正确率：_____/10
词数：170
难度：★★★☆☆
建议用时：10分钟
实际用时：_____
答案页码：140

阅读短文，用括号内所给单词的适当形式填空，使短文通顺，意思完整。

(1)_____
(2)_____
(3)_____
(4)_____
(5)_____
(6)_____
(7)_____
(8)_____
(9)_____
(10)_____

Sunday
[拓展阅读]

Treasure Stolen from Old Summer Palace Returns Home After 160-Year Odyssey

体裁：记叙文　　题材：传统文化　　词数：153
难度：★★★☆☆　　建议用时：6分钟　　实际用时：_____

　　A famous bronze sculpture（青铜雕塑）of a horse's head, which was looted in 1860 from the Old Summer Palace, or Yuanmingyuan, finally returned home on Dec 1, 2020. Not only is the horse head the first of the twelve animal-head sculptures to be returned to Yuanmingyuan, but it is also the first important cultural relic（遗迹）from the Old Summer Palace to be returned to and housed at its original site.

　　It was bought by the late Macao business magnate and philanthropist Stanley Ho Hung-sun in 2007 and was donated to the National Cultural Heritage Administration in November 2019. It was recently transferred to the authorities（当局）responsible for the Yuanmingyuan ruins, also reflecting（反映）Ho's wishes.

　　Seven of the twelve sculptures have so far been returned to China. In addition to the horse's head, the other six are also in Beijing, at the National Museum of China and the Poly Art Museum.

Week Ten 环境环保

Monday [完形填空]

体裁：说明文
题材：环境环保
正确率：_____ /10
词数：164
难度：★★★☆☆
建议用时：10 分钟
实际用时：_____
答案页码：141

NASA: 2020 Was One of the Hottest Years on Record

2020 was one of the hottest years in recorded history. The year __1__ an important marker（标志）of the long-term warming caused by human activities producing greenhouse gases（温室气体）.

__2__ hotspots（热点）in 2020 was Siberia（西伯利亚）. Broad areas of warmth and localized（局部的）hotspots are both linked to the long-term warming. A __3__ analysis（分析）of the role of global warming in Siberia's heat found that such extremes（极端）would __4__ around once every 80,000 years without human-made warming.

That __5__ heat records in recent years were led by long-term warming again, which was a basis（基础）for more such __6__. A 2017 analysis noted that __7__ the late 19th century and 1980, __8__ records for the hottest year would happen about every 8 __9__ 11 years. Since 1981, it has been occurring（发生）about every 3 to 4 years. So 2020's high ranking was __10__ —and was another example of how far the earth's climate（气候）has been away from its natural course（进程）.

1. A. provided   B. had
   C. grew   D. bought
2. A. Most of   B. Lots of
   C. One of   D. Many of
3. A. difficult   B. sad
   C. terrible   D. recent
4. A. take   B. make
   C. happen   D. miss
5. A. high   B. increasing
   C. slow   D. open
6. A. records   B. letters
   C. examples   D. news
7. A. from   B. with
   C. between   D. among
8. A. old   B. new
   C. different   D. same
9. A. of   B. at
   C. in   D. to
10. A. seen   B. expected
    C. said   D. interviewed

Tuesday
[阅读理解 A]

What Will Climate Change Look like near Me?

> 体裁：——
> 题材：环境环保
> 正确率：____/3
> 词数：134
> 难度：★★☆☆
> 建议用时：4 分钟
> 实际用时：____
> 答案页码：141

Dr. Lizzie: I think it's really frightening (可怕的). It's really a wake-up call as to what we're talking about here. We have already seen the impacts of climate change.

Lucy: To some people, warming weather may not seem like such a big deal. But even the smallest change in climate can cause terrible consequences (后果).

Dr. Lizzie: Farming has been described as being on the front line of climate change, the first to feel its influences. This year was a bad one for British farms.

Tom: What about farming?

Dr. Lizzie: Not even a pandemic (流行病) could stop its step.

Lucy: Are we too late to avoid dangerous warming?

Tom: The global warming depends on a number of factors (因素). The most important one is the amount of greenhouse gases (温室气体) produced in the coming years.

Lucy: In the future, what will most probably change the global warming?

1. According to the conversation, "Not even a pandemic could stop its step" probably means _____.
   A. global warming may be avoided
   B. it is impossible to avoid global warming
   C. a pandemic causes global warming to get worse
   D. global warming can be avoided by the pandemic

2. What might be the relationship of the three persons?
   A. Doctor and patients.
   B. Writer and publishers.
   C. Driver and passengers.
   D. Teacher and students.

3. They are talking about _____.
   A. farming
   B. weather
   C. global warming
   D. an animal house

Wednesday
[阅读理解 B]

Economy Along the Yangtze River

体裁：说明文
题材：环境环保
正确率：_____ /5
词数：170
难度：★★★☆☆
建议用时：6分钟
实际用时：_____
答案页码：142

China has a new development plan for the Yangtze River Economic Belt (长江经济带) for the next five years. To have green and sustainable (可持续的) development, more efforts will be made to encourage and support provinces and cities along the Yangtze River to develop new industries and high-level manufacturing clusters (制造业产业群) with international competitiveness (竞争力).

It covers around 21 percent of China's total land area and more than 40 percent of China's total population. In the next step, China will pay attention to the economic development and the protection and restoration (恢复) of ecological environment (生态环境) along the Yangtze River.

China has already made big progress in the economic development of the economic belt. Data showed that the economy of the Belt accounted for (占比) 46.5 percent of the total in 2019. During the first nine months of 2020, the number rose to 46.6 percent. In terms of transportation and connectivity (交通运输和互联互通), the economic belt's railway network grew to 43,700 kilometers as of last November, and the high-speed rail network reached 15,400 kilometers.

1. China has a new five-year plan along the Yangtze River for _____.
   A. green and sustainable development
   B. encouraging cities
   C. supporting new industries
   D. higher international competitiveness

2. From the second paragraph, we can know that the Yangtze River Economic Belt _____.
   A. is only a small area
   B. is an important area
   C. has the smallest population
   D. needs more economic help from other areas

3. Which of the following is mentioned in the passage?
   a. Economy.   b. Farming.
   c. Transportation. d. Internet.
   A. ac   B. ab
   C. bc   D. bd

4. How will the area deal with the economy and development?
   A. The area is only trying to develop economy.
   B. The area is developing the economy and protecting the environment.
   C. The area is developing the economy but doesn't protect the environment.
   D. The area has a plan to protect the environment so that it can slow down the development of the economy.

5. The last paragraph shows that the area's economy _____.
   A. was not always good
   B. rose to 46.6% in September
   C. went well in 2019 and 2020
   D. was almost a third of the total in China

Thursday
[阅读理解 C]

A Glacial Flood in India

体裁：记叙文
题材：环境环保
正确率：_____/5
词数：146
难度：★★★☆☆
建议用时：6分钟
实际用时：_____
答案页码：__142__

A recent tragedy（悲剧）in the northern state of India has left more than 38 people dead and 170 missing.

On Sunday, February 8, a large avalanche（雪崩）came breaking a hydroelectric dam（水电大坝）. It caused a terrible flood that destroyed（摧毁）many villages along the Alaknanda and Dhauliganga Rivers.

Scientists later found that the avalanche originated（源于）from a "hanging" glacier（冰川）that had broken off in the Himalayan（喜马拉雅）region of Uttarakhand. The exact reason why the glacier fell is unclear, but scientists say it is possible that global warming played a role.

Experts believe that the high temperatures led to the excessive melting（过度融化）of snow and ice. This is extremely dangerous. The melting of glacial ice can also create large glacial lakes. If the glaciers reach a certain breaking point, they could release（释放）millions of tons（吨）of water from these lakes roaring（咆哮）down the mountains. Accidents may happen.

1. Where did the tragedy happen?
   A. In the Himalayan region.
   B. In the Uttarakhand.
   C. In the northern state of India.
   D. All above.
2. According to the passage, _____ destroyed many villages.
   A. a large avalanche
   B. a terrible flood
   C. a hydroelectric dam
   D. the breaking of the hydroelectric dam
3. What is the origin of avalanches?
   A. Global warming.
   B. The breaking of "hanging" glacier.
   C. The Himalayan region of Uttarakhand.
   D. It is unclear.
4. Which of the following is true?
   A. The affected villages got the help from the scientists.
   B. Experts make sure that the glacier fell because of global warming.
   C. The melting of glacial ice can create new safe lakes.
   D. The breaking of the glacial lakes may cause the accident.
5. What's the main idea of this passage?
   A. A tragedy happened in India.
   B. Global warming is causing snow and ice to melt.
   C. What caused the tragedy in India.
   D. A sad story of an Indian village.

Friday
[任务型阅读 D]

Three Signs for "New Arctic"

Experts reminded a "new normal（常态）" is settling over the Arctic（北极）. It's already not the same place it was a few decades（十年）ago, and it won't be the same place a few more decades into the future. __1__ Many changes are happening before our eyes.

__2__

Arctic sea ice hit its lowest extent（范围）in September, at the end of the summer melting（融化）season. Scientists say the low sea ice extent and unusual high temperatures formed a bad cycle this year.

__3__

This year was a record-breaking summer for wildfires in the Arctic Circle. High temperatures and a lot of dry fuel（燃料）were the main reasons. The region is now experiencing some of the fastest climate warming on the planet.

__4__

Climate change is affecting（影响）plant and animal life in the Arctic Ocean, from the bottom of the food chain（食物链）up. Tiny algae（极细小的藻类）form the basis（基础）of the Arctic's marine（海洋）ecosystem. __5__

阅读短文，从下列选项中选出能填入文中空白处的最佳选项，选项中有一项为多余选项。

A. Missing Snow
B. Melting（融化）Sea Ice
C. Record Wildfires
D. Influenced Ecosystems
E. It's not good news for everyone.
F. Temperatures are rising at least twice as fast as the global average.

Saturday
[短文填空]

On the Front Line of Climate Change

Across the world, poor people are among those worst hit by climate (气候) change and natural disasters (自然灾害), resource (资源) shortage and poverty (贫穷) resulting from climate. This is because their lives (1)_____(be) often more dependent on weather and nature.

In China, there is (2)_____(grow) awareness (意识) about the vulnerability (脆弱) of women facing climate change, especially in rural areas. In certain areas, women (3)_____(make) up to 70 percent of the rural labor force (农村劳动力).

However, despite (尽管) (4)_____(increase) participation (参与) in agricultural production (农业生产), rural women have less access to resources. Data (5)_____(show) that more rural women than men do not have their (6)_____(name) on land. Moreover, a survey shows that the income of (7)_____(work) rural women is only 56 percent that of working rural men. That (8)_____(mean) rural women have a (9)_____(bad) material basis (物质基础) to adapt to (适应) climate change than men. In addition, stopped by household work, women (10)_____(has) less access to information such as early weather warnings (警告) than men have.

体裁：议论文
题材：环境环保
正确率：_____/10
词数：153
难度：★★★☆☆
建议用时：10 分钟
实际用时：_____
答案页码： 143

阅读短文，用括号内所给单词的适当形式填空，使短文通顺，意思完整。

(1)_____
(2)_____
(3)_____
(4)_____
(5)_____
(6)_____
(7)_____
(8)_____
(9)_____
(10)_____

Sunday
[拓展阅读]

Students Show Thanks with Traditional Laba Porridge

体裁：记叙文　　题材：传统文化　　词数：166
难度：★★★☆☆　　建议用时：6分钟　　实际用时：_____

Eight foreign students from Kyrgyzstan（吉尔吉斯斯坦）, Pakistan（巴基斯坦） and other countries cooked Laba congee（腊八粥）—a thick rice porridge—on Wednesday to express thanks to the teachers who in 2020 helped them get through the coronavirus pandemic（新冠肺炎疫情）.

Laba Festival falls on the eighth day of the 12th month on the Chinese lunar（农历的） calendar. It's traditional to cook porridge. It is made by boiling rice in water until it takes on a pudding-like consistency（布丁般的稠度）. It is shared with family and friends to welcome the new year.

In China, food and festivals are often linked, and the food carries good wishes. International students cooked the Laba congee together to thank their teachers for helping them spend the year 2020 safely and in good health.

One teacher said, "We are also happy to share congee with our students. They may not speak Chinese, but I can feel their sincerity（真诚）. This is not only a bowl of congee but also a symbol of their love for China."

Week Eleven 旅行交通

Monday
[完形填空]

体裁：记叙文
题材：旅行交通
正确率：_____/10
词数：190
难度：★★★☆☆
建议用时：10 分钟
实际用时：_____
答案页码：145

21-Year-Old Rows Across Atlantic, Sets Record

Last Saturday morning, Jasmine Harrison became the youngest woman to row（划船）alone across the ocean. The 21-year-old swimming teacher spent just over 70 __1__ rowing across the Atlantic Ocean.

Ms. Harrison didn't have lots of __2__ in rowing across the ocean. She got the idea three years ago __3__ she saw the end of the 2017 Talisker Whisky Atlantic Challenge.

It wasn't __4__. Every day, Ms. Harrison would row for about 12 hours. She had to push her 250-kilogram __5__ across the ocean. Ms. Harrison had a phone, so she could __6__ with families and friends every day. But she still had to spend __7__ time all by herself. During the journey, her speaker fell in the water __8__ she could no longer listen to her music.

There was danger, too. __9__, her boat was turned over（翻转）by large waves. The first time, she hurt her elbow（肘）quite badly. Another time, she nearly ran into a ship.

Somehow, she kept going. On February 20, after 70 days, 3 hours and 48 minutes, she __10__ the island of Antigua—the end of the journey.

1. A. years   B. days
   C. hours   D. minutes
2. A. experience   B. time
   C. money   D. space
3. A. why   B. what
   C. where   D. when
4. A. difficult   B. happy
   C. easy   D. sad
5. A. car   B. boat
   C. bike   D. food
6. A. play   B. talk
   C. dance   D. sing
7. A. little   B. no
   C. much   D. few
8. A. but   B. and
   C. or   D. because
9. A. Once   B. Twice
   C. Three times D. Four times
10. A. reached   B. left
    C. passed   D. stayed

Tuesday
[阅读理解 A]

Climbing Toward the Good Life

体裁：记叙文
题材：旅行交通
正确率：_____ /5
词数：172
难度：★★★☆☆
建议用时：6分钟
实际用时：_____
答案页码：145

Mose Subure and five other young villagers（村民）from the "cliff village"（"悬崖村"）started working early. They bought all the things that were used for building their house, and planned to go back to the village through a steel ladder（钢梯）.

The "cliff village" is in Southwest China's Sichuan Province. It is in a mountain. At the end of 2016, with the construction（建设）of the steel ladders, the travel conditions became better. The introduction（引进）of the Internet also changed the village. In 2017, a short video of women climbing the steel ladder in the "cliff village" became popular on the Internet.

In May 2020, 344 villagers moved to new homes with the help of the government and the living conditions of these families have become much better.

The villagers have moved down the mountain, but the village has received a lot of visitors. Mose Subure and five other young villagers spotted this chance and started a partnership（合作关系）in a plan to build a homestay（家庭旅馆）in November last year.

1. Mose Subure and five other villagers bought the things to build the _____.
   A. bridge   B. house
   C. road   D. school
2. The "cliff village" is in the _____ of China.
   A. north   B. south
   C. northwest   D. southwest
3. The word "spotted" in the last paragraph means _____ in Chinese.
   A. 发现   B. 失去
   C. 反对   D. 完善
4. What can we infer from the passage?
   A. Climbing the steel ladder was popular in China.
   B. The villagers built the steel ladder by themselves.
   C. Mose Subure didn't want to move down the mountain.
   D. People in the "cliff village" are moving toward a good life.
5. Which of the following is true?
   A. Visitors went to the "cliff village" through the steel ladder.
   B. The villagers moved to new homes by themselves.
   C. The life changed little in the "cliff village".
   D. People in the "cliff village" made much money.

Wednesday
[阅读理解 B]

The Best Title Wanted

Due to the COVID-19, many people have stopped traveling abroad, so domestic travel has become popular.

This year, the Garze Tibetan Autonomous Prefecture (甘孜藏族自治州) has become a popular place for travelers.

Garze's popularity was boosted (促进) by Tamdrin, whose name in Mandarin is Ding Zhen, a 20-year-old from the Tibetan ethnic group in Sichuan. He has gone viral on the Internet for his good looks and later helped the tourism in Sichuan to develop by posting (发布) short videos.

In early December, ticket sales to Daocheng Yading in Garze and some other scenic spots (景点) jumped more than 50% year-on-year. These places are located (位于) about a 12-hour drive from Chengdu Shuangliu International Airport, so travel there has driven car rentals (出租). During the period, car rentals in the area increased more than 100% year-on-year.

"More travelers come to Garze after the COVID-19 has been under better control in China," said Wu Ruoshan at the Tourism Research Center, China Academy of Social Sciences.

体裁：记叙文
题材：旅行交通
正确率：_____/5
词数：161
难度：★★★☆☆
建议用时：6 分钟
实际用时：_____
答案页码：146

---

1. According to the passage, _____ has become popular among tourists.
   A. Garze   B. Tibet
   C. Sichuan   D. Tamdrin
2. Which of the following is not true about Ding Zhen?
   A. He is a young boy.
   B. He is good-looking.
   C. He is from Tibet.
   D. He is also named Tamdrin.
3. How did Ding Zhen help the tourism in Sichuan to develop?
   A. By becoming a tour guide.
   B. By making short videos.
   C. By providing local food.
   D. By selling tickets.
4. According to Paragraph 4, why did the car rentals in the airport increase?
   A. Because tourists liked traveling by cars.
   B. Because traveling by cars was very cheap.
   C. Because the car drivers were very kind to tourists.
   D. Because the scenic spots were far from the airport.
5. What is the best title of this passage?
   A. Ding Zhen Boosts Tourism in Sichuan
   B. A New Popular Place for Travelers
   C. Traveling Has Become Popular
   D. Better Service Attracts Travelers

Thursday
[阅读理解 C]

Digital Technologies Make Travel Safer and More Convenient

体裁：记叙文
题材：旅行交通
正确率：_____ /5
词数：175
难度：★★★☆☆
建议用时：6 分钟
实际用时：_____
答案页码：147

During this year's Spring Festival holiday, the use of digital technologies（技术）in tourism has brought convenience（便利）to visitors.

During the holiday, the West Lake, a popular scenic spot in the city of Hangzhou, capital of East China's Zhejiang Province, saw more than 1.66 million visitors. Cameras were used to control tourist flow on Broken Bridge, an important scenic spot of the West Lake, during the peak（高峰时期的）holiday period.

During last year's National Day holiday, the West Lake used an LED screen showing some information, including the route（路线）map of bus travel and the real-time flow of visitors on Broken Bridge.

Qiandao Lake, another popular tourist destination in Zhejiang, received 78,500 tourists during the Spring Festival holiday this year. Tourists can book（预约）on the Internet and choose a proper time and route. They can enter the scenic spot directly after scanning a QR code（二维码）.

The tourism industry continues to face challenges due to the COVID-19, but thanks to digital technologies, travel is safer and more convenient during these difficult times.

阅读短文，判断正（A）误（B）。

1. The West Lake is in the west of China.
2. The workers can use cameras to control the tourist flow on Broken Bridge.
3. You can get the route map of bus travel on an LED screen at the West Lake.
4. Qiandao Lake received more tourists than the West Lake during this year's Spring Festival holiday.
5. You can book on the Internet if you want to visit Qiandao Lake.

Friday
[任务型阅读 D]

Cutting Travel Time to Guangzhou

Guangdong Province has decided to build two high-speed Maglev (磁悬浮) lines. __1__, several hundred km/h faster than bullet trains.

The two maglev lines will connect the Guangdong Province to Beijing and to Shanghai. __2__, the province's capital. This will help the city to play a leading (领先的) role in South China's high-speed railway network.

__3__, and between Beijing and Guangzhou to less than four hours. That's less than half the time of current (当前的) high-speed trains.

The plan also mentioned a line connecting Shanghai, Shenzhen and Guangzhou. __4__. However, according to the government, the part between Guangzhou and Shenzhen probably will be the first to be built.

__5__, according to the Shenzhen Development and Reform Commission. It can help to ease the pressure (压力) on regular and bullet trains in the area.

阅读短文，从下列选项中选出能填入文中空白处的最佳选项。

A. The maglev lines will cut the travel time between Shanghai and Guangzhou to less than three hours

B. Maglev trains can run 600 kilometers per hour

C. That line has not been built yet

D. The two lines will meet in Guangzhou

E. The maglev line between Guangzhou and Shenzhen will be built

Saturday
[短文填空]

Americans Continue to Fly During the COVID-19

Although a pandemic (流行病) is still spreading in the world, Americans continue to fly.

The Transportation Security Administration (TSA) reported that Wednesday (1)_____(be) the busiest day for domestic carriers (国内航空) since the COVID-19 (2)_____(begin) ravaging (摧毁) the U.S. in mid-March. Nearly 1.2 million Americans (3)_____(fly) on Dec. 23, according to TSA data.

"If you choose to travel around this holiday, please (4)_____(wear) a mask," said TSA spokeswoman (女发言人) Lisa Farbstein.

The Centers for Disease Control and Prevention (CDC) is advising travelers to take precautions (预防) during the holiday season.

"Travel may increase your chance of spreading and (5)_____(get) COVID-19," said the agency on its website. "CDC continues to recommend (建议) staying home because this is the best way to (6)_____(protect) yourself and others this year."

But that (7)_____(stop) many people from flying. "My mom (8)_____(need) my help," Brownlee, an Alabama resident, (9)_____(tell) The Associated Press earlier this week on his way to Oregon. "I know that God has got me. He is not (10)_____(go) to let me get sick."

体裁：记叙文
题材：旅行交通
正确率：_____ /10
词数：177
难度：★★★☆☆
建议用时：10 分钟
实际用时：_____
答案页码：148

阅读短文，用括号内所给单词的适当形式填空，使短文通顺，意思完整。

(1)_____
(2)_____
(3)_____
(4)_____
(5)_____
(6)_____
(7)_____
(8)_____
(9)_____
(10)_____

Sunday
[拓展阅读]

Things You May Not Know About Rain Water

体裁：说明文	题材：传统文化	词数：177
难度：★★★☆☆	建议用时：6 分钟	实际用时：_____

The traditional Chinese lunar calendar divides the year into 24 solar terms (二十四节气). Rain Water (雨水) starts on Feb 18 this year.

Rain Water signals the increase in rainfall and rise in temperature. With its arrival, a lively spring starts: the river water defreezes, and trees and grass turn green again.

According to an old Chinese saying, the rainfall in spring is as precious (宝贵的) as oil. In northern China, the spring drought (干旱) is common and the rainfall of this season accounts for only 10% to 15% of average (平均的) rainfall in a year.

Therefore, Rain Water is an important period for irrigation (灌溉) when the day gets warmer and rainfall increases.

Besides, it will be cold again during Rain Water period. It is strongly advised not to take off the thick coats too early and to keep warm, especially for the elderly and children.

The wet and damp weather during Rain Water period is considered harmful for people's spleen (脾) and stomach according to Chinese medical practice. Therefore, a bowl of nutritious porridge (粥) is the best choice to stay healthy.

Week Twelve 文化风俗、异国风情

Monday
[完形填空]

体裁：记叙文
题材：文化风俗
正确率：_____ /7
词数：147
难度：★★★☆☆
建议用时：7 分钟
实际用时：_____
答案页码：149

Chinese Opera Cartoon Festival Kicks Off on Thursday

阅读短文，从方框中选择合适的单词填空，使短文通顺，意思完整。其中有两个单词为多余选项。

public
cartoons
like
watching
enjoy
choose
in
looking
because

The art festival of Chinese opera cartoons will kick off (开始) in Beijing Thursday and run until Feb 26.

Classical Chinese operas chosen from 360 types of opera in China, are made into (1)_____, and will be exhibited (展览) to the (2)_____. The festival is organized (组织) by the Culture and Tourism Bureau of Beijing's Chaoyang district and the Chaoyang Cultural Center.

Many activities related to the theme, (3)_____ exhibition of original posters and manuscripts, and opera costume and aria analysis, will be held during the festival.

(4)_____ the festival is mainly held online, people can take part in the activities by (5)_____ videos on online short-video platforms like Douyin and Huoshan Video. People also can (6)_____ a 360-degree panoramic (全景的) view of the activities online. By clicking (点击) a mouse or using a mobile phone, people can (7)_____ any angle (角度) they like to view the activities at home.

Tuesday
[阅读理解 A]

How Does a Bus Driver Spend His Chinese New Year's Eve?

体裁：记叙文
题材：文化风俗
正确率：_____/5
词数：204
难度：★★★☆☆
建议用时：6分钟
实际用时：_____
答案页码：149

While most people on Chinese New Year's Eve focus on their big reunion dinners (团圆饭), in the case of Meng Dapeng, a bus driver in Beijing, it is a normal working day. The day consists of (由……组成) finishing a full inspection of the vehicle, keeping a cautious (谨慎的) eye on things and taking his passengers from stop to stop, a routine Meng has stuck to for 10 years.

Meng has a special, deeper, emotional connection (联系) with being a bus driver: His father was one as well.

"When I was a kid, my father was always working on lunar New Year's Eve. So, for my family, the time of the reunion dinner was changed to the next morning, on the first day of the new year," he said. After his father retired (退休), the family was finally able to spend New Year's Eve together.

Several years later, however, Meng became a bus driver. "So most years, one member is absent at our New Year's Eve dinner table; we're used to it," Meng said, smilingly.

In his spare time, Meng is busy studying safe driving and passenger psychology (心理), and plans to publish a collection of articles.

1. Meng Dapeng works in _____.
   A. Shanghai   B. Beijing
   C. Guangzhou   D. Wuhan
2. The underlined word "inspection" means _____ in Chinese.
   A. 启动   B. 驾驶
   C. 检查   D. 观看
3. According to the passage, what does a bus driver need to do for his work?
   A. Finishing a full inspection of the vehicle.
   B. Keeping a cautious eye on things.
   C. Taking his passengers from stop to stop.
   D. A, B and C.
4. Why does Meng Dapeng have a special, deeper, emotional connection with being a bus driver?
   A. Because he wants to work on lunar New Year's Eve.
   B. Because he likes driving.
   C. Because his father was a bus driver.
   D. Because he wants to publish a collection of articles.
5. We can infer from the passage that _____.
   A. Meng Dapeng has a big reunion dinner on Chinese New Year's Eve
   B. Meng Dapeng loves his work
   C. Meng Dapeng has been a bus driver for 9 years
   D. Meng Dapeng didn't have a reunion dinner when he was a kid

Wednesday
[阅读理解 B]

What Is the Thanksgiving like During the COVID-19?

Judy Woodruff: Today we'll have a talk about Thanksgiving this year. As we reported, public health officials are concerned (担心的) that too many people will travel this holiday to be with family. Tens of millions have decided to stay at home. Before the holiday begins, we gathered (收集) voices to hear their different thoughts about Thanksgiving this year.

Phil Wright: Thanksgiving at our house changes (变化) year to year. In the past we had as many as 20-25 people.

Selena: Sometimes, we will do turkey. Sometimes, we will do other things that are special to us.

Jacqui Falluca: My family gets together every year, usually at my aunt's house.

Phil Wright: We're going to reach out to everybody that couldn't be with us. It's just very important that everybody stays healthy, because we have made it for many months.

Selena: I want to be very cautious (谨慎的) myself, because I have a new baby, about five months old.

Jacqui Falluca: My husband and I are very active in the community, so I work as a nurse and he has to travel for work. we didn't think it would be safe to be around all of the big family.

1. According to the dialogue, how many people may decide to stay at home during the holiday?
   A. 200,000   B. 30,000,000
   C. 20,000   D. 1,000,000
2. Where does Jacqui Falluca's family usually get together?
   A. At her aunt's house.
   B. At their house.
   C. At her grandfather's house.
   D. At her friend's house.
3. Why does Selena want to be very cautious?
   A. Because she has been cautious for many months.
   B. Because she and her husband are very active in the community.
   C. Because she has a new baby.
   D. Because she thinks it's very important for everybody to stay healthy.
4. Does Jacqui Falluca think it safe to live in a big family?
   A. Yes, she does.
   B. No, she doesn't.
   C. Yes, she did.
   D. No, she didn't.
5. What can we know from the dialogue?
   A. Phil Wright won't reach out to everybody that couldn't be with him.
   B. Jacqui Falluca is a nurse and her husband has to travel for work.
   C. Public health officials don't care whether people will travel this holiday.
   D. Selena will cook chicken on Thanksgiving Day.

Thursday
[阅读理解 C]

The Best Title Wanted

A total of 300 pieces of painted sculptures (雕塑) themed on the 12 Chinese zodiac (属相) signs will be exhibited online from January 23.

The sculptures are chosen from more than 1,000 artworks, and will be on display (展览) through the website as well as the official WeChat (微信) account of the exhibition (展览) due to COVID-19.

The exhibition's title is "'2021 Year of the Ox' Chinese Zodiac Painted Sculpture Annual Invitation Exhibition", and it is held by the Chinese Folk Artists Association, and organized by the Painted Sculpture Professional Committee and the China Intangible Cultural Heritage Art Design and Research Institute (中国非遗艺术设计研究院).

During the opening ceremony (典礼), an art seminar (研讨会) with the theme of zodiac painted sculpture will also be held online.

The Chinese zodiac is a special culture and national memory that has <u>accompanied</u> the Chinese people for thousands of years. It is not only the crystallization (结晶化) of the wisdom of the Chinese nation, but also a valuable cultural resource in China.

体裁：记叙文
题材：文化风俗
正确率：_____/5
词数：164
难度：★★★☆☆
建议用时：6分钟
实际用时：_____
答案页码：150

---

1. According to the first paragraph, when will the exhibition start?
   A. On January 23.   B. On July 23.
   C. On April 23.   D. On March 13.

2. The sculptures will be on display through _____.
   A. the website
   B. the official WeChat account of the exhibition
   C. both A and B
   D. TV and radio

3. The exhibition is held by _____.
   A. the Painted Sculpture Professional Committee
   B. the China Intangible Cultural Heritage Art Design and Research Institute
   C. the Chinese Folk Artists Association
   D. an art seminar themed "2021 Year of the Ox"

4. According to the passage, what does the underlined word "accompanied" most probably mean?
   A. 安慰   B. 陪伴
   C. 鼓励   D. 忍受

5. What's the best title of this passage?
   A. Painted Sculptures on Chinese Zodiac on Display Online
   B. A Special Culture and National Memory in China
   C. 2021 Year of the Ox
   D. The Wisdom of the Chinese Nation

Friday
[任务型阅读 D]

Old Photos Shed New Light on Yuanmingyuan's Former Glory

体裁：继续文
题材：文化风俗
正确率：_____/5
词数：162
难度：★★★☆☆
建议用时：6分钟
实际用时：_____
答案页码：151

Referring to（参考）historical documents, archaeological（考古学的）research, scattered ruins（废墟）and ancient artworks presenting original scenes, people have to rely on their imagination to get an impression（印象）of the past beauty of Yuanmingyuan, or the Old Summer Palace, in Beijing. But they may now be able to get a clearer picture of its former glory（壮丽）.

On Tuesday, the administration of the Yuanmingyuan ruins shared more than 360 old photos, which were collected from all over the world in recent years. Taken after invading Anglo-French allied forces looted（洗劫）and burned Yuanmingyuan, these photos record the time before the past royal resort（度假胜地）fell into ruin over the following years.

Most of the photos had never been publicly displayed, and around 100 of them will be exhibited over the next month at the Zhengjue Temple of the Yuanmingyuan Ruins Park.

"These findings will help people get a better understanding of how Yuanmingyuan has changed throughout history," said Li Xiangyang, deputy（副的）director of the administration.

阅读短文，回答下面 1~5 小题。

1. How many old photos have been shared by the administration of the Yuanmingyuan ruins?
_____
_____

2. 根据短文内容填空（在空格处填入一个单词）。
_____ photos had been publicly displayed, and around 100 of them will be exhibited over the next month at the Zhengjue Temple of the Yuanmingyuan Ruins Park.

3. When will the photos be exhibited at the Zhengjue Temple of the Yuanmingyuan Ruins Park?
_____
_____

4. Will these findings be helpful for people to understand how Yuanmingyuan has changed throughout history?
_____
_____

5. 请将画线句子翻译成中文。
_____

Saturday
[短文填空]

Henan Beauty

A dance production set in Tang era (时代) becomes popular (1)_____(quick) online at a Spring Festival gala (盛会), Chen Nan reports.

The dance (2)_____(start) with a scene where a group of young women are on their way (3)_____ a banquet (宴会). The women act like they are (4)_____(play) musical instruments such as the bamboo flute, hand drum and pipa as they walk through (5)_____ garden, laughing along the way.

The piece's title is *A Tang Dynasty Banquet*. It (6)_____(be) less than six minutes long. "The performance (7)_____(bring) us back to the Tang Dynasty, which is beautiful and amazing. The dancers play the maids (侍女) so (8)_____(good) that it feels as if they are real Tang Dynasty maids from the painting," one viewer (9)_____(write) on Sina Weibo.

A Tang Dynasty Banquet is choreographed (为……编舞) and performed by artists of Zhengzhou Song and Dance Theater. It was first shown during the 12th Lotus Awards, the (10)_____(high) dance awards in China, in Luoyang, Central China's Henan province, on Oct 16. The production is inspired (启发) by the tangsancai displayed at a museum in Luoyang, especially the figurines (小雕像) of instrument-players and dancers.

Sunday
[拓展阅读]

Traditional Operas Increasingly Staged in Old Courtyards

体裁：记叙文　　题材：传统文化　　词数：167
难度：★★★☆☆　　建议用时：6分钟　　实际用时：_____

　　For many lovers of traditional Kunqu Opera, the Peony Pavilion, a century-old mansion（宅第）in Kunming, has been a go-to place to enjoy the classical（古典的）romance.

　　Kunqu, a Chinese opera form with a history of hundreds of years, is listed by UNESCO as an intangible cultural heritage（非物质文化遗产）.

　　In recent years, more and more producers（制作人）have chosen to stage traditional operas in historical places such as old courtyards, a move proven popular among young people who try to reconnect with their cultural roots.

　　Like Kunqu, Gui Opera, a traditional opera form that originated（发源）about 200 years ago in the city of Guilin, has been popular again in recent years. "In 2019 alone, the play was staged more than 200 times at the courtyard, with an almost full house each time," said Zhou Qiang, a producer of the performance.

　　Liu Hui, director of a traditional opera research center in Guilin, said, "Connecting the traditional opera with old courtyards meets the trend of retro（复古的）fashion in China."

Week Thirteen 文学艺术

Monday
[完形填空]

体裁：记叙文
题材：文学艺术
正确率：_____/15
词数：190
难度：★★★★☆
建议用时：16 分钟
实际用时：_____
答案页码：153

App Writes New Chapter in Reading

Now more people like reading e-books on their phones or computers. __1__ people are reading paper books. This trend (趋势) __2__ worse because of the COVID-19 pandemic (流行病). Retail (零售) book sales __3__ by 5.08% in 2020. It's the first fall in twenty years.

At __4__ a time, the launch (推出) of a literature (文学) app Xiao Niao Aves seems both timely and __5__. The app was launched in December 2020. Articles are mostly written by "good writers". One can read a part of the articles but will have to __6__ 12 yuan ($1.85) to read the first three __7__. If you want to read __8__ year's articles, you have to pay 588 yuan. Many people would think that it's too __9__. However, Yang Ying, the editor-in-chief (主编), says that subscription (订阅) levels __10__ the first month are better than __11__.

"In fact, I don't know __12__ we have a good future, but there are so many Chinese __13__, so even if one __14__ 10,000 of them would like to pay for __15__ literature, the future for us is optimistic (乐观的)," she says.

1. A. More   B. Further
   C. Less   D. Fewer
2. A. begins   B. feels
   C. becomes D. covers
3. A. rose   B. dropped
   C. entered D. closed
4. A. such   B. any
   C. that   D. this
5. A. hopeful B. different
   C. dangerous D. important
6. A. pay   B. cost
   C. spend   D. take
7. A. books   B. pieces
   C. paragraphs D. lines
8. A. a part of B. some
   C. a whole D. all
9. A. cheap   B. expensive
   C. wonderful D. special
10. A. before B. after
    C. during D. on
11. A. wanted B. expected
    C. explained D. worried
12. A. that   B. which
    C. because D. if
13. A. readers B. writers
    C. articles D. languages
14. A. of   B. out of
    C. between D. from
15. A. fun   B. foreign
    C. serious D. popular

Tuesday
[阅读理解 A]

2020 Top 2 Art Exhibits in China

Six Centuries at the Forbidden City（紫禁城）
- Held in: The Palace Museum
- Time: Sept 10–Nov 15
- Rank（排名）: 1st
- There were over 400 cultural relics（遗物）at the exhibition. This exhibition was very important because it marked（标志）the 600th anniversary（周年纪念日）of the Forbidden City. 24 emperors（皇帝）lived there during the Ming (1368–1644) and Qing (1644–1911) dynasties（朝代）. The area of the Forbidden City is 720,000 square meters. Within it, there are 1,050 buildings.

Jade（碧玉）from Hongshan
- Held in: National Museum of China（中国国家博物馆）
- Time: Oct 30–Jan 3
- Rank: 2nd
- The history of Hongshan culture is 5,000–6,500 years long. More than 160 jade objects（物件）were showed at the exhibition. These objects help people today understand the social ranks, ceremonies（仪式）and customs（风俗）of the Hongshan culture.

---

1. The Forbidden City has a history of _____ years.
   A. 160   B. 600
   C. 5,000   D. 6,500
2. What can you NOT learn at the exhibition Jade from Hongshan?
   A. Social ranks of the Hongshan culture.
   B. Ceremonies of the Hongshan culture.
   C. Customs of the Hongshan culture.
   D. Emperors in the Hongshan culture.
3. If you are free on Dec 10, which exhibition(s) can you go to?
   A. Six Centuries at the Forbidden City.
   B. Jade from Hongshan.
   C. Both A and B.
   D. Neither A or B.
4. Which of the following is TRUE?
   A: The history of the Qing dynasty was from 1368 to 1644.
   B. 42 emperors lived in the Forbidden City.
   C. Over 100 jade objects were showed at Jade from Hongshan.
   D. The exhibition Jade from Hongshan ranks higher than the other.

Wednesday
[阅读理解 B]

Wuhan Gets Back on Its Musical Feet

体裁：记叙文
题材：文学艺术
正确率：_____ /4
词数：177
难度：★★★☆☆
建议用时：5分钟
实际用时：_____
答案页码：154

Zhu Ning is the founder and owner of VOX, the oldest and one of the best-known live music venues (场地) in Wuhan. On Jan 19, 2020, he went back his hometown of Sichuan Province, to celebrate Spring Festival with his family. He planned to return to Wuhan after the holiday. However, because of the pandemic (流行病), Wuhan was locked down on Jan 23, 2020. Zhu had to close VOX.

"Everything happened so fast. For the first time in 15 years, VOX closed for several months. We didn't know if it would open again," Zhu said.

A year later, life in Wuhan returned to normal and VOX reopened. "Although we have to cut (削减) the number of shows, bands are eager (渴望的) to perform," Zhu said.

Audience (观众) members are offered face masks before they enter the venue. All tickets are sold online, and the number of audience is limited to about 80. Zhu said that from September to December, 85 shows were staged (上演) at the venue by bands from Wuhan and other parts of the country.

1. The underlined word "live" in Paragraph 1 probably means _____ in Chinese.
   A. 生活 B. 活的
   C. 现场的 D. 生动的
2. When was Wuhan locked down in 2020?
   A. On Jan 19. B. On Jan 23.
   C. On Jan 15. D. On Jan 20.
3. Which of the following was NOT done after VOX reopened?
   A. Offering audience face masks.
   B. Limiting audience number.
   C. Selling tickets online.
   D. Adding the number of shows.
4. Which of the following is NOT true about VOX?
   A. VOX is a place to listen to live music.
   B. VOX had been closed for many months before.
   C. VOX is loved by many bands.
   D. Shows at VOX decreased after it reopened.

Thursday
[阅读理解 C]

Masters of the Zisha Pots

Whether your favorite tea is in green or black, the best color of the teapot (茶壶) is purple. Because that is the color of the teapots which are produced (生产) in the city of Yixing, Jiangsu Province. Most people in China know that it produces the best teapots.

Thousands of craftspeople (工匠) make those teapots in that city. Nobody knows exactly how many teapots and cups are produced in Yixing. But everybody knows that the price of those teapots and cups are very high. At an auction (拍卖会) in Beijing in 2015, the price of a 10-piece Zisha tea set reached 92 million yuan ($14.3 million). It was made by Gu Jingzhou.

Gu was one of seven craftspeople in the 1950s. Officers of Yixing government offered him a job to train those young craftspeople. Now the seven—six men and a woman—are widely known as the "seven great masters of Zisha".

Today there are 30 master craftspeople in Yixing who are known as national masters of Zisha art. More than 100 craftspeople are called "masters of Jiangsu Province".

体裁：记叙文
题材：文学艺术
正确率：_____ /4
词数：183
难度：★★★☆☆
建议用时：5 分钟
实际用时：_____
答案页码：155

---

1. The underlined word "it" refers to _____.
   A. Yixing city
   B. Jiangsu Province
   C. craftsperson
   D. Gu Jingzhou

2. "national masters of Zisha art" refers to _____.
   A. Gu Jingzhou and his students
   B. 30 master craftspeople in Yixing
   C. 100 craftspeople in Jiangsu Province
   D. seven craftspeople in the 1950s

3. Which is NOT true about Zisha teapots?
   A. Zisha teapots produced in Yixing are the best teapots.
   B. Zisha teapots produced in Yixing are very expensive.
   C. Gu Jingzhou still is the best Zisha craftsman in Yixing.
   D. There are many people who make Zisha teapots in Yixing.

4. What does the passage mainly discuss?
   A. Zisha pots and Zisha craftspeople in Yixing.
   B. Zisha pots produced in Jiangsu Province.
   C. Zisha master Gu Jingzhou.
   D. Zisha pots in the 1950s.

Friday
[任务型阅读 D]

Women's Written Language

体裁：说明文
题材：文学艺术
正确率：_____/5
词数：173
难度：★★★☆☆
建议用时：6分钟
实际用时：_____
答案页码：156

Nv Shu (in English: Women's Written Language) is the world's only known written language for women. A thousand years ago, it was a popular language in Jiangyong county, Hunan Province. Now, Zhou Na, a North China artist, is trying to popularize（普及）it worldwide.

The language is different from traditional Chinese writings. It is based on a local（当地的）language in Jiangyong county. It is written in the styles of poems（诗）. They are mostly published（出版）on beautiful papers, books, fans（扇子）and silk scarves. They are believed to carry women's secrets.

Zhou says that she learned Nv Shu from her grandfather's sister. The first character（文字）that she learned to write was in Nv Shu. However, she didn't know the mystery of the language in her childhood. She has recently finished her Nv Shu writings. "Because the books on Nv Shu are difficult to find in the market, I hope that the publications hit the market in the first half of the year."

阅读短文，回答下面 1~5 小题。

1. Where was Nv Shu popular many years ago?
_____
_____

2. What language is Nv Shu based on?
_____
_____

3. Did Zhou Na know that Nv Shu was a special language when she was a child?
_____
_____

4. Why does Zhou want to publish her Nv Shu writings?
_____
_____

5. Would you like to learn how to write in Nv Shu? And why?
_____
_____

Saturday
[短文填空]

Rice-Straw Dragon Dance

Rice-straw dragon dance (舞草把龙) is a special dance (1)_____ Longwan town, Hubei Province. The dragon's body is usually made of cloth, with bamboo as (2)_____(it) "bones". People from Longwan town usually perform (表演) dragon dance to celebrate the Longtaitou Festival, (3)_____ Dragon Head-raising Festival every year.

The history of the town's rice-straw dragon dance is very long. Dragon is (4)_____(more) legendary (传奇的) creature (生物) in Chinese culture. It symbolizes (象征) power, strength and good luck. So, people (5)_____(believe) that performing dragon dance on Longtaitou Festival can make bad things (6)_____(go) away and bring good luck.

Zhang Jinpan, 80, comes from Longwan town. At the age of 15, he (7)_____(become) a farmer after primary (初级的) school. Then, he learned the (8)_____(skill) of making dragons with rice straw and performing dragon dances from his father. He remembers (9)_____ people would perform dragon dance to drive away illness, (10)_____ medical (医疗的) care was limited in the past. Now only a few people know how to make rice-straw dragon or perform dragon dance.

体裁：说明文
题材：文学艺术
正确率：_____/10
词数：170
难度：★★★☆☆
建议用时：10 分钟
实际用时：_____
答案页码：156

阅读短文，在短文空缺处填入适当的单词，或用括号内所给单词的适当形式填空。

(1)_____
(2)_____
(3)_____
(4)_____
(5)_____
(6)_____
(7)_____
(8)_____
(9)_____
(10)_____

Sunday [拓展阅读]

Little New Year

体裁：说明文　　题材：传统文化　　词数：184
难度：★★★☆☆　　建议用时：6分钟　　实际用时：_____

Little New Year (Chinese: Xiaonian), is usually a week before the lunar（农历的）New Year. It is also known as the Festival of the Kitchen God（灶神节）. Here are five things you should know about the Little New Year.

1. Offer sacrifices to Kitchen God

On that day, people offer the Kitchen God delicious food, hoping that he will only say good things about the family when he goes to heaven to make his report（报告）. But now, very few families still do that.

2. House cleaning

Between Laba Festival and Little New Year, families in China do a thorough（彻底的）house cleaning, sweeping（扫）out the old to welcome the New Year.

3. Eat Guandong candy

Guandong candy is a sticky traditional snack that Chinese people eat on the Festival of the Kitchen God.

4. Paste（粘贴）paper-cuts to windows

On the Little New Year, old couplets（对联）and paper-cuts from the last Spring Festival are taken down, and new ones are pasted up.

5. Bath and hair-cut

As the old Chinese saying goes, whether they're rich or poor, people often have a haircut before the Spring Festival.

Week Fourteen 新闻速递

Monday
[完形填空]

China Spending 400b Yuan on Fighting COVID-19

体裁：记叙文
题材：新闻速递
正确率：_____ /10
词数：149
难度：★★★★☆
建议用时：12 分钟
实际用时：_____
答案页码：158

China spent more than 400 billion（十亿）yuan ($61.73 billion) on fighting COVID-19 by the end of November 2020.

The fiscal system（财政体系）has __1__ funds（资金）in the first place for fighting COVID-19 so that people will not be scared by the __2__ of medical treatment, said Finance Minister（财政部部长）Liu Kun in an online speech. __3__ people can get the funds, Liu added, local governments will not be hampered（阻碍）by the cost of __4__ treatment and epidemic（疫情）control.

The fiscal system has found ways to lower the __5__ of the epidemic on the economy when facing the great __6__ in 2020, Liu said.

China set a 2020 fiscal deficit（赤字）of at least 3.6 __7__ of GDP（国内生产总值）, and it is __8__ than the last year's 2.8 percent. It has __9__ 1 trillion（万亿）yuan of government bonds（债券）for COVID-19 control in order to provide more __10__ for companies and individuals（个人）.

1. A. put   B. made
   C. stayed   D. run
2. A. number   B. cost
   C. dollar   D. wallet
3. A. And   B. So
   C. Because   D. But
4. A. healthy   B. local
   C. private   D. medical
5. A. hope   B. influence
   C. speed   D. attention
6. A. difficulty B. surprise
   C. development D. exercise
7. A. points   B. price
   C. yuan   D. percent
8. A. lower   B. higher
   C. low   D. high
9. A. given out B. given away
   C. given in D. given back
10. A. signs   B. gifts
    C. money   D. food

Tuesday
[阅读理解 A]

The Best Title Wanted

China will build more than 600,000 5G base stations in 2021 as the nation speeds up the development of wireless (无线的) technology, according to the Ministry of Industry and Information Technology (工信部).

China had built more than 718,000 5G base stations as of mid-December in 2020, and 5G signals were <u>available</u> in more than 300 cities.

The nation will promote the building and using of 5G networks in an orderly manner, speed up 5G coverage in major cities and advance building and sharing of 5G base stations among telecom operators (电信运营商), Xiao Yaqing, minister of industry and information technology, said at a meeting on Monday.

More efforts will be made to carry out industrial 5G network pilot (试点的) projects by focusing on 10 key industries and forming 20 typical industrial application scenarios (场景), Xiao said, without offering more details.

The 5G rollout (试运行) plan for next year will lay a good basis for deeper integration (融合) of the digital and real economies, help stabilize (使稳定) investment (投资) and speed up industrial upgrades, experts said.

体裁：记叙文
题材：新闻速递
正确率：_____/5
词数：166
难度：★★★★☆
建议用时：7分钟
实际用时：_____
答案页码：159

---

1. According to the passage, China had built _____ 5G base stations as of mid-December in 2020.
   A. about 600,000   B. less than 781,000
   C. over 718,000   D. more than 71,800

2. The underlined word "available" means _____ in Chinese.
   A. 可用的   B. 缺乏的
   C. 免费的   D. 珍贵的

3. According to Xiao Yaqing, how many typical industrial application scenarios will be formed?
   A. Twenty.   B. Ten.
   C. Five.   D. Thirty.

4. From the passage, we can know that _____.
   A. the 5G rollout plan is helpful to digital and real economies
   B. the nation will speed up 5G coverage in small cities
   C. Xiao Yaqing offered no details about 5G network pilot projects
   D. the nation will not promote the building and using of 5G networks

5. The best title of this passage probably is _____.
   A. The Advantages of Building 5G Base Stations
   B. China to Build More 5G Base Stations During 2021
   C. The Development of Digital and Real Economies in China
   D. The Development of Major Cities in China

Wednesday
[阅读理解 B]

Tianwen-1 Is the 1st Chinese Spacecraft to Reach Mars

体裁：记叙文
题材：新闻速递
正确率：_____/5
词数：179
难度：★★★★☆
建议用时：7 分钟
实际用时：_____
答案页码：159

China's Tianwen-1 robotic probe (探测器) entered a Martian (火星的) orbit (轨道) on Wednesday night, becoming the first Chinese spacecraft to reach Mars.

The probe's engine (引擎) was fired at 7:52 pm and worked for about 15 minutes to slow down the probe and help it be caught by Martian gravity (重力).

Then the probe moved into an orbit with a perigee (近地点) of about 400 kilometers and a circling period of 10 days, then started flying around the planet according to the China National Space Administration. The move was difficult because it required the probe to slow down within 10 minutes from the <u>ultrafast</u> speed of 28 km/s to about 1 km/s.

Tianwen-1, the country's first independent Mars mission (任务), was launched by a Long March 5 heavy-lift carrier rocket (长征五号遥四运载火箭) on July 23 from the Wenchang Space Launch Center in Hainan Province, starting the nation's planet exploration program. It was the world's 46th Mars exploration mission since October 1960, when the former Soviet Union (苏联) launched the first Mars-bound spacecraft. Only 18 of those missions were successful.

1. How long did the probe's engine work after it was fired?
   A. 15 minutes.
   B. 15 seconds.
   C. About 15 minutes.
   D. About 15 seconds.
2. The underlined word "ultrafast" most probably means _____ in Chinese.
   A. 极慢的   B. 极快的
   C. 极其的   D. 特别的
3. When was Tianwen-1 launched from the Wenchang Space Launch Center?
   A. On July 20.   B. On June 23.
   C. On April 23.   D. On July 23.
4. How many times did the Mars exploration missions succeed?
   A. Twenty-three.   B. Eighteen.
   C. Five.   D. One.
5. Which of the following is true?
   A. The probe moved into an orbit with a perigee of about 40 kilometers.
   B. Tianwen-1 was China's first independent Mars mission.
   C. Tianwen-1 was the world's 56th Mars exploration mission.
   D. The former Soviet Union launched the first spacecraft.

Thursday
[阅读理解 C]

China Urges Global Unity on Climate Measures

China has called for（提倡）all countries to join forces and take action on climate adaptation（适应）and work to achieve new progress on global climate governance（治理；管理）, as 2021 marks the comprehensive implementation（全面落实）of the Paris Agreement on climate change.

Vice-Premier Han Zheng made the remark on Monday when addressing the Climate Adaptation Summit（峰会）2021 via video link in Beijing. The response to climate change, a common <u>challenge</u> facing humanity, requires considering both mitigation（减缓）and adaptation, he said.

In order to actively carry out（执行；实现）the Paris Agreement, Han said that developed countries should offer more financial and technical support to developing countries.

He also called on all countries to make and carry out national adaptation plans according to their national realities. This would make their adaptation measures more effective（有效的）, he said.

The summit came after Han had addressed the One Planet Summit, which focused on global climate and environmental governance, earlier this month.

体裁：记叙文
题材：新闻速递
正确率：_____/5
词数：151
难度：★★★★☆
建议用时：7 分钟
实际用时：_____
答案页码：160

---

1. What has China called for other countries to do?
   A. Join forces and take action on climate adaptation.
   B. Work for new changes on the Paris Agreement.
   C. Achieve the implementation of the Paris Agreement.
   D. Have a meeting on climate change in Paris.

2. The underlined word "challenge" most probably means _____ in Chinese.
   A. 机会   B. 挑战   C. 向往   D. 改变

3. Han Zheng thought that _____ countries should help _____ countries in terms of technology.
   A. developing; developed
   B. developed; developed
   C. developed; developing
   D. developing; developing

4. From the passage, what can we know about Han Zheng?
   A. He thought all countries should make and carry out national adaptation plans.
   B. He believed all adaptation measures would be very effective.
   C. He cared little about global climate and environmental governance.
   D. He held the One Planet Summit.

5. What does the passage mainly discuss?
   A. China advises all countries to work together on climate adaptation.
   B. Developed countries should help developing countries.
   C. Other countries ask China to take actions on climate change.
   D. We should actively carry out the Paris Agreement.

Friday
[任务型阅读 D]

Shanghai Museum Holding an Ox Art Show

A new Chinese zodiac (生肖) show on the ox in ancient Chinese art opened on Feb 2, followed by a series of seven exhibitions at the Shanghai Museum for the year 2021.

Four objects stood in glass cases in the hall and four other pieces were displayed in the different showrooms at the Shanghai Museum. The zodiac exhibition featured eight objects related to the ox, the symbolic (象征的) animal for the Year 2021.

The museum hoped visitors could take a journey of discovery through the showrooms, to understand the wide representation (代表) of oxen in ancient Chinese culture, according to Chu Xin, deputy director (副主任) of the exhibition department at the Shanghai Museum. The ox is important in Chinese art because the animal is closely related to two important issues in traditional Chinese society: farming and rituals (仪式).

While six of the sculptures (雕塑), paintings and jade (玉制的) objects with oxen on them were chosen from the collection of the Shanghai Museum, two objects from the Republic of Korea were borrowed from the National Museum of Korea.

阅读短文，回答下面 1~5 小题。

1. Where did the Chinese zodiac show open?
_____
_____

2. How many objects were displayed in the glass cases in the hall?
_____
_____

3. According to Chu Xin, what could visitors do by visiting the showrooms?
_____
_____

4. Why is the ox important in Chinese art?
_____
_____

5. Were all the objects displayed from China?
_____
_____

Saturday
[短文填空]

Thousands of Ancient Tombs Found near Xi'an

According to the news post on Monday by the Shaanxi Provincial Administration of Cultural Heritage, more than 3,500 ancient tombs of (1)_____ dynasties（朝代）have been discovered on the construction site（建筑工地）of Xi'an Xianyang International Airport.

From Feb 4 to 17, more than 60 members of an excavation（挖掘）(2)_____ lived near the airport, and together with 900 workers, celebrated the Spring Festival (3)_____. They gave up the (4)_____ and kept on excavating to make the project go smoothly.

"Within the work area of the project, a total of 4,600 cultural relics（文物）were (5)_____, including 3,500 ancient tombs," the administration said in the news. "Such a large (6)_____ and scale means the excavation will be quite (7)_____."

No more details about the excavation have been released.

As of Wednesday afternoon, posts on the topic has been viewed 34 million (8)_____.

As the (9)_____ of 13 dynasties throughout Chinese history, Xi'an and its archaeological（考古的）discoveries have often (10)_____ the headlines.

阅读短文，从方框中选择合适的单词填空，使短文通顺，意思完整。

discovered
hit
team
times
capital
different
holiday
difficult
number
locally

Sunday
[拓展阅读]

The Tongliang Dragon Dance

体裁：说明文　　题材：传统文化　　词数：174
难度：★★★☆☆　建议用时：6分钟　　实际用时：_____

The Tongliang dragon (龙) dance surprised people when it showed in New York City's Times Square on New Year's Eve. A colorful 15-meter-long dragon made of paper, nylon (尼龙) silk, bamboo and wooden poles jumped, rolled and hovered (盘旋) to traditional folk songs as it was controlled by eight performers (表演者).

In China, the dragon dance has been a major festival activity during Lunar New Year for over 1,000 years. Tongliang, a district in Southwest China's Chongqing, is home to the country's best dragon-dance show. The best-known is the Tongliang fire-dragon dance. Fire that comes out from the dragon's mouth and body forms a spectacular (壮观的) show.

The Tongliang dragon dance has been performed at such major events like China's National Day celebrations, the 2008 Beijing Olympics and the 2010 Shanghai World Expo. And dragon-dance has been performed in more than 30 countries and regions, including the United States, Britain, France, Australia, Turkey, Japan and the Republic of Korea. And this ancient tradition will continue to fly into the future.

答案解析 / 词汇碎片 / 重难句讲解

Week One

Monday [完形填空]

【答案解析】

1. B。考查冠词辨析。此处表示泛指，故填 a 或者 an；空格后的 unusual 为元音音素开头，应填 an，故选 B。

2. C。考查动词辨析。A 项意为"听"，B 项意为"制作；使得"；C 项意为"想；认为"，D 项意为"看"。think 常与 of 连用，意为"考虑；想起"，所以 C 项符合语义，故选 C。

3. B。考查上下文语义。空格所在句子的前半句提到 The idea of cloning was understood（人们理解克隆的概念），后半句提到 it was hard to carry out for many animals（很难将它在许多动物的身上实现），前后构成转折关系，故选 B。

4. C。考查名词辨析。A 项意为"科学家"，B 项意为"人们"，C 项意为"动物"，D 项意为"婴儿"。空格前面提到了克隆在动物身上很难实现，但接着又举了克隆羊"多莉"的例子，所以"动物"符合语义，故选 C。

5. C。考查动词辨析。A 项意为"写"，B 项意为"唱歌"，C 项意为"谈话"，D 项意为"玩耍"。C 项与 about 连用意为"讨论"，代入文中后符合语义，故选 C。

6. C。考查副词辨析。A 项意为"恰好"，B 项意为"缓慢地"，C 项意为"终于；最后"，D 项意为"明显地"。空格所在句子的前面提到美国鱼类及野生动物管理局从 2013 年以来就一直在讨论克隆黑足雪貂，"终于；最后"代入后符合语义，故选 C。

7. B。考查介词辨析。表示"在……国家"时，一般用"in+国家名"，故选 B。

8. B。考查形容词辨析。A 项意为"生病的"，B 项意为"健康的"，C 项意为"难过的"，D 项意为"和蔼的"。文章第一段第一句提到 a healthy black-footed ferret（一只健康的黑足雪貂），这只黑足雪貂就是伊丽莎白·安，且空格后面提到雪貂 enjoys spending her days（享受生活），故选 B。

9. B。考查名词辨析。A 项意为"孩子"，B 项意为"姐妹"，C 项意为"朋友"，D 项意为"家人"。空格处和前面的 brothers 并列，B 项 sisters 和 brothers 构成短语 brothers and sisters，意为"兄弟姐妹"，故选 B。

10. D。考查动词辨析。A 项意为"改变"，B 项意为"停止"，C 项意为"离开"，D 项意为"传播"。根据上文的 she will probably have babies（它可能会有孩子）和 her children will have babies（它的孩子也会繁衍后代）可知伊丽莎白·安的基因会传播开来，故选 D。

【词汇碎片】

scientist *n.* 科学家
die *v.* 死亡；凋零
store *v.* 贮藏

【重难句讲解】

（第二段第二句）

In the 1980s, samples from a ferret named Willa were stored in the "Frozen Zoo". 20 世纪 80 年代，一只名叫韦拉的雪貂的样本被存放在"冷冻动物园"里。

本句是一个简单句，句子的主干是 samples were stored in the "Frozen Zoo"，from a ferret 和 named Willa 作后置定语，分别修饰 samples 和 a ferret，翻译时把定语放在其修饰的名词前面。In the 1980s 作时间状语。

Tuesday [阅读理解 A]

【答案解析】

1. B。细节理解题。根据第二段第一句中的China took a leading role in the number of such companies（中国在这类公司数量上占据领先地位）可知，此处应是"数量"最多，故选B。

2. B。细节理解题。第三段列举了中国各种不同的人工智能公司的例子，说明人工智能公司的种类很多，故选B。

3. B。细节理解题。根据第三段中的Chinese government...help AI develop in the country（中国政府……促进国内人工智能的发展）可知中国政府支持人工智能的发展，故选B。

4. D。推理判断题。最后一段提到，目前有很多机器人在工厂工作，而且在疫情期间，人工智能在医疗领域得到了快速发展，这说明技术给人们提供了许多帮助，故选D。

5. A。态度观点题。全文主要讲述了中国人工智能领域的发展现状及其发展前景，根据文章对中国人工智能的介绍，可知作者对中国人工智能的发展是有信心的，所以A项最有可能是作者的观点，故选A。

【词汇碎片】

country n. 国家
billion num. 十亿
expect v. 期待；预测

【重难句讲解】

（第三段第三句）

It is expected that China's face recognition market share will account for 44.59 percent of the world's total by 2023. 预计到2023年，中国的人脸识别市场份额将占全球总额的44.59%。

本句是一个复合句，包含主语从句。It作形式主语，真正的主语是后面that引导的主语从句。It is expected that... 是固定句型，意为"预计……"。

Wednesday [阅读理解 B]

【答案解析】

1. D。细节理解题。根据题干中的关键词popular定位到第一段，从mobile payment has become popular in China可知移动支付在中国很普遍，故选D。

2. A。词义猜测题。画线单词所在句子的主干是The proportion reached 85%，由后面的百分比85%可推测proportion表示"比例；占比"，故选A。

3. C。推理判断题。第二段第三句提到2020年使用扫码支付的人群的比例达85%，说明扫码支付是一种很重要的支付方式，所以C项正确。A项和D项中的everyone都过于绝对；第二段第三句提到2020年使用扫码支付的人相比2019年有所增长，B项不符合原文，故排除；故选C。

4. B。细节理解题。根据题干中的关键词post-1995 generation定位到第三段，从People from the post-1995 generation were the most active users...especially the men（95后是最活跃的使用群体……尤其是男性）可知使用移动支付的男性比女性多，故选B。

5. B。细节理解题。根据最后一段的第一句可知移动支付流行的原因是多方面的，所以B项正确。最后一段还提到直播在消费者中很受欢迎，且部分用户通过直播购买生活必需品，A、C两项与原文不符，D项属于无中生有，故选B。

【词汇碎片】

technology n. 技术
reach v. 达到；延伸
reason n. 原因；理由

【重难句讲解】

（第二段第四句）

The report said Chinese people used mobile payment three times a day on average. 报告称，中国人平均每天使用三次移动支付。

本句是一个复合句，包含宾语从句，主句是The report said, Chinese people used mobile payment three times a day on average 是省略了 that 的宾语从句，作 said 的宾语。three times a day 是固定搭配，意为"一天三次"。

Thursday [阅读理解 C]

【答案解析】

1. B。细节理解题。根据题干中的关键信息 find answers 定位到第一段第一句，从 because it needed a lot of time and efforts to find the right answers to the problems（因为找出问题的正确答案需要花费许多时间和精力）可知需要花费很多时间，故选 B。

2. C。细节理解题。解答本题可采用排除法，根据第二段中的 her seven subjects（她的七门功课）、the last year of junior high school（初中的最后一年）和 sleep is important to me（睡眠对我来说很重要）可知 A、B、D 三项正确，故选 C。

3. A。词义猜测题。画线单词所在段落的第一句提到她在完成家庭作业后还需要多学习一个小时，可知额外学习一个小时就意味着睡眠时间少一个小时，由此推测画线单词意为"缺乏；短缺"，故选 A。

4. A。推理判断题。第三段最后一句提到了这种装置的使用方法，学生只需要拍下错题的照片，装置上就会显示答案，由此可以推知该装置的使用方法很简单，故选 A。

5. C。主旨大意题。本文主要讲述技术让学习变得更简单了，C 项"技术在学习中的应用"符合文章大意，故选 C。

【词汇碎片】

useful *adj.* 有用的
subject *n.* 学科；科目
important *adj.* 重要的

【重难句讲解】

（第三段第一句）

But hope is coming for Yimeng and her friends in the form of an intelligent question answering device. 但是对于一梦和她的朋友们来说，智能答题装置正在给她们带来希望。

本句是一个简单句，句子的主干是 hope is coming。for Yimeng and her friends 和 in the form of an intelligent question answering device 分别作对象状语和方式状语，其中 in the form of 为固定搭配，意为"以……的形式"。

Friday [任务型阅读 D]

【答案解析】

1. B。空格前面一句在介绍 microprocessors（微处理器），后面一句在介绍微处理器的用途，所以可推测空格处的内容仍然与微处理器有关，选项中只有 B 项提到了微处理器，故选 B。

2. D。空格后面列举了三个汽车运行方面的细节，可知空格处是一个总结概括性的句子，D 项 Chips control many things（芯片控制很多方面）符合上下文关系，且其中的 control 与空格后面的 controlling 对应，故选 D。

3. C。空格后面提到汽车制造商们无法生产他们计划生产的汽车，这是一种结果，可知空格处是原因，C 项 But now car makers don't have enough chips（但是现在汽车制造商们没有足够多的芯片）符合上下文关系，故选 C。

4. E。空格前面提到由于疫情，汽车制造商们关闭了工厂，空格后面提到汽车制造商们停止购买芯片。E 项 Since they weren't making cars（因为他们不生产汽车了）起到了连接上下文的作用，故选 E。

5. A。空格前面提到汽车制造商遭遇困境，这使得芯片制造商停止为汽车制造芯片，A 项 They began selling lots of chips to other kinds of companies（他们开始向其他行业的公司出售大量芯片）符合语义，故选 A。

【词汇碎片】

part *n.* 部分；零件
control *v.* 控制

【重难句讲解】

（第二段第一句）

Tiny computers, called microprocessors, are very important in modern cars. 被称为微处理器的微型计算机在

现代汽车中非常重要。

　　本句是一个简单句，句子的主干是 Tiny computers are very important in modern cars, called microprocessors 作后置定语修饰 Tiny computers。

Saturday [短文填空]

●【答案解析】

（1）several。空格后为复数名词 successes，所以空格处应填入修饰名词的形容词，将所给形容词代入后，只有 several 符合句意，意为"几次成功"，故填 several。

（2）simply。空格所在句句意为："天问一号"不会_____绕火星轨道运行。空格处修饰动词 orbit，应该填副词。下文提到"天问一号"将向火星地表发送火星车，由此可知形容词 simple 的副词形式 simply 符合句意，意为"仅仅"，故填 simply。

（3）months。根据语境判断 for a few_____作时间状语，month 符合句意。空格前面有 a few 修饰，故填名词 month 的复数形式 months。

（4）size。空格所在句句意为："天问一号"的火星车只有高尔夫球般_____。size 意为"尺寸"，符合句意，故填 size。

（5）countries。根据空格前的 many 可知空格处应该填入名词的复数形式。下文提到了 the U.S.，country 意为"国家"，正好与之呼应，故填 countries。

（6）And。空格前面提到很多国家都尝试过登陆火星，但只有美国成功了，后面提到甚至美国的登陆也失败过，两者之间呈递进关系，故填 and。

（7）plans。空格所在句缺少谓语，应该填动词。plan 意为"计划"，符合句意，因为主语 China 是第三人称单数形式，故填 plans。

（8）wide。空格处修饰名词 area，应该填形容词。本句提到中国航天局在选择火星着陆点，wide 意为"宽阔的"，符合句意，故填 wide。

（9）landed。空格所在句缺少谓语，应该填动词，同时根据时间状语 in 1976 可知要用一般过去时。landed 代入文中后意为"维京 2 号着陆器着陆"，符合句意，故填 landed。

（10）for。look for 为固定搭配，意为"寻找"，故填 for。

●【词汇碎片】

recently *adv*. 最近
succeed in 在……方面取得成功
fail *v*. 失败

●【重难句讲解】

（第三段第一句）

Landing on Mars is something many countries have tried and failed at. 火星着陆是很多国家尝试过但都失败了的事情。

　　本句是一个复合句，包含定语从句。主句是 Landing on Mars is something，many countries have tried and failed at 是定语从句，省略了引导词 that，修饰 something。

（第四段第二句）

China's space agency has chosen a wide area called Utopia Planitia for landing the rover. 中国航天局选择了一个叫作乌托邦平原的宽阔区域来进行火星车的着陆。

　　本句是一个简单句，句子的主干是 China's space agency has chosen a wide area，called Utopia Planitia 作后置定语修饰 area，for landing the rover 作目的状语。

Sunday [拓展阅读]

●【词汇碎片】

protect *v*. 保护
invention *n*. 发明
image *n*. 图像，影像

Week Two

Monday [完形填空]

【答案解析】

1. D。考查固定搭配。live a... life 是固定搭配，意为"过着……生活"。故选 D。
2. B。考查形容词辨析和上下文语义。A 项意为"有趣的"，B 项意为"受欢迎的"，C 项意为"美好的"，D 项意为"重要的"。由文章开头提到的 Famous 可知，蔡志忠先生的漫画是非常有名的，又由空格后的 around the world（全世界）可知，此处应填表达"受欢迎的""普及的"等意思的词。故选 B。
3. A。考查形容词辨析。A 项意为"不同的"，B 项作形容词时意为"和蔼的，宽容的"，也可作名词意为"种类"，但一般要与 of 搭配，C 项意为"困难的"，D 项意为"相同的"。由上文可知，蔡志忠先生的漫画非常受欢迎，因此被翻译成 26 种不同的语言，供全球的读者阅读。故选 A。
4. A。考查动词辨析。A 项意为"工作"，B 项意为"坐"，C 项意为"锻炼"，D 项意为"学习"。由第三段前两句可知，蔡志忠先生的作息时间表很特殊，他下午 5 点上床睡觉，凌晨 1 点醒来。然后，从凌晨 1 点到下午 2 点之间，他应该是在"工作"。故选 A。
5. B。考查代词辨析。A 项意为"没有什么"，B 项意为"所有；一切"，C 项意为"任何事物"，D 项意为"一些事物"。由空格前的 When you are really focused（当你真正专注时）可知，当人们专注于某件事时，周围的一切都是安静的。故选 B。
6. C。考查上下文语义。空格前的 This 指代上文中的 When you are really focused... slow down，空格所在句句意为：这就是_____ 我喜欢在_____ 起床。why 表示原因，符合语境，故选 C。
7. C。考查名词辨析和上下文语义。A 项意为"上午"，B 项意为"下午"，C 项意为"夜晚"，D 项意为"天；白昼"。从第三段描述的蔡志忠先生的作息时间表可知，蔡志忠先生喜欢在半夜起来工作，因此空格处应填 night。故选 C。

8. A。考查上下文语义。由上下文可知，此处是漫画家和作家的对比，蔡志忠先生本身就是一个漫画家，因此此处应填 We。故选 A。
9. B。考查动词辨析。A 项意为"想象"，B 项意为"写"，C 项意为"猜测"，D 项意为"讲话；发言"。空格所在句的 They 指代上文的"作家"，这些作家必须一个字接一个字地"写"。故选 B。
10. D。考查连词辨析。And 前后文一般为并列关系，意为"和"；But 前后文一般为转折关系，意为"但是"；Because 前后文一般为因果关系，意为"因为"；Although 前后文一般为让步关系，意为"虽然"。从下文的 old（老了）和 still works hard（仍然努力工作）可知，此处连词应表示让步关系。故选 D。

【词汇碎片】

create *v.* 创造
special *adj.* 特殊的
quiet *adj.* 安静的
middle *n.* 中间

【重难句讲解】

（第二段第一句）

Born in 1948 in Taiwan, Tsai has been creating comic books that have been popular around the world since 1984. 蔡先生于 1948 年出生在中国台湾，自 1984 年以来一直在创作漫画，他的漫画在全世界广受欢迎。

本句是一个复合句，主句是 Tsai has been creating comic books。句首的 Born in 1948 in Taiwan 是状语，that have been... world 是 that 引导的定语从句，修饰 comic books，句末的 since 1984 是时间状语。

Tuesday [阅读理解 A]

【答案解析】

1. C。细节理解题。根据题干中的关键词 medals 计算每位运动员的奖牌数,可知武大靖是 1 枚,刘佳宇是 1 枚,于淑梅是 5 枚,谷爱凌是 2 枚,故选 C。

2. D。细节理解题。根据题干中的关键信息 Wu Dajing and Liu Jiayu 定位到人物对应的表格,可知武大靖和刘佳宇两人均参加了 2018 年的奥运会,且分别获得了金牌和银牌,故选 D。

3. C。细节理解题。根据题干中的关键信息 Wu Dajing and Gu Ailing 定位到人物对应的表格,可知武大靖在奥运会上为中国赢得了第一枚男子个人冰上运动项目的金牌,而谷爱凌也在极限运动项目上为中国赢得了第一枚金牌,故选 C。

4. D。细节理解题。根据题干中的关键词 Gu Ailing 定位到人物对应的表格,可知谷爱凌在 2021 年 1 月 29 日赢得了第一枚极限运动项目的金牌,在 2021 年 1 月 30 日赢得了第二枚金牌,因此 D 项"她于 2021 年 1 月 30 日获得 2 枚金牌"错误。谷爱凌虽然在美国出生,但是她代表中国参加比赛,故 A 项和 B 项正确。武大靖出生于 1994 年,刘佳宇出生于 1992 年,于淑梅出生于 1975 年,谷爱凌出生于 2003 年,因此谷爱凌是他们四个中年龄最小的一个,C 项正确。故选 D。

【词汇碎片】

medal *n.* 奖牌
champion *n.* 冠军

【重难句讲解】

In 1996, she took part in 5 events and won 2 gold, 1 silver and 2 bronze medals. 1996 年,她参加了 5 项赛事,获得了 2 枚金牌、1 枚银牌和 2 枚铜牌。

本句是一个由 and 连接的并列句。第一个并列句中的 took part in 为固定搭配,意为"参加"。第二个并列句中,谓语动词 won 前省略了主语 she,2 gold, 1 silver and 2 bronze medals 为 and 连接的三个并列宾语。

Wednesday [阅读理解 B]

【答案解析】

1. B。细节理解题。根据题干中的关键词 first scarf 定位到第二段,可知陈秀兰是在 16 岁时制作了第一条围巾,故选 B。

2. B。细节理解题。根据题干中的关键信息 sell her embroidery works 定位到第三段第一句,可知陈秀兰是骑着摩托车去售卖她的刺绣产品的,故选 B。

3. C。细节理解题。根据题干中的关键词 online 定位到第四段第一句,可知陈秀兰在网上售卖她的产品很难,是因为她从未学过如何使用计算机,故选 C。

4. A。主旨大意题。本篇文章主要讲述了陈秀兰对刺绣手工艺的执着追求,并希望刺绣这种传统手工艺得以传承。因此,A 项"坚持我们的梦想"与主题相符。B 项和 C 项太过片面,D 项在文中无相关内容,故选 A。

【词汇碎片】

owner *n.* 所有者
education *n.* 教育
youth *n.* 青(少)年时期
carry forward 发扬;推进

【重难句讲解】

(第四段第一句)

Without enough education in her youth, Chen said that it's hard for her to sell her works online because she has never learned to use a computer. 陈秀兰说,由于年轻时没有得到足够的教育,在网上售卖她的产品对她来说很难,因为她从未学过如何使用计算机。

本句是一个复合句,主句的句子主干是 Chen said that... , that it's hard for her... use a computer 是 that 引导的宾语从句,作 said 的宾语,其中还包含一个 because 引导的原因状语从句,句首的 Without enough education in her youth 作原因状语。

Thursday [阅读理解 C]

【答案解析】

1. B。细节理解题。根据题干中的关键词 childhood 和 dream 定位到第二段,由第二句和第三句可知王梓漪童年的梦想是做一名职业的高尔夫球手,第三句中的 childhood dream 指代的就是第二句中的 become a professional golfer,故选 B。

2. D。词义猜测题。画线单词所在句提到王梓漪在中国女子职业高尔夫球巡回赛中获得冠军,破折号是对前面的内容做进一步介绍,具体讲述了王梓漪在哪场巡回比赛中获得的冠军,所以可推测 Challenge 应与赛事有关,故选 D。

3. A。细节理解题。根据题干中的关键词 politics 定位到第二段最后两句,可知王梓漪放弃成为一名职业的高尔夫球手的梦想,决定学习政治学,因为她意识到自己对政治学比对运动更感兴趣,故选 A。

4. C。细节理解题。由第一段王梓漪在高尔夫球运动中取得的成绩可知,她非常擅长打高尔夫球,故 A 项正确;由第二段最后一句可知,王梓漪对政治学比对运动更感兴趣,故 B 项正确;由最后一段最后一句 In golf, I'm always facing loss, and it helps me to face difficulties(在高尔夫球运动中,我总是面临失败,这有助于我面对困难)可知,高尔夫球教会了她如何面对失败,故 D 项正确;C 项属于偷换概念,最后一段第一句中的 years of hard work(努力练习了很多年)指王梓漪学习打高尔夫球很多年,不是学习政治学,C 项错误。根据题目要求,故选 C。

【词汇碎片】

challenge *n.* 挑战赛;挑战
finish *v.* 完成
decide *v.* 决定
realize *v.* 认识到

【重难句讲解】

(第二段第四句)

She realized that she had a deeper interest and passion for politics than for sport. 她意识到自己对政治学的兴趣和热情比对体育的更强烈。

本句是一个复合句,主句的句子主干是 She realized that...,that 引导宾语从句,作 realized 的宾语。形容词比较级 + than 表示"比……更……"。

(第三段第一句)

My friends and coaches feel sorry for me because I gave up the golf career after years of hard work. 我的朋友和教练为我感到遗憾,因为我努力练习了很多年,最终却放弃了高尔夫球职业。

本句是一个复合句,主句的句子主干是 My friends and coaches feel sorry for me,后面是 because 引导的原因状语从句。feel sorry for 表示"为……感到可惜(难过)",动词词组 gave up 的原形为 give up,意为"放弃"。

Friday [任务型阅读 D]

【答案解析】

1. At the age of 12. 根据题干中的关键信息 have the idea of collecting old porcelain pieces 定位到第二段第一句,可知余学云从 12 岁就有了收集瓷器的想法。

2. About 30 million yuan. 根据题干中的关键信息 spend in porcelain ware 定位到第三段第一句,可知在过去的 30 年里,余学云大概花了 3 千万在瓷器上。

3. At first she couldn't understand him, but as she grew up, she learned a lot from him. 根据文章最后一段最后两句可知,余学云的大女儿起初不明白为什么父亲把钱全花在这种爱好上,但随着她慢慢长大,她渐渐理解了,并且从父亲身上学到了很多。

4. Yes, I will. Because it will make me happy./No, I will not. Because I will spend some money on something more important.(根据自己的真实想法合理作答即可。)

【词汇碎片】

remember *v.* 记得
soil *n.* 土壤

million *num.* 百万
use up 花光，用完
hobby *n.* 业余爱好

● 【重难句讲解】

（第二段第一句）

Yu remembered that he first had the idea of collecting porcelain pieces at the age of 12. 余学云记得，他第一次萌生收藏瓷器的想法是在12岁的时候。

本句是一个复合句，主句的句子主干是 Yu remembered that...，that 引导宾语从句，作 remembered 的宾语，of collecting porcelain pieces 作后置定语，修饰 idea，at the age of 12 是时间状语。

（第四段第二句）

At first, she couldn't understand why her father used up his money in such a hobby. 起初，她不明白为什么父亲要把钱全花在这种爱好上。

本句是一个复合句，主句的句子主干是 she couldn't understand why...，why 引导宾语从句。句首的 At first 作时间状语。

Saturday [短文填空]

● 【答案解析】

（1）traveled。空格所在句子有主语，但是缺少谓语，由此可知空格处应该填入一个动词，根据文章第一段提到的 traveled to 84 countries（游历了84个国家），可知该空应填 travel，又因时间是2012年，须用过去式，故填 traveled。

（2）no。空格所在句子为 There be 句型，由第二段倒数第二句可知，古巴很多地方没有网络，所以空格所在句要表达的是，在古巴，除了大酒店，其他地方都连不上互联网，故填 no。

（3）lots。lots of 为固定搭配，意为"很多"，故填 lots。

（4）computer。空格前为不定冠词，所以该空应填名词，空格后面提到房主买了一台电脑，故填 computer。

（5）see。空格后面提到 perspective（视角），由此可知空格处应填入表达"看；看待"意思的词，故填 see。

（6）first。空格后面提到 start his exploration（开始他的探索），由此可知空格处应填入表达"第一"意思的词，for the first time 为固定搭配，意为"第一次"，故填 first。

（7）Besides。空格后面为并列的动名词短语，且句子并没有缺少主语，所以空格处需要填入一个介词，又因空格所在句的主句中出现了 also，可知空格处应填入表达"除了……（还）"意思的介词，故填 Besides。

（8）running/to run。空格后面的句子提到 Running in a city（在城市里跑步），由此可知空格处应该填入表示"跑步"的词，like 后面可以接 to do 或 doing，故填 running/to run。

● 【词汇碎片】

travel *v.* 旅行
instrument *n.* 乐器
computer *n.* 电脑；计算机

● 【重难句讲解】

（第三段的直接引语）

One of the most meaningful things about traveling is that you can see the world with a fresh perspective. 旅行最有意义的一点就是，你可以用全新的视角看世界。

本句是一个复合句，主句的句子主干是 One of the most meaningful things is that...，about traveling 作后置定语，修饰主语 One of the most meaningful things，系动词 is 后面是 that 引导的表语从句。

（第四段第三句）

Running in a city, which I have not visited before, allows me to see something new and soak in its sights, sounds and smells. 在一个我以前从未去过的城市里跑步，可以让我看到一些新事物，沉浸在它的景色、声音和气味中。

本句是一个复合句，主句是 Running in a city allows me... and smells，两个逗号之间的句子是 which 引导的定

语从句，修饰 city。allow sb. to do sth. 是 allow 的常见用法，意为"允许某人做某事"，soak in 为固定用法，意为"沉浸于"。

set out 出发；开始
remember v. 记起；牢记

Sunday [拓展阅读]

【词汇碎片】

be good for 有益于；对……有好处

Week Three

Monday [完形填空]

【答案解析】

1. A。考查名词辨析。A项意为"结果",B项意为"方式",C项意为"理由",D项意为"目的"。代入原文后,"结果"更符合语义,故选A。

2. C。考查动词短语辨析。A项意为"起飞;脱下",B项意为"下(车)",C项意为"关闭(电源)",D项意为"切断;中断"。cameras属于电子产品,将其关闭要用turn off,故选C。

3. D。考查形容词辨析。A项意为"无聊的",B项意为"愤怒的",C项意为"困难的",D项意为"紧张的"。代入原文后,"紧张的"更符合语义,故选D。

4. B。考查代词辨析。A项意为"一个",B项意为"另一个",C项意为"其他的",D项意为"哪一个"。在前文中出现了One student, Another student表示"另一名学生",故选B。

5. B。考查条件状语从句。A项意为"如果不;除非",B项意为"如果",C项意为"虽然",D项意为"即使"。这里是该学生提出的一种假设:如果关闭摄像头,他能更加专注地学习。所以该句为条件状语从句,故选B。

6. B。考查动词辨析。A项意为"制作",B项意为"鼓励",C项意为"造成;导致",D项意为"控制"。代入原文后,"鼓励"更符合语义,且后文出现了B项encourage的名词形式encouragement,故选B。

7. A。考查上下文语义。空格前面提到老师要鼓励学生打开摄像头,空格后面提到老师不能强迫学生,所以此处的上下文语义出现了转折,故选A。

8. D。考查动词辨析。A项接to意为"同意",B项接to意为"回答",C项接to意为"选择",D项接to意为"向……解释"。代入原文后,"向……解释"更符合语义,故选D。

9. D。考查宾语从句。空格所在句是so引导的结果状语从句,对逗号前面的句子进行解释,而understand后面缺少宾语。why表示原因,代入原文后意为"这样学生就能更好地明白老师要求他们这样做的原因",故选D。

10. D。考查介词辨析。A项意为"在……里面",B项意为"在……上面",C项意为"去;向",D项意为"用;和……一起",这里表示"用麦克风发言",故选D。

【词汇碎片】

focus v. 集中(注意力)
force v. 强迫

【重难句讲解】

(第一段)

Two Cornell University teachers have found that most students don't like to show their faces on video during online classes because they are worried about how they look. 康奈尔大学的两位老师发现,大多数学生在网络课程中不喜欢通过视频露脸,因为他们对自己的样貌有所顾虑。

本句是一个复合句,句子的主干是Two Cornell University teachers have found that...,为主谓宾结构,that引导的宾语从句作found的宾语,because引导原因状语从句,原因状语从句中还包含一个how引导的宾语从句,作worried about的宾语。

Tuesday [阅读理解A]

【答案解析】

1. C。细节理解题。根据题干中的关键词make toys定位到第一段第一句,可知张先生用纸板为其女儿制作玩具,故选C。

2. D。细节理解题。根据my daughter always asks me to make one(我的女儿总是要我做一个玩具)可知A项错误;根据His daughter prefers these cardboard toys to video games(比起电子游戏,他的女儿更喜欢

这些纸板玩具）可知 B 项错误；根据 In Zhang's eyes, everything can have a hard cardboard copy（在张先生的眼中，所有东西都可以用硬纸板做出复制品来）可知 C 项错误；根据 some classic video games... be played in the real world（一些经典的电子游戏……可以在现实世界中玩）可知 D 项正确，故选 D。

3. C。词义猜测题。画线单词的后文提到技术带来的影响：difficulty in concentration（难以集中注意力）。由此可以推测 negative 为带有负面感情色彩的词汇，故排除 A、B 两项。由于画线单词修饰的是 effects（影响），故 C 项相较于 D 项来说更合适，故选 C。

4. A。主旨大意题。本篇文章主要讲述一位父亲用废弃的纸板为其女儿制作玩具的故事，这是一种新的亲子相处方法，B 项和 D 项的内容过于片面，C 项与文中 encourage them to use screens less（鼓励孩子们少使用屏幕）正好相反。故选 A。

【词汇碎片】

make from 由……制成
creative *adj.* 有创造力的
friendly *adj.* 友好的
prefer *v.* 偏爱

【重难句讲解】

（第三段）

He hopes that his video can provide a creative solution for parents, especially fathers, on how to enjoy a quality time with their children and encourage them to use screens less. 他希望自己的视频可以为家长（尤其是父亲）提供一个创造性的解决方案，帮助他们与孩子一起享受美好时光，并鼓励孩子们少使用屏幕。

本句是一个复合句，句子的主干是 He hopes that...，为主谓宾结构。that 引导的宾语从句充当 hopes 的宾语；provide sth. for sb. 为固定用法，意为"提供某物给某人"；especially fathers 为插入语，对句意进行补充；how to 加动词原形充当介词 on 的逻辑宾语。

Wednesday [阅读理解 B]

【答案解析】

1. B。细节理解题。根据 China has made great progress in special education in the past ten years（在过去的十年中，中国在特殊教育方面取得了重大进展）可知，中国的特殊教育比以前更好了，故选 B。

2. A。细节理解题。根据题干中的关键信息 with serious disabilities 定位到第二段最后一句，但是这里没有提供具体的数据，因此我们需要自行计算，去掉前面的 49%、21.5% 和 0.48%，最后得出结果为 29.02%，故选 A。

3. C。细节理解题。根据题干中的关键信息 special schools necessary 定位到第三段第三句，可知特殊学校是必要的，因为普通学校目前无法给有特殊需求的学生提供更好的学习体验，所以 C 项正确。文中并没有提到特殊学校更受家长欢迎，故排除 A 项；文中提到普通学校拒绝接受有特殊需求的学生，但这只是假设，且不符合题意，故排除 B 项；普通学校目前并不具备满足特殊需求学生的教育资源和能力，故排除 D 项。故选 C。

4. C。推理判断题。最后一段中作者提到有特殊需求的学生有权接受教育，但是目前的普通学校还不具备给这些学生提供教育的资源和能力。如果这个问题得到解决，中国的特殊教育将更进一步发展，所以可以推测作者接下来可能会介绍帮助普通学校解决这个问题的办法，故选 C。

【词汇碎片】

the number of... ……的数量
receive *v.* 接受
be able to 能够
necessary *adj.* 必要的

【重难句讲解】

（第三段第四句）

And if this problem can be solved, special education will go further towards the right direction. 如果这个问题能够得到解决，那么特殊教育将朝着正确的方向进一步发展。

本句是一个复合句，句子的主干是 special education will go，为主谓结构；if 引导一个条件状语从句。在 if 引导的条件状语从句中，主句用一般将来时的时候，从句用一般现在时。

Thursday [阅读理解 C]

【答案解析】

1. A。细节理解题。根据题干中的关键词 photography 定位到表格的第一行第一列，可知学生要了解摄影的话应该去 The Maihaugen Gallery（迈豪根画廊），故选 A。

2. C。细节理解题。根据题干中的关键词 ships 定位到表格的第四行第一列，可知学生要看关于船的展览的话应该去 Hart Nautical Gallery（哈特航海画廊），地址在 55 Massachusetts Avenue（马萨诸塞大道 55 号），故选 C。

3. B。细节理解题。根据题干中的关键信息 7:00 pm on Thursday 可知看展的时间为星期四晚上 7 点，这个时候还没闭馆的只有 List Visual Arts Center（李斯特视觉艺术中心），故选 B。

4. D。细节理解题。根据题干中的关键词 the MIT Museum 定位到表格的第三行，题目问的是 the MIT Museum（麻省理工学院博物馆）的门票费用，成人 10 美元，18 岁以下青少年 5 美元，加起来是 15 美元，故选 D。

【词汇碎片】

store v. 储藏；储存
collect v. 收藏
all kinds of 各种各样的

【重难句讲解】

It is a creative laboratory that provides students and artists with a space to do artistic experiment and collects lots of sculptures by artists such as Henry Moore, Anish Kapoor, Cai Guoqiang and Alexander Calder. 这是一个创意实验室，为学生和艺术家提供进行艺术实验的空间，并收藏了亨利·摩尔、艾尼斯·卡普尔、蔡国强和亚历山大·卡尔德等艺术家创作的大量雕塑作品。

本句是一个复合句，句子的主干是 It is a creative laboratory。that 引导的定语从句修饰先行词 laboratory，that 在从句中充当主语；provide sb. with sth. 为固定用法，意为"为某人提供某物"。

Friday [任务型阅读 D]

【答案解析】

1. He was 12 years old. 根据题干中的关键信息 the youngest winner 定位到文章第一段第一句，可知这时索利·拉斐尔是 12 岁。

2. It's about political wisdom, environmental consciousness and the importance of social consciousness. 根据题干中的关键词 *Australian Air* 定位到文章第一段第一句和第二句，可知这首诗主要与政治智慧、环保意识和社会意识的重要性有关。

3. Because it encouraged more students to create poetry. 根据题干中的关键信息 Solli's first book 定位到文章第二段第三句，可知索利的第一本书因鼓励更多的学生进行诗歌创作而广受赞誉。

4. Solli's poems are powerful and warm. 根据题干中的关键信息 Solli's poems 定位到第三段第一句，这里提到索利喜欢撰写有力且温暖的诗歌，可知索利的诗歌特点就是"有力而温暖的"。

5. 这个活跃的青少年随着全球青年运动的发展而成长，并为年轻人展示了成功的可能性。

【词汇碎片】

winner n. 获胜者
perform v. 表演
praise n. 赞誉；赞赏
important adj. 重要的

【重难句讲解】

（第一段第一句）

At 12 years of age, Solli Raphael became the youngest winner of the Australian Poetry Slam held at the Sydney Opera House after he performed *Australian Air*. 时年12岁的索利·拉斐尔，凭借对（诗歌）《澳大利亚的空气》进行的表演，成为在悉尼歌剧院举办的澳大利亚诗歌大满贯的最年轻的获奖者。

本句是一个包含时间状语从句的复合句。after 引导时间状语从句；of the Australian Poetry Slam 作后置定语，修饰 winner；held at the Sydney Opera House 作后置定语，修饰 Australian Poetry Slam。

Saturday [短文填空]

【答案解析】

（1）a。空格前面主语和谓语完整，后面是一个形容词修饰的名词，由此考虑空格处缺少冠词，language 是可数名词，故填 a。

（2）tips。空格后文出现 The first tip（第一个技巧）和 The second tip（第二个技巧），由此可知空格处应该填入表示"技巧"的词，故填 tips。

（3）is。The first tip 为第三人称单数，且此处时态为一般现在时，故填 is。

（4）problems。空格后文出现了 about this problem，由此可推测这里应该填入 problems，且 have problems with 为常见搭配，意为"在……（方面）有问题"，故填 problems。

（5）when。空格前后都为完整的句子，由此可知这里需要填入一个连接词，以表示从属、并列、转折等关系。空格前后的两个句子在时间上有同时进行的关系，所以考虑这里是时间状语从句，故填 when。

（6）attention。pay attention to 为固定搭配，意为"注意；重视"，故填 attention。

（7）about。think about 为固定搭配，意为"思考；想一想"，故填 about。

（8）other。空格前面以 order 作为关键词举例，但在真实的对话中还会有别的关键词，所以空格处需要填入一个表示"别的；其他的"的词，故填 other。

【词汇碎片】

carry on 进行
difficult *adj.* 困难的
try *v.* 尝试；试图

【重难句讲解】

（第三段第二句）

The second tip is to prepare a list of those words and try to listen to them when a customer begins talking with you. 第二个技巧是准备那些单词的列表，并在客户开始与你交谈时试图听到它们。

本句是一个复合句，包含一个 when 引导的时间状语从句。to prepare a list of those words and try to listen to them 为动词不定式短语，作 be 动词 is 的表语，try to do sth. 意为"试图做某事"。

Sunday [拓展阅读]

【词汇碎片】

make up 组成；编造
order *n.* 顺序；命令

Week Four

Monday [完形填空]

【答案解析】

1. C。考查连词辨析。A项意为"因此",B项意为"或者",C项意为"但是",D项意为"因为"。根据第一段可知,人们都在新的一年里决定提升自己。空格所在句指出,汤姆·范德比尔特没有等到新的一年才开始提升自己,这里的语义发生转折,因此用But。上下文没有因果的逻辑关系,故排除A项和D项。这里也没有二选一的含义,故排除B项。故选C。

2. B。考查动词辨析。A项意为"控制",B项意为"观看",C项意为"讨论",D项意为"听到"。首先空格处填入的动词后面应搭配sb. do,故可排除A项和C项。而根据句意,这里应指看女儿学习下棋,而不是听女儿学习下棋,排除D项,故选B。

3. A。考查动词辨析和上下文语义。A项意为"决定",B项意为"拒绝",C项意为"忘记",D项意为"需要"。空格所在句意为:他_____加入她的行列。下文都在说他学习新的技能,可知这里只有A项符合上下文语义,故选A。B项与上下文语义相反,故排除。C项和D项均不符合语义,故排除。

4. B。考查动词短语辨析。A项意为"出发;着手进行",B项意为"开始",C项意为"重新开始",D项意为"动身前往"。B项代入后符合语义,故选B。

5. C。考查名词辨析。A项意为"活动",B项意为"练习",C项意为"技能",D项意为"方法"。根据后文可知,他想要的是掌握技能,故选C。

6. D。考查名词辨析。A项意为"头;领导人",head teacher表示"校长";B项意为"钢琴",piano teacher表示"钢琴老师";C项意为"艺术",art teacher表示"艺术老师";D项意为"声音",voice teacher表示"声乐老师"。空格前面指出他是为了学习唱歌,可知他找的是声乐老师,故选D。

7. D。考查形容词辨析。A项意为"遗憾的",B项意为"自豪的",C项意为"有害的",D项意为"快乐的"。空格所在句意为:你应该敞开心扉,把它当成一次_____的经历。A项和C项表示消极的感情色彩,可直接排除。B项和D项代入后,D项更符合语义,故选D。

8. A。考查冠词辨析。根据句意可知这里特指上文提到的声乐老师,因此填定冠词,故选A。

9. A。考查名词辨析。A项意为"关键",B项意为"原因",C项意为"例子",D项意为"乐趣"。空格后面提到将注意力从自己身上转移出去,可以看出这里说的是学习新事物的方法或关键,故选A。

10. B。考查介词辨析。A项意为"从……起",B项意为"与……;随着",C项意为"在……之后",D项意为"在……之前"。空格所在句没有表达一种前后状态或者开始的状态,且后半句意为"他学会了……",说明他是在过程中学会了某种技巧,因此这里表示"在冲浪的过程中",B项代入后符合语义,故选B。

11. B。考查名词辨析。A项意为"警卫员",B项意为"冲浪板",C项意为"教练",D项意为"地面"。上文提到转移注意力,因此这里说的是在冲浪过程中,注意力不能放在自己的双脚或者_____上。B项符合语义,故选B。

12. C。考查名词辨析和上下文语义。A项意为"帽子",B项意为"鞋子",C项意为"球",D项意为"瓶子"。空格所在句意为:他们观察_____被抛出时达到的顶点。根据前文可知,这里说的应该是抛球,故选C。

13. D。考查固定搭配。win... prize(s)为固定搭配,意为"获得……奖项",故选D。

14. A。考查形容词辨析。A项意为"快乐的",B项意为"悲伤的",C项意为"生气的",D项意为"紧张的"。下文提到finding delight(寻找快乐),故根据语境,这里说的应该是做这些事情使他快乐,故选A。

15. C。考查动词辨析。A项意为"成功",succeed in doing sth. 表示"成功做某事",但此处既无法与表示时间的2021形成搭配,也不符合语义,故排除;B项意为"享受"，enjoy doing sth. 表示"享受做某事"，无法与2021形成搭配，故排除；C项意为"花费"，spend time (in) doing sth. 表示"花时间做某事"，符合语义；D项意为"浪费"，waste time (in) doing sth. 表示"浪费时间做某事"，与语义相反，故排除。故选C。

【词汇碎片】

improve *v.* 提高水平；改进
experience *n.* 经历
encourage *v.* 鼓励

【重难句讲解】

（第四段第三句）

When he started juggling, he found that jugglers didn't look at the balls; they watched the apex where balls are thrown. 当他开始玩杂耍时，他发现杂耍演员不看球；他们观察球被抛出时达到的顶点。

本句是一个复合句。When引导时间状语从句，that引导的宾语从句作found的宾语；宾语从句中包含由分号连接的两个并列句，第二个并列句中包含where引导的定语从句，修饰apex。

Tuesday [阅读理解 A]

【答案解析】

1. C。推理判断题。根据题干中的关键词The Pack定位到第一个产品。第二句提到学生能学到的技能有说、听、读、写。①"如何用英语谈论一些话题"是"说"方面的技能。②"如何观察说话的人"在文中未涉及。③"如何给一位女商人发送电子邮件"为Business Skills中能学到的技能。④"如何理解他们听到的内容"是"听"方面的技能。故选C。

2. B。细节理解题。根据题干中的关键词The Pack定位到第一个产品，其中提到该产品有5 levels（5个级别）和Over 20 lessons per level（每个级别的课程均超过20节），可知一共有100多节课，故选B。

3. A。细节理解题。根据所给选项定位到第二、三个产品。从第二个产品中的Practical ideas for lessons on e-mail...（关于电子邮件……课程的实用理念）可知A项正确。第三个产品中提到hundreds of fantastic games（数百个精彩的游戏），而不是一百种游戏，故排除C项；B项和D项文中均未提及，故排除。故选A。

4. D。推理判断题。这篇文章是一则广告，最有可能来自杂志（或电子杂志），只有D项符合要求。A项"电影海报"，B项"笔记本"，C项"教科书"均可排除。故选D。

5. C。推理判断题。这篇文章最有可能写给老师，因为文章开头提到了这是介绍给老师的三个产品，目的是帮助老师更好地授课，故选C。

【词汇碎片】

prepare *v.* 使做好准备

Wednesday [阅读理解 B]

【答案解析】

1. B。细节理解题。根据第二段最后一句可知赵彬觉得他所做的事情是有价值的，B项中的was of worth意为"具有价值"，为原文was valued的同义替换，故B项正确。A项原文未提及，故排除；第三段提到在雨天顾客会给赵彬发短信，而不是赵彬给顾客发短信，故排除C项；D项原文未提及，故排除。故选B。

2. A。细节理解题。根据题干中的关键词hobby定位到第四段第二句，这里介绍了赵彬的业余爱好是摄影，故选A。

3. D。词义猜测题。画线单词所在的句子意为"他相信，无论日常_____有多繁重，人们仍然需要梦想和爱好"，且画线单词由heavy修饰，A项、B项和C项所给的词义与heavy不搭，D项代入后意为"工作负荷重"，符合文意，故选D。

4. B。文章排序题。根据第四段的描述可知，赵彬做外卖员之前是在博物馆做安保人员，所以第一项应为①；然后新冠肺炎疫情来袭，外卖人员受到了人们更多的尊重和理解，因此第二项应为②；文章最后提到赵彬心爱的武汉回来了，

113

即武汉恢复了生机，因此③为最后一项，所以正确顺序为①②③，故选B。
5. A。主旨大意题。本文第一至三段主要讲述赵彬的身份是一位外卖员及其在工作上的事情；第四至六段介绍了赵彬的兴趣爱好是拍照，并用照片记录所在城市中的人们，所以这篇文章主要讲述的就是一位喜欢拍照的外卖员，故选A。

• 【词汇碎片】

take up 开始从事
no matter 不论怎样

• 【重难句讲解】

（第一段第二句）

He and other local deliverymen worked day and night with no time off and often forgot about meals during the days when the coronavirus was raging. 他和其他的当地外卖员在新冠肺炎疫情肆虐的日子里不分昼夜地工作，经常忘记吃饭。

本句是一个复合句。句子的主干是 He and other local deliverymen worked... and often forgot about meals，forgot about meals 与 worked day and night 为并列的谓语结构。when 引导的是定语从句，修饰 days。day and night 为固定用法，意为"不分昼夜"。

Thursday [阅读理解C]

• 【答案解析】

1. D。细节理解题。根据第一段第一句和第二句可知王教授上了一堂两个小时的在线数学课，故选D。
2. C。细节理解题。第一段第三句提到参加王教授在线课程的学生都没有听到他在讲什么，故A项"没有学生参加他的网络课程"是错误的，排除；B项"很少有学生在他的课上认真听讲"属于无中生有，故排除；第一段第二句提到王教授的麦克风处于关闭状态，因此他上课的视频没有声音，故C项符合题意；第一段最后一句提到教授使用iPad进行在线授课，而不是普通电脑，故D项错误，排除。故选C。
3. B。细节理解题。根据第二段第二句可知，学生通过挥舞手臂和打电话来提醒教授，故选B。
4. A。词义猜测题。画线单词的后面有 so 引导的目的状语从句，表示"这样他的学生就不会错过那堂课了"，也就是说他会重新讲一遍那堂课，因此"重做"符合句意，故选A。
5. B。态度观点题。根据第二段末尾的 I took a class under him before and he taught well. I feel bad for him（我以前上过他的课，他教得很好。我为他感到难过）可知，一位学生认为教授本来可以教得很好，因此她对此感到难过。根据 bad 可知应选择带有负面情绪的词汇，故可排除D项"激动的"。而A项和C项均为教授的情绪，故可排除。B项意为"难过的；沮丧的"符合句意，故选B。

• 【词汇碎片】

attend v. 出席
wave v. 挥动；摆动

• 【重难句讲解】

（第一段第三句）

This meant that none of the students attending his online class heard what he was talking about. 这意味着，参加他的在线课程的学生都没有听到他在讲什么。

本句是一个复合句。主句是 This meant that...，为主谓宾结构，that 引导宾语从句。宾语从句中，attending his online class 为现在分词短语作后置定语，修饰 students，what 引导的宾语从句作 heard 的宾语。

Friday [任务型阅读D]

• 【答案解析】

1. D。本空位于第二段句首，首句一般是该段的中心句。因此解答本题需要看第二段的内容。第二段主要讲的是教育方面出现的一些现象，这些现象可能是导致不及格的学生人数增多的原因，而文章第一段指出不及格的学生人数增多，很明显第二段是在解释这种问题产生的原因，将D项代入文中，符合文意，故选 D。
2. C。本空位于两个段落之间，是个过渡段，起承上启下的作用。上文说明了不及格的学生人数增加的原因，下文举了具体的例子来说明不及格的学生人数增加，因此本空还是与不及格的学生人数增加有关，C 项符合文意，故选 C。
3. A。本空位于第四段最后一句，需要联系空格前的内容。空格前举了一所学校学生成绩的例子，因此尾句应该在解释说明这个例子中的现象，只有 A 项在解释这种现象，与此相关，故选 A。
4. E。本空后面一句出现了 Other schools，因此本空应该在说 schools，选项中只有 E 项出现了 schools。将 E 项代入原文，符合语义和上下文逻辑，故选 E。
5. B。本空后面一句 They have been urged to find different ways of teaching（被敦促寻找不同的教学方法）中的 They 应指代某类与教育相关的人或机构。B 项、D 项和 E 项分别出现了老师、教育工作者和学校，将这三个选项代入文中，只有 B 项符合文意，故选 B。

● 【词汇碎片】

report v. 报告
notice v. 注意；留意
fall behind 落后

● 【重难句讲解】

（第一段）

School districts across the United States have reported the number of students failing classes has risen many times higher than usual numbers. 美国各学区报告称，不及格的学生人数比平时高出了许多倍。

本句是一个复合句。主句主干为 School districts have reported...，为主谓宾结构，宾语为省略了 that 的宾语从句，作 reported 的宾语。宾语从句中，failing classes 为现在分词短语，作 student 的后置定语。

（第二段第三句）

And teachers who do not see their students in person have fewer ways to notice who is falling behind. 而那些不能当面见到学生的老师也没有什么方法去注意哪个学生落后了。

本句是一个复合句。主句主干为 teachers have fewer ways to notice...，为主谓宾结构，teachers 后面为 who 引导的定语从句，修饰 teachers；notice 后面为 who 引导的宾语从句，作 notice 的宾语。

Saturday [短文填空]

● 【答案解析】

（1）blood。根据句意"张宇琦和刘宇琦虽然没有_____ 关系，却因_____ 爱好——收藏火车模型而结缘"可知，这里说的是两个没有血缘关系的人，故填 blood。

（2）shared。根据文章第一段可知，两人喜爱的东西都是火车，因此收藏火车模型应为其共同爱好，因此这里需要填 share 的过去分词形式，作定语，表示"共同的"，故填 shared。

（3）brothers。根据句意可知，人们称他们为"高铁兄弟"，这里需要填 brother 的复数形式，故填 brothers。

（4）grew。这里应为固定搭配 grow up，表示"成长，长大"。这里的时态为一般过去时，需要填 grow 的过去式，故填 grew。

（5）beginning。at the beginning 为固定搭配，意为"一开始"。这里需要将 begin 转变为动名词形式，故填 beginning。

（6）know。根据句意"在进一步_____对方之后"可知，二人应该是在互相了解之后发现对方喜欢收藏火车模型的，故填 know。

（7）spare。根据句意"他们发现二人都喜欢在_____时间收藏火车模型"可知这里说的是业余时间、空闲时间，故填 spare。

（8）them。both of... 为常见用法，意为"两者都"，这里需要将 they 转变成宾格形式，故填 them。

（9）experiences。根据句意"分享火车模型的收藏_____"可知他们分享的是一次次关于收藏火车模型的经历，故这里可填入 experience。experience 指"经历"时是可数名词，故填其复数形式 experiences。

（10）after。该句的前半句提到的"精检细修，保障动车的安全运行"是 at work（在工作中）；后半句提到他们分享收藏火车模型的经历，这应该是在工作后，即下班后，故填 after。

【词汇碎片】

relationship *n.* 关系
connect *v.* 连接
model *n.* 模型

【重难句讲解】

（第二段第一句）

Zhang Yuqi and Liu Yuqi, who have no blood relationship, are connected by their shared hobby—collecting model trains. 张宇琦和刘宇琦虽然没有血缘关系，却因共同的爱好——收藏火车模型而结缘。

本句是一个复合句。主句主干为 Zhang Yuqi and Liu Yuqi are connected by their shared hobby。who 引导的定语从句 who have no blood relationship 修饰 Zhang Yuqi and Liu Yuqi。破折号后面的 collecting model trains 为 hobby 的同位语。

Sunday [拓展阅读]

【词汇碎片】

light *v.* 点着
fever *n.* 发烧，发热

Week Five

Monday [完形填空]

【答案解析】

1. B。考查动词辨析。A 项意为"庆祝",B 项意为"举办",C 项意为"建议",D 项意为"开始"。空格所在句的意思是:2 月 26 日晚 8 点,中国中央电视台 _____ 一年一度的元宵节联欢晚会。根据语境可知应选 B。

2. A。考查形容词辨析。A 项意为"年轻的",B 项意为"完美的",C 项意为"小的",D 项意为"勇敢的"。根据句子结构可知,所填词修饰 Chinese artists(中国艺术家),且与前面的 old 为并列关系,所以此处的意思应该是"中国的老艺术家和青年艺术家",故选 A。

3. C。考查固定搭配。be popular with... 为固定搭配,意为"受……欢迎",故选 C。

4. B。考查名词辨析。A 项意为"名字",B 项意为"主题",C 项意为"单元",D 项意为"清单"。将以上四个选项分别代入文中可知,只有 B 项符合文意,故选 B。

5. C。考查名词辨析。A 项意为"碎片",B 项意为"手表",C 项意为"次数",D 项意为"符号"。times 在这里表示次数,为可数名词,符合语境,故选 C。

6. A。考查介词辨析。A 项意为"在……上面",B 项意为"在……下面",C 项意为"穿过;贯穿",D 项意为"在……中"。on the Internet 是固定搭配,表示"在网上",故选 A。

7. B。考查名词辨析。A 项意为"开头;开端",B 项意为"结尾",C 项意为"开头;开端",D 项意为"休息;暂停"。空格所在句的意思是:元宵节标志着春节的 _____。根据生活常识可知,元宵节是春节的最后一天,故此处应填入 end,故选 B。

8. C。考查指示代词辨析。A 项意为"那个",B 项意为"这些",C 项意为"今;这个",D 项意为"那些"。this year 表示"今年",且此处时态为一般现在时,C 项符合语境,也符合时态要求,故选 C。

9. D。考查形容词辨析。A 项意为"无聊的",B 项意为"美丽的",C 项意为"安全的",D 项意为"重要的"。空格所在句的意思是:作为中国最 _____ 的传统节日之一。众所周知,元宵节是中国一个很重要的节日,故选 D。

10. B。考查动词辨析。A 项意为"清洁",B 项意为"吃",C 项意为"画",D 项意为"观看"。根据常识,中国人在元宵节这一天要吃元宵,故选 B。

11. C。考查固定搭配。be made of 表示"由……制成",一般指的是看得到原材料的情况,符合要求;be made to 表示"被要求做",不符合文意;be made from 表示"由……制成",一般指的是看不见原材料的情况,不符合文意;be made by 表示"由……制造",后面常跟动作的执行者,也不符合文意。故选 C。

12. D。考查词组辨析。A 项意为"例如",后面加例子时一般要用逗号隔开,故排除 A 项;B 项意为"也",代入文中不符合文意;C 项意为"只要",用于引导条件状语从句,故排除;D 项意为"例如",用于列举事物,一般位于被列举的事物和前面的名词之间,后面一般不加逗号。将 D 项代入文中符合文意,故选 D。

13. A。考查名词辨析。A 项意为"形状",B 项意为"尺寸",C 项意为"长度",D 项意为"颜色"。空格所在句的意思是:元宵圆圆的 _____ 代表着家庭团聚。"圆圆的"表示元宵的形状,B、C、D 三项代入文中均不符合文意,均排除,故选 A。

14. C。考查动词辨析。A 项意为"放置",B 项意为"带走",C 项意为"带来",D 项意为"购买"。这里说的应该是吃元宵能给家人带来幸福和好运,故选 C。

15. D。考查代词辨析。根据句子结构可知,所填词修饰 family(家庭),故选形容词性物主代词,意为"他们的家庭",故选 D。

【词汇碎片】

festival *n.* 节日
popular *adj.* 受喜爱的;受欢迎的

【重难句讲解】

（第三段第二句）

Articles with the topic about Lantern Festival have been viewed more than 1.1 billion times, with over 5 million comments on the Internet. 与元宵节主题相关的文章浏览量超过11亿次，网上的点评超过500万条。

本句是一个简单句，句子主干为 Articles have been viewed。with the topic about Lantern Festival 作后置定语，修饰主语 Articles。

Tuesday [阅读理解 A]

【答案解析】

1. C。细节理解题。第一段第一句提到 Hao Lei is one of the most famous actresses in Chinese art films（郝蕾是中国艺术电影中最著名的女演员之一），故选 C。

2. D。细节理解题。由第二段第一句中的 veteran actors and directors shared their experiences in filmmaking（资深演员和导演分享了他们在电影制作方面的经历）可知，D 项正确，experienced 与 veteran 词义相近，都表示"经验丰富的"。故选 D。

3. B。细节理解题。根据第三段第一句 Hao said that the best way to learn acting is reading books in an interview with CGTN（郝蕾在接受中国国际电视台采访时表示，学习表演最好的方法就是读书）可知 B 项符合原文。A 项具有干扰性，郝蕾提到修佛有帮助只是针对她自身来说的，并不能推断出她认为修佛是学习表演最好的方法。故选 B。

4. C。词义猜测题。画线单词所在句子的意思是：但现在佛教帮助我从更高的 _____ 看待工作和生活。前文提到 Learning Buddhism helps me become open-minded and tolerant（学佛帮助我变得开明、宽容。）也就是说，学佛让郝蕾的思想境界更高了，因此她应该是能从更高的角度看待工作和生活。故选 C。

5. D。细节理解题。由第一段可知郝蕾参演的作品叫 *Seventeen no Cry*，故 A 项错误。文中提到郝蕾接受了 CGTN 的采访，而不是 CCTV，故排除 B 项。C 项与第三段第二句提到的 Today's young people don't like reading（现在的年轻人不喜欢读书）相悖，故排除。文章末段提到佛教对郝蕾的一些积极影响，也就是说，郝蕾认为学佛是有帮助的，故选 D。

【词汇碎片】

famous *adj.* 著名的
act *v.* 扮演；行动

【重难句讲解】

（第二段第一句）

She was invited to attend a masterclass, where veteran actors and directors shared their experiences in filmmaking on Friday in Sanya, China's Hainan Province. 周五，她受邀参加了在中国海南省三亚市举办的一个大师班，资深演员和导演分享了他们在电影制作方面的经历。

本句是一个复合句，主句是 She was invited to attend a masterclass。where 引导的定语从句修饰先行词 masterclass，且 where 在从句中充当地点状语。in filmmaking 是后置定语，修饰 experiences。on Friday 是时间状语，in Sanya, China's Hainan Province 是地点状语。

Wednesday [阅读理解 B]

【答案解析】

1. B。细节理解题。第二段提到了票房收入的主要贡献者和其各自的票房收入。对比可知，《你好，李焕英》票房最高，即贡献最大，故选 B。

2. C。细节理解题。由第二段最后一句中的 comedy drama *Endgame*, have also each earned more than 300 million yuan in revenue（喜剧《人潮汹涌》也都各自创造了超过3亿元的票房收入）可知，喜剧《人潮汹涌》的票房超过3亿元。故选 C。

3. B。推理判断题。由文章最后一段中的"2021年的票房收入在2月16日就超过100亿元，比2020年快了230天，2020年的票房收入在10月3日才达到这个数字"可推知，2021年2月的收益比2020年2月的高。故选B。

4. C。细节理解题。总览全文，A项"中国的票房收入在2月创下历史新高"符合文意，故A项表述正确。由第二段可知，《熊出没：狂野大陆》是一部动画片，故B项表述正确。第二段提到，《新神榜：哪吒重生》创造了超过3亿元的票房收入，故C项与文意不符。根据文章最后一段第一句the total box office revenue for the seven-day Spring Festival holiday over Feb 11-17 stood at 7.8 billion yuan（从2月11日到17日，春节7天假期的总票房收入达到78亿元）可知，D项表述正确。综上，本题选C。

5. A。主旨大意题。文章第一段指出中国2月份的票房收入创下新高；第二段提到了为票房收入做了主要贡献的几部电影，并介绍了其各自的票房收入；第三段简要提到了2月份春节假期间的票房收入。综上所述，本文第一段为主旨段，其余两段都只是对其进行补充说明的。故选A项"中国的票房收入在2月创下历史新高"。B项"春节7天假期的总票房收入"只是2月份票房收入的一部分，故排除。C项《刺杀小说家》创造了超过3亿元的收入"只是第二段中提及的一个细节，无法概括全文，故排除。D项"票房收入的主要贡献者"范围太大，且只是文中的例证，故排除。综上所述，本题选A。

【词汇碎片】

billion *num.* 十亿
single *adj.* 单一的，单个的
pocket *v.* 把……放进口袋

【重难句讲解】

（第三段第二句）

Moreover, the revenue in 2021 was over 10 billion yuan on Feb 16, 230 days earlier than 2020, in which the revenue reached this number on Oct 3. 此外，2021年的票房收入在2月16日就超过100亿元，比2020年快了230天，2020年的票房收入在10月3日才达到这个数字。

本句是一个复合句，in which引导的定语从句修饰先行词2020，in which在从句中充当时间状语。

Thursday [阅读理解C]

【答案解析】

1. B。细节理解题。第一段提到周杰伦的最新电影即将上映，紧接着第二段第一句就提到了该电影的英文名字，即 *Nezha*（《叱咤风云》）。故选B。

2. A。词义猜测题。前文提到这部电影的英文名是 *Nezha*（《叱咤风云》），后文指出该电影围绕三个赛车手展开，并未提到古代人物"哪吒"，也就是说，电影与"哪吒"这个人物没什么联系，故A项正确，代入原文后意为：这部电影本身与古代人物哪吒没有任何关系。

3. A。细节理解题。由第二段第三句中的Centering on three young racers（围绕着三位年轻的赛车手）可知，A项正确。故选A。

4. D。细节理解题。由第三段第一句中的Directed by Chen Yi-xian（由陈奕先执导）可知，D项正确。故选D。

5. B。细节理解题。A项"电影中三个年轻的赛车手轻而易举地追求荣誉"与第二段第三句中的facing up to difficulties and pursuing honor on the tracks（在赛道上勇敢地面对困难和追求荣誉）意思相悖，故排除。B项"制作该电影花费巨大"与第四段中的up to more than 400 million yuan（高达4亿元）相符，故B项正确。C项"周杰伦未出演《头文字D》"与最后一段中的Chou starred in...racing film, *Initial D*（周杰伦主演了……街头赛车电影《头文字D》）相悖，故排除。D项"该影片中有个角色叫哪吒"在文中并未提及，故排除。

【词汇碎片】

interestingly *adv.* 有趣地
center *v.* 把……放在中心；居中

【重难句讲解】

（第四段）

It's reported that with a budget up to more than

400 million yuan ($61.8 million), the film used some expensive racing cars for the action scenes, accounting for about 80 percent of the whole content. 据报道，这部电影的预算高达 4 亿元（6 180 万美元），且在动作场景中使用了一些昂贵的赛车，这些动作场景约占全部内容的 80%。

本句是一个复合句，It's reported that... 意为"据说……"，此处 It 为形式主语，真正的主语是 that 引导的从句。在英语中，在不便或不必指明某看法、说法或消息的来源时，往往使用"It + be 动词 + 过去分词 + that 引导的从句"的句式结构。

Friday [任务型阅读 D]

●【答案解析】

1. A。空格后面的句子提到 It's adapted from an online novel. My idol Hu Yitian plays the leading role in it（它改编自一部网络小说。我的偶像胡一天主演的）。这充分说明迈克对于这部剧是了解的，故选 A。

2. D。空格后紧接着提到 It depicts the pursuit of dreams and the love story of Wu Bai and Ai Qing, two robot fighting competitors（它讲述了机器人格斗选手吴白和艾情对梦想的追求和他们的爱情故事）。由此可知，这里问的是这部剧的内容，故选 D。

3. B。由空格前后的句子可知，听者应该是对以上所听到的内容感兴趣，故选 B。

4. C。空格后面提到了人名，所以空格处询问的应该是"谁"，故选 C。

5. A。空格后面的回答提到了这部剧的相关剧情以及编剧写这部剧的目的，故选 A。

●【词汇碎片】

online *adj.* 在线的
robot *n.* 机器人

●【重难句讲解】

And it's said that professional companies in the robot fighting industry were invited to build the competition venue, design competition rules and guide the actors and actresses on how to operate in the competitions. 据悉，剧组还邀请了机器人格斗行业的专业公司搭建比赛场地，设计比赛规则，指导男女演员如何在比赛中操作。

本句是一个复合句，it's said that... 意为"据说……"，其中 it 是形式主语，真正的主语是 that 引导的主语从句。不定式短语 to build the competition venue... operate in the competitions 为目的状语。

Saturday [短文填空]

●【答案解析】

（1）through。根据句子结构可知，空格前句子结构完整，不缺成分。through 在此处为介词，意为"通过"，符合语境，且介词短语 through Ms. Wallace's memories 作方式状语。故填 through。

（2）little。下一段第一句提到 When Biggie was young（大个小子年轻的时候），所以这段应该说的是大个小子的童年时期，故填 little。

（3）play。"play+ 乐器名"表示"弹奏……（乐器）"，故填 play。

（4）shy。由空格后的 He would get mad if his friends told anyone he knew how to rap（如果他的朋友告诉某个人他会说唱，他就会生气）可知，大个小子很害羞，故填 shy。

（5）time。根据句子结构可知，空格处所填词由前面的形容词性物主代词 our 修饰，故空格处所填词为名词，time 在此处表示"时代"，符合语境和词性要求。故填 time。

●【词汇碎片】

grow *v.* 成长
role *n.* 角色；作用

【重难句讲解】

（第四段第二句）

He would get mad if his friends told anyone he knew how to rap. 如果他的朋友告诉某个人他会说唱，他就会生气。

本句是一个复合句，主句是 He would get mad，此处的时态为过去将来时，if 引导的是条件状语从句，从句时态为一般过去时。

Sunday [拓展阅读]

【词汇碎片】

decide *v.* 决定
practice *v.* 练习；实践
proper *adj.* 合适的

Week Six

Monday [完形填空]

【答案解析】

1. A。考查连词辨析。A项意为"但是",B项意为"在……之前",C项意为"和",D项意为"当……时"。空格前提到张向阳在康复后重返工作岗位,空格后有否定词not,根据空格前后内容可知,此处表达转折含义。故选A。

2. B。考查形容词辨析。A项意为"艰难的",B项意为"容易的",C项意为"酷的",D项意为"紧张的"。根据空格前后内容可知,康复后重返工作岗位,但心理上恢复正常还是不容易的。将四个选项代入文中,B项最符合上下文语义。故选B。

3. C。考查动词辨析。A项意为"大笑",B项意为"微笑",C项意为"说话",D项意为"靠近"。根据空格前后内容可知,当人们和她说话时会和她保持距离。将其他三项代入文中后句意不通。故选C。

4. D。考查介词辨析。A项意为"为了",B项意为"通过",C项意为"在……上面",D项意为"没有"。空格前指出人们与她保持距离,空格后提到她假装很好。根据空格前后内容可知,她没有和任何人提起自己受到的冷遇,D项符合语境。故选D。

5. B。考查代词辨析。A项意为"任何事",B项意为"每件事",C项意为"一些事",D项意为"没有什么事"。根据语境可知,此处要表达的是张向阳假装一切正常,只有B项符合上下文语义。故选B。

6. C。考查形容词辨析。A项意为"伤心的",B项意为"高兴的",C项意为"忙碌的",D项意为"疯狂的;狂怒的"。此处说的是即使受到了冷遇,还是要假装一切都好,照看病人,让自己忙碌起来,只有C项符合文意。故选C。

7. A。考查关系副词辨析。A项意为"怎么",B项意为"当……时",C项意为"为什么",D项意为"在哪里"。根据空格后的内容可知,这里表达的是她的感受是怎样的。故选A。

8. D。考查固定搭配。A项意为"东西",B项意为"经历",C项意为"感觉",D项意为"次数"。it was the first time (that)... 意为"这是第一次……",代入文中后此句意为"这是我第一次感到有人关心我",符合上下文语义。故选D。

9. C。考查动词辨析。A项意为"制作;使得",B项意为"使",C项意为"设法;努力",D项意为"提供"。C项代入文中后句意为"将努力提升人们的心理健康水平",符合文意。故选C。

10. B。考查动词辨析。A项意为"拉;吸引",B项意为"增加",C项意为"(使)后退",D项意为"拉;拖"。将四个选项代入文中,只有B项符合文意,表示"增加治疗人数"。故选B。

【词汇碎片】

difficulty *n.* 困难
treatment *n.* 治疗;疗法

【重难句讲解】

(第四段)

According to the Healthy China 2030 plan, China will try to better people's health psychologically, as the country aims to increase the number of treatment of depression by 80 percent by 2030. 根据"健康中国2030"计划,中国将努力提升人们的心理健康水平,因为中国的目标是到2030年将抑郁症的治疗人数增加80%。

本句是一个复合句,主句是China will try to better people's health psychologically,是主谓宾结构,后面是as引导的原因状语从句。

Tuesday [阅读理解 A]

【答案解析】

1. A。根据第一段中的one in ten people is to suffer from hearing loss by 2050(预计到2050年,每10人中就有

1人会遭受听力损失）可知，到2050年，每10人中就有1人会遭受听力损失，也就是10%，故正确。

2. B。根据第二段中的But in the United States, around 20 percent of America's adult is already experiencing some level of hearing loss（但是在美国，大约20%的美国成年人已经在经历一定程度的听力损失）可知，大约有20%的美国成年人正遭受听力损失，本题说的是一半，也就是50%，故错误。

3. B。根据第五段About 20 percent of American adults aged from 20 to 69 have some trouble with hearing and almost 28.8 million could benefit from the use of hearing aids（在20~69岁的美国成年人中，大约有20%的人有听力障碍，将近2 880万人可以从助听器的使用中受益）可知，在20~69岁之间的美国成年人中，大约有20%的人听力有问题。而本题将年龄段改为20~59岁，且将有听力问题的人数改为需要使用助听器的人数，故错误。

4. A。根据最后一段中的turn up the sound of the television（把电视的音量调大）可知，有听力障碍的人看电视时通常会把音量开得很大，故正确。

5. B。根据最后一段中的cannot hear the door bell（听不到门铃声）可知，听不见门铃声也是听力损失的一种表现，而本题说这不是个大问题，与文意不符，故错误。

【词汇碎片】

WHO 世界卫生组织
information *n.* 信息
repeat *v.* 重复

【重难句讲解】

（第四段）

We might use mouth movements and body language to understand what somebody is saying or help us fill in the blanks when we miss some information. 当我们漏掉一些信息时，我们可能会利用嘴部动作和肢体语言来理解别人在说什么，或者帮助我们填补空白。

本句是一个复合句，主句的主干是We might use mouth movements and body language，是主谓宾结构，what和when分别引导宾语从句和状语从句。

Wednesday [阅读理解 B]

【答案解析】

1. D。细节理解题。第二段第一句提到Herd immunity is when a large number of people in a community will either have recovered from infection or been vaccinated（群体免疫是指一个社区中的大量人群要么已经从感染中恢复过来，要么已经接种疫苗），D项与原文相符。故选D。

2. D。细节理解题。根据第三段中的Once people are sick or receive the vaccine, they start to develop antibodies（一旦人们生病或接种疫苗，他们就开始产生抗体）可知，生病或接种疫苗能够使人产生抗体。故选D。

3. B。细节理解题。根据第三段中的Experts think the number of people with antibodies needs to reach 70 percent or more for herd immunity（专家认为，为了实现群体免疫，带有抗体的人的数量需要达到70%或更多）可知，人群中至少要有70%的人携带抗体才算达到群体免疫。故选B。

4. C。推理判断题。第四段提到，群体免疫需要在全球范围内实现，但是一些地区与新冠病毒的斗争时间会更长，也就是说，一些国家可能会优先达到群体免疫的状态，故C项正确。A项、B项和D项都过于绝对，故均错误。故选C。

5. D。主旨大意题。第一段开头提到的That is the question说明题目为问句，排除A项和C项。文章讲了群体免疫的概念，如何达到群体免疫，以及达到群体免疫的判断标准，只有D项最合适。故选D。

【词汇碎片】

government *n.* 政府
community *n.* 团体

【重难句讲解】

（第二段第一句）

Herd immunity is when a large number of people in a community will either have recovered from infection or been vaccinated. 群体免疫是指一个社区中的大量人群要么已经从感染中恢复过来，要么已经接种疫苗。

本句是一个复合句。Herd immunity 为主句的主语，when 引导的表语从句对主语进行解释说明。either... or... 译为"要么……要么……"。

Thursday [阅读理解 C]

【答案解析】

1. B。细节理解题。根据第一段 The coronavirus has influenced... what we eat（冠状病毒几乎影响了……我们吃的东西）可知，本文讲的是新冠肺炎疫情对人们饮食的影响。故选 B。

2. D。细节理解题。根据第二段第三句 Home cooking activity is up everywhere for restaurants and other food shops are closed（由于餐馆和其他食品商店都关门了，家庭烹饪活动到处都在增加）可知，疫情期间更多的人开始自己做饭，所以疫情暴发之前人们关于吃饭地点的选择更多。故选 D。

3. C。细节理解题。根据第二段第四句 People are increasingly trying new foods in their own kitchens（越来越多的人在自己的厨房里尝试新的食物）可知，越来越多的人吃自己做的饭，故 C 项正确。A 项为强干扰项，但是家庭烹饪才是重点，健康食物并非本文重点讲述对象。故选 C。

4. D。推理判断题。根据最后一段中的 Some experts think that changes in the way we eat also come from having more time to think about how food comes to our tables（一些专家认为，饮食方式的改变也源于我们有更多的时间去思考食物是如何被端上我们的餐桌的）可知，在新冠肺炎疫情期间，人们改变了他们的一些饮食习惯，所以 D 项符合文意。其余三项的表述都过于绝对且不

符合文意，故错误。故选 D。

5. B。主旨大意题。本文说的是受疫情影响，人们居家制作家庭美食，并因此尝试了新的食物和口味，是关于健康生活类的文章。故选 B。

【词汇碎片】

influence *v.* 影响
kitchen *n.* 厨房

【重难句讲解】

（第四段第一句）

Some experts think that changes in the way we eat also come from having more time to think about how food comes to our tables. 一些专家认为，饮食方式的改变也源于我们有更多的时间去思考食物是如何被端上我们的餐桌的。

本句是一个复合句，主句的主干为 Some experts think that...，为主谓宾结构，that 引导的宾语从句作 think 的宾语。

Friday [任务型阅读 D]

【答案解析】

1. Five. 阅读全文可知，本文共提到了五个国家，分别是瑞士、日本、德国、意大利和俄罗斯。

2. Fish, miso soup, and rice are all represented in a traditional Japanese dish. 根据第三段中的 A traditional Japanese dish? Fish, miso soup, and rice are all represented（传统的日本料理？鱼、味噌汤和米饭都是代表）可知，鱼、味噌汤和米饭都是传统的日本料理。

3. They will take coffee for breakfast. 根据最后一段第二、三句 Italians are almost too busy for breakfast. In coffee bars, guests take their espresso at the beginning of the day（意大利人几乎忙得连早餐都没时间吃。在咖啡吧，客人们在一天开始的时候会喝一杯意式浓咖啡）可知，意大利人很忙的时候可能早餐就只喝咖啡。

4. Yes, they are. 根据最后一段第四句 On weekdays, breakfasts are simpler in Russia: Caviar is spread across black bread（在工作日，俄罗斯的早餐更简单：将鱼子酱涂抹在黑面包上）可知，答案是肯定的。

5. I usually have an egg and a glass of milk for breakfast. 合理作答即可。

• 【词汇碎片】

traditional *adj.* 传统的；惯例的
Germany *n.* 德国

• 【重难句讲解】

（第一段）

When it comes to breakfast foods around the world, there are as many ways to enjoy the first meal of the day as there are to say "good morning." 当谈到世界各地的早餐食品时，享受一天中第一顿饭的方式就和说"早上好"的方式一样多。

本句是一个复合句，主句是 there be 句型，主句中的 as many as 意为"和……一样多"，When 引导时间状语从句。

Saturday [短文填空]

• 【答案解析】

1. D。根据第一段中的 Like many people around the world, I am waiting for a COVID vaccine（和世界上很多人一样，我正等待着接种新冠疫苗）及 My sister says she doesn't trust it（我的姐姐说她不相信疫苗）可知，此处填入的句子应为转折句，D 项代入原文后符合上下文语境，故选 D。

2. E。根据下文中的 First, it's not necessary to change their minds（第一，没有必要改变他们的想法）可知，下文是作者罗列的一些观点，故空格处应为下文的总起句，故选 E。

3. F。根据第三段中的 Third 及后面的 Fifth 可知，此处缺少的是第四个观点，故选 F。

4. C。根据第四段中的 Sixth, for forgetful types, simple reminders... can be useful（第六，对于健忘的人来说，简单的提醒……可能是有效的）可知，此处讲的是提醒的方式，C 项中的短信和语音信息均为提醒方式，故选 C。

5. B。根据第四段中的 A 2019 study showed that daily reminders to complete drug treatment greatly increased good results（2019 年的一项研究表明，每天提醒患者完成药物治疗大大提高了治疗效果）和 You'd think that would be bad, but it was useful（你可能会认为这样不好，但它是有帮助的）可知，提醒是有效的，所以还要继续这一方式，故选 B。

• 【词汇碎片】

historical *adj.* 历史的
treatment *n.* 治疗

• 【重难句讲解】

（第三段第四句）

Offering more hours and having more people know that there is no cost are two ways to improve the number. 给予更多时间和确保公众知道可以免费接种是增加接种人数的两种方法。

本句是一个复合句，句子的主语为 Offering more hours and having more people know that there is no cost，that 引导一个宾语从句作 know 的宾语，系动词为 are，表语为 two ways。to improve the number 为动词不定式短语，作后置定语修饰 two ways。

Sunday [拓展阅读]

• 【词汇碎片】

popular *adj.* 受欢迎的
traditional *adj.* 传统的

【重难句讲解】

（第二段第二句）

For example, coffee, which has become more and more popular in China, is one beverage that many cannot do without today. 例如，在中国越来越受欢迎的咖啡，是今天许多人都离不开的饮料。

本句是一个复合句。主句的主干为 coffee is one beverage，第二个逗号后的 which 引导定语从句，修饰主语 coffee。that 引导定语从句，修饰表语 beverage。

Week Seven

Monday [完形填空]

【答案解析】

1. A。考查上下文语义。A项表示转折，B项表示并列，C项表示选择，D项表示因果。空格前的句子指出，游泳池通常是在五月至九月营业；空格后的句子指出，今年秋天和冬天也开放了。由此可知，前后两句为转折关系。故选A。

2. C。考查连词辨析。A项意为"在……之后"，B项意为"自从"，C项意为"在……之前"，D项意为"当……的时候"。空格所在句提到1月封城，以及户外游泳池都被允许营业。根据句意可知，应该是在新冠肺炎疫情导致封城之前，户外游泳池被允许营业，故C项正确。将其他选项代入文中后，意思均不符合逻辑，故均排除。故选C。

3. B。考查动词辨析。A项意为"降低"，B项意为"增加"，C项意为"发明"，D项意为"介意"。空格所在句的大意为：在过去的几年中，冷水游泳的流行度在英国_____。根据下文可知，冷水游泳在英国是越来越流行，故B项符合文意。其他选项填入后均与文意不符，故均排除。故选B。

4. C。考查代词辨析。A项意为"这些"，B项意为"那些"，C项意为"一些"，D项意为"所有"。空格所在句意为：在_____地方，例如约克郡的沃夫河，这一新趋势……足以用来洗澡。these和those一般指代上文或下文出现过的地方，且不止一个，由于上下文没有出现特定的几个地方，故排除A项和B项，"在一些地方"符合文意；"在所有地方"不符合文意，故排除D项。故选C。

5. B。考查动词短语辨析。A项意为"构成；编造"，B项意为"确保"，C项意为"由……制成"，D项意为"辨认出"。空格所在句意为：这一新趋势促使环保团队_____这些地方的水未被污染，并干净到足以用来洗澡。将四个选项分别代入文中，只有B项符合逻辑，故选B。

6. D。考查代词辨析。A项意为"其他的"；B项意为"另一个；再一个"；C项意为"另一个"，通常与one一起使用；D项意为"其他人"，一般与some一起连用，表示"一些人……；另一些人/其他人……"。空格所在句的分号前面出现了Some，且根据谓语动词可知，空格处应填入复数名词，只有others符合文意。故选D。

7. B。考查介词辨析。in后面接年份、月份等；on后面接具体的某一天；at后面接时间点；during后面接一段时间。空格后为几个并列的节日，具体到了某一天，用介词on。故选B。

8. C。考查动词辨析。空格所在句意为：英国每年都有人被相机拍到_____进冰水中。A项意为"看"，B项意为"爬"，C项意为"跳"，D项意为"移动"，将四个选项代入文中，只有C项最符合文意。故选C。

9. D。考查副词辨析。A项意为"快乐地"，B项意为"快速地"，C项意为"突然地"，D项意为"缓慢地"。根据Likewise可知，前面的建议与后面的建议意思一致，后面的建议为"逐渐使身体暖和起来"，因此前面的副词应该与gradually意思相近，该空填入"缓慢地"最符合文意。故选D。

10. A。考查名词辨析。A项意为"天气"，B项意为"水"，C项意为"水池"，D项意为"河"。下文提到了保罗·戴维斯对于天气的预测，故他应该是一名研究天气的科学家。故选A。

【词汇碎片】

allow v. 允许
pollution n. 污染
regular adj. 定期的

【重难句讲解】

（第五段第三句）

Paul Davies, a scientist who studies the weather, said the forecast indicates "the likelihood of the cold weather continuing through January". 保罗·戴维斯是一名研究天气的科学家，他表示，预测显示"冷天气可能会在整个一月份延续"。

本句是一个复合句,包含定语从句和宾语从句。Paul Davies said... 是主句的主干,a scientist 是 Paul Davies 的同位语,后面的 who 引导定语从句,修饰 scientist。said 后面是省略了 that 的宾语从句,该宾语从句中的 of the cold weather continuing through January 是后置定语,修饰 likelihood。

Tuesday [阅读理解 A]

【答案解析】

1. B。细节理解题。根据题干中的关键信息 10 years ago 定位到第二段第一句和第二句,可知在 10 年前,黎志伟是一名攀岩运动员,故选 B。

2. C。细节理解题。根据第二段最后两句 But Mr. Lai couldn't stop his love for climbing. He found a way... to climb again(但是,黎先生无法停止自己对攀登的热爱。他想到了一个……再次攀爬的办法)可知,黎先生再次攀登是因为无法停止自己对攀登的热爱,故选 C。

3. B。推理判断题。A 项和 C 项在文中未提及,故排除;根据文章大意可知,黎先生出车祸后,仍然坐轮椅攀登,由此可推知,他是一个很坚强的人,所以 B 项正确;第三段最后一句提到黎先生不得不放弃,由此可知,沿着摩天大楼攀登并不容易,故 D 项错误。故选 B。

4. D。语篇理解题。画线词所在句子的前面提到黎先生帮助残疾人的事情,结合句意:如果残疾人士能带来机会、希望和光明,那他们不必被视为弱者。由此可知,这句话中的 they 指代残疾人士,即 the disabled,故选 D。

5. A。主旨大意题。文章通过讲述身患残疾的黎先生坐轮椅攀登摩天大楼并帮助其他残疾人士的事情,告诉我们残疾人士不一定很脆弱,所以 A 项正确。B 项以偏概全,C 项与文意相反,D 项过于绝对,且这三项并不是文章想要表达的中心思想,故均排除。故选 A。

【词汇碎片】

climb *v.* 爬;攀登
rock *n.* 岩石
injured *adj.* 受伤的
disabled *adj.* 残疾的

【重难句讲解】

(第一段第二句)

Mr. Lai, who can't move his legs, was tied into his wheelchair as he climbed. 因为双腿无法移动,黎先生攀登时将自己拴在了轮椅上。

本句是一个复合句,包含定语从句和时间状语从句。Mr. Lai was tied into his wheelchair 是主句,who 引导的定语从句修饰 Mr. Lai,as 引导时间状语从句。

(第四段第二句)

He also raised over $700,000 for a charity that is working to help others who have been paralyzed. 他还为一个慈善团体筹集了 70 多万美元的善款,将用于帮助其他瘫痪的病人。

本句是一个复合句,包含两个定语从句。He also raised over $700,000 for a charity 是主句,that 引导的定语从句修饰 charity,who 引导的定语从句修饰 others。

Wednesday [阅读理解 B]

【答案解析】

1. C。细节理解题。根据题干中的关键词 ten climbers 定位到第一段,可知 10 名攀登者来自尼泊尔,故选 C。

2. D。细节理解题。根据第二段第三句可知攀登者有被冰块砸中的危险。文中虽然提到了有被冰块砸中的危险,但没有提及是否有很多人被冰块砸中,故 A 项错误;根据第三段第二句中的 it looked as if the climbers would have to give up after a strong storm broke some tents and important tools(在一场强风暴毁坏了帐篷和重要的登山装备后,攀登者们看起来似乎不得不放弃)可知,攀登并不顺利,故 B 项错误;根据最后一段第四句 It was a joint record—no single person was being named the first climber to get to the summit(这是一项共同达成的纪录——没有单独的个人被提名为首位到达顶峰的人)可知

C项错误；根据最后一段最后一句中的history made for Nepal（为尼泊尔创造了历史）可知，这对于他们的国家来说是巨大的荣耀，故选D。

3. A。细节理解题。根据题干中的关键信息 nine Sherpas 定位到第四段第一句和第二句，由原文可知夏尔巴人住在喜马拉雅山区，他们因登山技术而出名。因此 Purja 选夏尔巴人是因为他们的攀登技术，所以 A 项正确。B 项内容正确，但这并不是 Purja 选他们的原因，故排除。C 项和 D 项文中均未提及，故排除。故选 A。

4. B。词义猜测题。根据第三段第一句中的 60 climbers raced to be the first to reach its top in winter（60 名攀登者比赛，争先成为首位冬天登顶 K2 的人）可知攀登者们是比赛看谁第一个到达山顶。由此可推测画线单词 summit 与 top 应为同义词，因此 summit 在这里意为"顶峰"，故选 B。

5. B。主旨大意题。第一段提到 10 人成功登顶 K2，创造新的世界纪录；第二段介绍攀登 K2 的难度；第三段讲途中遇到的困难；最后一段讲 Purja 和其他九名尼泊尔夏尔巴人一起成功到达顶峰，并提到了他们的感想。A 项、C 项和 D 项以偏概全，只有 B 项的概括最为全面，故选 B。

● 【词汇碎片】

reach v. 到达
danger n. 危险
fail v. 失败

Thursday [阅读理解 C]

● 【答案解析】

1. A。根据第一段第一句中的 breaking is a sport like no other（霹雳舞是一项与众不同的运动）可知，Breaking is different from other sports 正确，故填 A。

2. B。根据第二段第三句和第四句 I'm really excited... I really want to win the gold medal（我真的很兴奋……我真的很想赢得金牌）可知，塔拉并没有赢得金牌，只是希望自己能在 2024 年的奥运会上赢得金牌，所以 B-girl Terra has won a gold medal in Olympics 错误，故填 B。

3. B。根据第二段第五句 One YouTube video of her breaking has nearly 22 million views（她跳霹雳舞的视频在油管上有近 2 200 万的播放量）可知，是一个视频有近 2 200 万的播放量，并非在油管上有 2 200 万粉丝。所以 Terra has 22 million followers on YouTube 错误，故填 B。

4. A。根据最后一段第一句 In a breaking competition, two dancers will take turns to perform their routine on a stage（在一场霹雳舞比赛中，两名舞者轮流在舞台上表演他们的一套动作）可知，在霹雳舞比赛中两位舞者彼此竞争，故 Two dancers compete with each other in a breaking competition 正确，故填 A。

5. B。根据最后一段最后两句 It is yet not known how the 2024 Olympic games will be arranged... possibly mixed-doubles games with both men and women（2024 年奥运会的比赛将如何安排还不知道……可能是男女双人混合比赛）可知，比赛的具体形式还不知道，故 It has announced that there will be separate men and women competitions 错误，故填 B。

● 【词汇碎片】

recently adv. 最近
announce v. 宣布
perform v. 表演

● 【重难句讲解】

（第一段第二句）

Breaking was recently announced as one of the Olympics sports for the first time when the Games will be held in Paris, France, in 2024. 最近，据宣布，霹雳舞将在 2024 年法国巴黎举行的奥运会上首次成为奥运会运动项目之一。

本句是一个复合句，包含时间状语从句。Breaking was recently announced as one of the Olympics sports 是主句。when 引导时间状语从句。

（第二段第六句）

Terra is known for the move that she spins on her head. 塔拉因她头顶地面旋转的动作而出名。

本句是一个复合句，包含定语从句。Terra is known for the move 是主句，that 引导的定语从句修饰 move。

Friday [任务型阅读 D]

【答案解析】

1. E。空格所在段落是对四处自由走动的介绍，第一句提到在包括挪威和瑞典在内的很多国家，有权四处走动是一种传统，后面应该继续介绍这种传统。E 项中的 tradition 与该段第一句中的 tradition 相呼应，其是对该段第一句的补充，故填 E。

2. D。空格所在段落的第一句意为：在苏格兰，一项法律允许人们自由地去他们想去的地方走动，只要他们遵守户外活动准则。在剩下的 6 个选项中，D 项与第一句形成对比，且下文提到有人向英国首相鲍里斯·约翰逊写信，要求扩大可以自由走动的区域，由此可推测上面应该提及在英国能自由走动的区域的情况，故填 D。

3. A。空格前面一句提到 walk around 8% of England's countryside（在英格兰 8% 的乡村区域走动），A 项意为：剩余 92% 的区域被商业、政府、私人庄园和大富豪所占有，刚好与 8% 的走动区域形成对照，故填 A。

4. C。总体来看，文章最后两段结构相似，最后一段介绍的是 Reason why people should not be allowed to walk around（人们不应该被允许四处走动的原因），C 项 Reason why people should be allowed to walk around（人们应该被允许四处走动的原因）刚好符合最后一段第一句的结构，故填 C。

5. G。根据分析可知，空格所在段落第一句指出本段介绍人们不被允许四处走动的原因，空格前面提到被围起来的地方对许多人来说是谋生之地，剩下的三个选项中，G 项 The right to walk around would damage their businesses（四处走动的权利会破坏他们的生意）是不应该允许人们四处走动的一大原因，且与空格前一句有联系，故填 G。

【词汇碎片】

right *n.* 权利
country *n.* 国家
obey *v.* 遵守
private *adj.* 私人的；私有的

【重难句讲解】

（第四段第一句）

In 2000, a law was passed, which made it legal to walk around 8% of England's countryside. 2000 年通过了一项法律，该法律使得在英格兰 8% 的乡村区域走动是合法的。

本句是一个复合句，包含定语从句。a law was passed 是主句，which 引导非限制性定语从句，并指代前面的主句。

Saturday [短文填空]

【答案解析】

（1）Playing。空格处的单词与后面的短语一起作主语，所给单词为动词，因此此处应填入动名词，故填 Playing。

（2）quietly。空格后面为动词 began，所以此处应填入副词，修饰 began，故填 quietly。

（3）noticed。空格所在句的前半句的时态为过去完成时，由 before 可知，此处也应使用动词的一般过去时态，故填 noticed。

（4）the。空格后面是序数词，序数词前面需要使用定冠词，故填 the。

（5）deeply。空格处的单词修饰后面的形容词 uncomfortable，修饰形容词要用副词，故填 deeply。

（6）used。空格所在句意为：许多人对国歌被用来伤害美国黑色和棕色人种的事情深感不舒服。根据句意可知，国歌被用来伤害人，需使用被动语态。被动语态的结构为"be 动词 + 动词的过去分词"，故填 used。

（7）decision。空格前面是所有格形式，后面是动词不定式作后置定语，因此空格处应填名词，故填 decision。

（8）response。空格前为冠词和形容词，因此空格处应填名词，故填 response。

（9）games。空格前为 all，后面接复数名词，故填 games。

（10）stresses。由分号前的句子可知，空格所在句的时态应为一般现在时。空格所在句的主语为 it，谓语动词应使用第三人称单数，故填 stresses。

● 【词汇碎片】

empty *adj.* 空的；无意义的
notice *v.* 注意
harm *v.* 伤害
pride *n.* 自豪

● 【重难句讲解】

（第四段第三句）

In a direct response to the Mavericks, Governor Dan Patrick announced he would speed up an act which would require the national anthem to be played at all games that receive public funding. 在对达拉斯小牛队的直接回应中，州长丹·帕特里克宣布他会加快一项法案的进程，该法案会要求在接受公共资助的赛事上奏国歌。

本句是一个复合句，包含一个宾语从句和两个定语从句。Governor Dan Patrick announced... 是主句的主干。he would speed up an act 是省略了 that 的宾语从句，which 引导定语从句，修饰 act，that 引导定语从句，修饰 games。

Sunday [拓展阅读]

● 【词汇碎片】

celebrate *v.* 庆祝
return *v.* 返回；回归
romantic *adj.* 浪漫的
chat with 聊天；闲谈

Week Eight

Monday [完形填空]

【答案解析】

1. A。考查介词辨析。A项后一般加原因，B项后一般跟的是对象，C项一般加表示时间或空间的词，D项一般表示伴随。空格所在句意为：它们容忍你的抚摸，也许只是_____一些好处，比如你给它们的食物和关注。根据句意可知，空格处需要填入表示"原因"的表达，B、C、D项均不符合文意，故均排除。故选A。

2. C。考查动词辨析。A项意为"需要"，B项意为"期待"，C项意为"厌恶"，D项意为"享受"。根据前面的cats aren't social（猫不喜欢社交）可知C项符合语境，故选C。

3. D。考查动词辨析。A项意为"给"，B项意为"制作"，C项意为"偷"，D项意为"得到"。空格所在句意为：如果你怀疑你的猫容忍你的抚摸只是为了再_____一口晚餐，那你可能猜对了。猫不能"给一口晚餐"或"做一口晚餐"，故A、B项均排除；"偷一口晚餐"属于过度推测，不符合文意。"得到一口晚餐"符合文意，故选D。

4. C。考查连词辨析。A项表示并列，B项表示选择，C项表示转折，D项表示因果。空格所在句意为：人们通常认为猫喜欢被抚摸，_____研究表明这可能会导致猫做出最消极的反应。根据句意可知，空格前后两句之间是转折的逻辑关系，故选C。

5. B。考查上下文语义。A项意为"人们"，B项意为"猫"，C项意为"研究者"，D项意为"动物"。空格前提到人们通常认为猫喜欢被抚摸，但这种抚摸猫的行为可能会导致一些消极的反应。结合语境可知，做出这些消极反应的主体是猫，故选B。

6. C。考查形容词辨析。A项意为"仔细的"，B项意为"兴奋的"，C项意为"生气的"，D项意为"幸福的"。空格所在句意为：那么，你应该注意哪些细微的_____信号呢？根据前面提到的negative responses（消极的反应）

可知，此处应填入一个表示负面意义的词，因此C项最符合文意，故选C。

7. B。考查动词辨析。A项意为"开始"，B项意为"停止"，C项意为"接受"，D项意为"喜欢"。空格所在句意为：它们也可能只是定住不动，或主动_____互动。根据句意可知，猫定住不动表示它们不想互动了，and连接的后半句的意思应与前半句一致，所以空格处应填入表示否定意义的词，只有B项符合文意，故选B。

8. C。考查状语从句。空格所在句意为：_____它们这么做，它们的耳朵不会笔直地竖立着。When表示"当……时"，引导时间状语从句，代入原文后符合语境，故选C。

9. A。考查形容词辨析。A项意为"消极的"，B项意为"鼓励的"，C项意为"受欢迎的"，D项意为"积极的"。前文提到猫在恼怒时的消极表现，空格所在句中的also表明该句描述的也是猫的消极行为。根据句意可知，只有A项符合文意，故选A。

10. D。考查动词辨析。A项意为"得到"，B项意为"想象"，C项意为"猜想"，D项意为"观察"。空格所在句意为：我_____过众多被抚摸的猫，它们经常发出这些细微的信号，但是人们通常注意不到这些信号。将四个选项分别代入原文，只有D项最符合文意，故选D。

【词汇碎片】

probably *adv.* 也许；很可能
research *n.* 研究
freeze *v.* 呆住不动；冻结
quite *adv.* 相当

【重难句讲解】

（第三段第四句）

When they're doing this, they're going to have ears that are not pointing directly forward. 当它们这么做时，它们的耳朵不会笔直地竖立着。

本句是一个复合句，they're going to have ears是主句，When引导时间状语从句，that引导的定语从句修饰ears。

Tuesday [阅读理解 A]

【答案解析】

1. B。细节理解题。根据第一段中的 an industrial plant that has been changed into a prison（一座已被改造成监狱的工厂）可知，工厂被改造成了监狱，故选 B。

2. A。词义猜测题。第二段中 transform 所在句的句意为：他希望将这个老旧的奴隶种植园_____一座新城。将四个选项分别代入原文，只有"转变"最符合文意，故选 A。

3. D。细节理解题。第二段第二句指出：McKissick wished the city would bring money and opportunity and change the leaving trend of black people（麦基西克希望这座城市能带来财富与机会，并改变大批黑人离开这里的趋势）。c 和 d 符合文意，故选 D。

4. B。细节理解题。第三段第一、二句指出：However, development stopped 10 years later... In the fourty years since, Soul City has been gradually forgotten（然而，十年以后，那里的发展就停滞不前了……从那以后的四十年里，灵魂之城就渐渐被遗忘了）。因此，发展停滞不前大约 40 年后，这座城市就被人们逐渐遗忘了，故选 B。

5. D。推理判断题。第三段第一句指出：development stopped 10 years later, and there were just 135 jobs（十年以后，那里的发展就停滞不前了，只有 135 个工作岗位），由此可知 A 项错误；第三段最后一句指出：Most people have never heard of it（大多数人都从未听说过这座城市），故 B 项错误；最后一段第一句指出：The history of Soul City is worth remembering（灵魂之城的历史值得被铭记），因此麦基西克的梦想并不是毫无影响的，故 C 项错误；最后一段最后一句指出：McKissick's unrealized dream encourages the fight for racial equality... the way（麦基西克没有实现的梦想激励人们为种族平等而奋斗，与仍在阻碍人们的社会、政治和经济力量斗争），由此可知美国人民应该通过麦基西克的梦想得到激励，故选 D。

【词汇碎片】

entertainment *n*. 娱乐
plant *n*. 工厂；车间
population *n*. 人口
continue *v*. 继续

【重难句讲解】

（第四段第二句）

McKissick's unrealized dream encourages the fight for racial equality and against the many social, political and economic forces that continue to stand in the way. 麦基西克没有实现的梦想激励人们为种族平等而奋斗，与仍在阻碍人们的社会、政治和经济力量斗争。

本句是一个复合句，McKissick's unrealized dream encourages the fight for racial equality and against the many social, political and economic forces 是主句，that 引导的定语从句修饰 forces，该定语从句为主谓结构，in the way 是地点状语。

Wednesday [阅读理解 B]

【答案解析】

1. A。细节理解题。文章第一段提到，大多数死于气候灾难的人都来自世界上最贫穷的国家，故选 A。

2. D。文章排序题。根据第二段中的 Rich countries... face serious climate risk, but they usually have the ability to deal with it（像美国和许多欧洲国家一样的富裕国家也面临着严峻的气候危机，但是他们通常都有能力应对）和 Average developed countries... have to act quickly to make the influence smaller（一般的发达国家也受其影响，他们必须快速行动以减轻影响），以及 developing countries suffer most from climate disasters（发展中国家所受的气候灾难的影响是最大的）可知，受影响最大的是发展中国家，其次是发达国家，最后是富裕国家，故选 D。

3. C。词义猜测题。第三段第三句的句意为：这些灾难_____了47.5万条生命，还造成了2.5万亿美元的经济损失。根据句意和标题中的Killed 475,000 People可知，claimed在文章中的意思为"夺走"，故选C。

4. C。细节理解题。第三段提到在2021年的报告中，气候灾难带来的经济损失是2.5万亿美元，而这还没有包括美国全部的数据。第三段最后一句提到，如果2021年的报告包括整个美国的数据，那么气候灾难带来的经济损失会比现在这个数字高出大约1万亿美元。因此，如果加上美国所有的数据，经济损失应该是 $2.5 trillion 加 $1 trillion，总共是 $3.5 trillion，故选C。

5. B。主旨大意题。最后一段指出：governments can be shaken by natural disasters, which often leads to greater social problems（政府会被自然灾难动摇，这通常会导致更严重的社会问题）。B项"气候灾难可能会导致社会问题"符合文意。A项过度推测，文中并未提及美国正在面临社会问题，故排除；C项意为"对一个国家来说，避免气候灾难是十分重要的"，文中并未提及避免气候灾难，故排除；D项"气候灾难已经在欧洲造成了严重的社会问题"在文中未被提及，故排除。故选B。

【词汇碎片】

country *n.* 国家
serious *adj.* 严重的
report *n.* 报告；报道

【重难句讲解】

（第三段最后一句）

If the whole U.S. data had been included in the 2021 report, the losses would have been about $1 trillion higher. 如果2021年的报告包括整个美国的数据，那么气候灾难带来的经济损失会比现在这个数字高出大约1万亿美元。

本句是一个复合句，the losses would have been about $1 trillion higher 是主句，If 引导条件状语从句。

Thursday [阅读理解 C]

【答案解析】

1. D。细节理解题。根据第一段中的 more than 70% of young people... think the Government and social media companies should do more to deal with false information online（超过70%的英国青少年认为，英国政府和社交媒体公司应该在处理互联网虚假信息方面采取更多行动）可知，D项正确，故选D。

2. B。细节理解题。根据第二段中的 48% were seeing false information online every day（48%的青少年每天都会在网上看到虚假信息）和 More than one in ten said they were seeing it at least six times a day（超过10%的青少年表示他们每天至少会看到六次虚假信息），以及46% of young people had believed false information online in the past year（46%的青少年在过去一年中相信过网上的虚假信息）可知，A项"网上有太多虚假信息"可从该段推测出来。B项"超过一半的青少年每天都会看到虚假信息"与48%不符。C项"将近一半的青少年相信过网上的虚假信息"符合文意。D项"互联网上的虚假信息对青少年有很大的影响"可从该段推测出来。因此只有B项不正确，故选B。

3. A。细节理解题。第三段指出：the Internet has become more important than ever... Because of lockdowns, many students have to learn online（互联网对青少年来说比以往任何时候都重要。因为封锁，许多学生不得不使用互联网学习）。由此可知，A项正确。B、C、D三项在文中均未被提及，故排除。故选A。

4. C。语篇理解题。These 前面提到：Each of these points includes ideas for what the Government... to improve the Internet（每个要点下面都包含了关于政府和社交媒体公司可以为改善互联网环境做些什么的意见）。These 所在句的句意为：_____包括将安全使用互联网纳入学校课程。由此可知，These指的是上一句中提到的ideas（意见），这些意见是英国互联网安全中心和英国青少年一起提出的，故选C。
5. B。主旨大意题。第一段提出，英国青少年认为政府和社交媒体公司应该为解决网络虚假信息采取更多行动；中间两段指出互联网上的虚假信息对英国青少年产生的影响；最后两段指出英国互联网安全中心与青少年合作，共同改善网络环境。B项最能概括全篇大意，A、C、D三项都只能概括文章的部分内容，故选B。

【词汇碎片】

government n. 政府
social adj. 社会的；社交的
company n. 公司

【重难句讲解】

（第五段第一句）

Each of these points includes ideas for what the Government and social media companies could do to improve the Internet. 每个要点下面都包含了关于政府和社交媒体公司可以为改善互联网环境做些什么的意见。

本句是一个复合句，Each of these points includes ideas 是主句。what 引导宾语从句，作介词 for 的宾语；to improve the Internet 是目的状语。

Friday [任务型阅读 D]

【答案解析】

1. To know where snowy owls go and what they do when they fly south. 根据第一段中的 people aren't sure where they go or what they do. Project Snowstorm is trying to solve these mysteries（人们就不能确定它们去了哪里，做了什么了。暴风雪项目正在努力解开这些疑团）可知，暴风雪项目是为了了解雪鸮向南迁徙时去了哪里，做了什么。
2. Catch a snowy owl; put a tiny backpack on the bird; receive location information from the tracker. 根据第三段中的 First... catch a snowy owl（首先……抓住一只雪鸮）、Then... put a tiny backpack on the bird（然后……给它戴上一个小背包）和 The solar-powered tracker transmits the bird's location back to scientists（这个太阳能追踪器将雪鸮的位置信息传回给科学家们）可知，追踪雪鸮的三个步骤是：首先抓住雪鸮，然后给它戴上背包，最后接收追踪器传回来的位置信息。
3. They stay by openings in the frozen Great Lakes. 根据第四段中的 many snowy owls to stay by openings in the frozen Great Lakes to hunt waterbirds such as ducks and geese（许多雪鸮都会守在冰封的北美五大湖的开口旁边来猎捕诸如鸭子和鹅之类的水禽）可知，雪鸮们是在冰封的北美五大湖有开口的地方捕猎。
4. Because they have to fly away from curious people. 根据第五段中的 snowy owls in some areas are making lots of short flights... that is because the birds have to fly away from curious people in populous areas（有些地区的雪鸮会进行多次短途飞行……这是因为在一些人口较多的地区，雪鸮不得不逃离充满好奇心的人类）可知，雪鸮进行多次短途飞行的原因是不得不逃离好奇的人们。
5. He suggests us to give the snowy owl some space if we can see one. 根据第五段最后一句 If you're lucky enough to see one, give it some space（如果你足够幸运，能看到一只雪鸮，请给它一些空间）可知，他建议我们如果看到了雪鸮，要给它空间。

【词汇碎片】

snowy adj. 下雪的；多雪的
solve v. 解决
catch v. 捕捉
enough adv. 足够地；充分地

Saturday [短文填空]

【答案解析】

（1）are。因为主语是 dogs，为第三人称复数，根据空格前的时间状语 recent（最近的）可知空格所在句的时态为一般现在时，故填 are。

（2）hearing。after only _____ it four times 是介词短语作时间状语，after 为介词，介词后面接动名词，故填 hearing。

（3）chose。根据文章可知，做实验是已经发生的事情，所以"选择"这个动作也已经发生了，故使用一般过去时，choose 的过去式为 chose，故填 chose。

（4）were given。因为实验已经发生了，所以应该使用一般过去时，且主语 dogs（狗）与谓语动词 give（给）之间为被动关系，所以应填一般过去时的被动语态，其结构为"was/were+ 过去分词"。这里的主语是 dogs，为复数，故 be 动词用 were，故填 were given。

（5）to fetch。be able to do sth. 是固定搭配，表示"能够做某事"，故填 to fetch。

（6）got。get 为系动词，表示"变得"，后面可以接形容词作表语。根据空格前的 was given 可知空格所在句的时态为一般过去时，故填 got。

（7）picking。空格前的 by 为介词，后面接动名词，故填 picking。

（8）seemed。根据空格前后的时态可知该句时态为一般过去时，故填 seemed。

（9）learn。空格前的 can 是情态动词，情态动词后面接动词原形，故填 learn。

（10）learning。根据句子结构可知，空格处需要填入一个主语，空格前的 rapid 为形容词，修饰名词，故用 learn 的动名词形式 learning 作主语，故填 learning。

【词汇碎片】

recent *adj.* 最近的
owner *n.* 主人；所有者
object *n.* 物体
similar *adj.* 相似的

【重难句讲解】

（第二段第二句）

For the first test, the dogs were given seven objects they knew the names of and one new object with a new name. 在第一个实验中，研究人员给了两只狗七件它们已经知道名字的物品和一件有着新名字的新物品。

本句是一个复合句，the dogs were given seven objects and one new object 是主句，为被动语态。they knew the names of 是省略了引导词的定语从句，修饰 seven objects。with a new name 是介词短语作后置定语，修饰 one new object。

（第四段第一句）

Such rapid learning seems to be similar to the way human children learn their vocabulary, at around two to three years of age. 如此快速的学习速度似乎和小孩两三岁时学词汇的情况类似。

本句是一个复合句，Such rapid learning seems to be similar to the way 是主句。human children learn their vocabulary 是省略了引导词的定语从句，修饰 the way。at around two to three years of age 是介词短语作时间状语。

Sunday［拓展阅读］

【词汇碎片】

celebrate *v.* 庆祝
dumpling *n.* 饺子
date *n.* 日期

【重难句讲解】

（第五段第四句）

The date for Chinese New Year is decided through the traditional Chinese lunar calendar. 中国春节的日期是通过中国传统的农历确定的。

本句是一个简单句，主干是 The date is decided，这里的谓语动词使用了被动语态。介词短语 for Chinese New Year 作后置定语修饰 The date。介词短语 through the traditional Chinese lunar calendar 作方式状语。

Week Nine

Monday [完形填空]

【答案解析】

1. B。考查介词辨析。根据空格后的 the Civil War（美国南北战争）可知，此处应填入一个表示"在……期间"的介词，B 项符合文意。故选 B。
2. D。考查定语从句。空格所在句子缺少主语，可排除 B 项，且空格前的先行词为 all，后面关系代词要用 that，故选 D。
3. D。考查介词辨析。for 表示目的，fight for 为固定搭配，意为"为了……而战"，故选 D。
4. C。考查动词辨析和上下文语义。A 项意为"制作"，B 项意为"跟随"，C 项意为"允许"，D 项意为"告诉"。根据上下文可知，此处讲的应该是"允许组建黑人军团"，故选 C。
5. C。考查介词短语辨析。at sea 为常用表达，意为"在海上"，符合文意。故选 C。
6. A。考查动词辨析。A 项意为"死亡"，B 项意为"生存"，C 项意为"哭泣"，D 项意为"受伤"，将四个选项代入文中，可知 A 项最符合文意。故选 A。
7. B。考查让步状语从句。空格所在句为 whether... or... 引导的让步状语从句，意为"不管是……还是……"，故选 B。
8. A。考查副词辨析。根据上下文可知，不管黑人的处境如何，他们都会像白人兄弟一样战斗，A 项 bravely 意为"勇敢地"，符合上下文语义。B 项 happily 意为"开心地"，C 项 hardly 意为"艰难地"，D 项 sadly 意为"难过地"，均与文中语义不符，故排除。故选 A。
9. C。考查动词辨析。A 项意为"说"，B 项意为"开始"，C 项意为"记住"，D 项意为"写"。将四个选项代入文中，只有 C 项符合文意，故选 C。
10. D。考查连词辨析和上下文语义。空格前面有 over（结束），空格后面有 beginning（开始），由此可知上下文语义发生转折，故选 D。

【词汇碎片】

allow v. 允许；准许
serve v. 服役；服务

【重难句讲解】

（第四段第二句）

Whether they were born free or broke their own chains, black soldiers proved they would fight as bravely as their white brothers. 不管他们是生来自由还是挣脱了自己的枷锁，黑人士兵证明了他们会像他们的白人兄弟一样勇敢地战斗。

本句是一个复合句，包含让步状语从句和宾语从句。black soldiers proved they would fight bravely 是句子主干，they would fight bravely 是省略了 that 的宾语从句的主干。whether... or... 引导让步状语从句。

Tuesday [阅读理解 A]

【答案解析】

1. A。细节理解题。根据 Red is a beloved color for Christmas and a lucky one for Chinese New Year（红色在圣诞节是受人喜爱的颜色，在中国新年是幸运的颜色）可知，人们在春节和圣诞节都喜欢红色，故选 A。
2. C。词义猜测题。birth 意为"出生"，前缀 re 表示"再一次"的意思，因此 rebirth 在这里意为"重生"，故选 C。
3. B。细节理解题。根据 Many Chinese New Year customs... such as decorating the Christmas tree（许多中国新年习俗……比如装饰圣诞树）可知，红对联、鞭炮在中国春节是可以带来好运的事物，装扮的圣诞树是西方认为可以带来好运的事物。数字 6 在中国是幸运数字，但文中未提及，故 d 不对，故选 B。
4. D。推理判断题。本文主要介绍了圣诞节和中国新年的许多共同之处，可推知其各自代表的文化也有共同点，故 D 项符合要求。A 项和 B 项均未在文章中提及，且根据常识判断均错误，故均排除。C 项中的 all 过于绝对，故排除。

故选 D。

5. D。主旨大意题。本文主要说明了圣诞节和中国新年的相似之处，故选 D。A 项指代所有的节日，过于宽泛，故排除；B 项只是简单地点明两个节日，并未指出具体的关系，故排除；C 项并非文章内容，故排除。

● 【词汇碎片】

interesting *adj.* 有趣的
tradition *n.* 惯例，传统

● 【重难句讲解】

While Chinese New Year signals the start of the new lunar year, Christmas once fell on the exact date of the winter solstice, the shortest day of the year in the Northern Hemisphere, being the "rebirth" of the sun. 中国新年标志着农历新年的开始，而圣诞节曾经恰逢冬至，这是北半球一年中白昼最短的一天，标志着太阳的"重生"。

本句是一个由 while 连接的并列句。Chinese New Year signals the start 是第一个分句的主干，Christmas fell on the exact date 是第二个分句的主干。While 作为并列连词，意为"而，然而"，表示前后的对比。

Wednesday [阅读理解 B]

● 【答案解析】

1. B。细节理解题。根据第一段中的 the dinosaurs... see a large rock getting bigger and bigger in the sky（恐龙……看到一块巨大的岩石在空中变得越来越大）和 the rock hit the ground（岩石撞击地面）可知，是一块陨石砸中地球导致恐龙灭绝。故选 B。

2. C。词义猜测题。根据画线单词后面的 they could have known the coming rock and perhaps made it miss the earth（它们就可以知道有岩石正在靠近，也许还可以使它偏离方向而不击中地球）和 astronomy can save lives（天文学可以拯救生命）可知，与天文学相关的能观察到正在靠近的陨石的物品就是望远镜，因此 telescopes 在这里意为"望远镜"，故选 C。

3. B。细节理解题。根据第三段第二句 If a risk is identified, we could use many skills so that it will miss the earth（如果发现一个危险体，我们可以使用各种方法使其偏离地球）可知，我们可以观察到正在靠近的陨石，并想办法让它偏离地球，从而避免陨石砸中地球。故选 B。

4. C。推理判断题。根据第三段第三句 But our advantage also brings a sense of responsibility for our earth（但我们的优势也带来了我们对地球的责任感）可知，人类对地球负有责任，想要保护好地球，故 C 项正确。A 项和 B 项在文中均未提及，故错误。D 项中的 all 过于绝对，故错误。故选 C。

5. D。主旨大意题。第一段讲述了陨石砸中地球导致恐龙灭绝，第二、三段讲述了人类可以如何避免此类灾难的发生。D 项符合文章大意，故选 D。

● 【词汇碎片】

similar *adj.* 相似的
general *adj.* 普遍的；普通的；总的

● 【重难句讲解】

（第三段第四句）

The biggest problem we face is how to live long rather than arrive at the brink of self-extinction through the technologies we use. 我们面临的最大问题是如何长期生存，而不是通过我们所使用的技术到达自我灭绝的边缘。

本句是一个复合句，包含定语从句和表语从句。主句为主系表结构，其中 The biggest problem 为主语，we face 是省略了 that 的定语从句，修饰 problem，is 是系动词，how 引导的表语从句对主语进行解释说明，we use 是省略了 that 的定语从句，修饰 technologies。

Thursday [阅读理解 C]

● 【答案解析】

1. A。细节理解题。根据第一段第二句 Costumes and

objects of dressing show technical progress and aesthetic changes（服饰和装饰物体现了技术的进步和审美的变化）和第三句 They also stand as evidence to the cultures, social values and class of society（它们也是文化、社会价值观和社会阶层的见证）可知，本文讲服饰的历史变化能体现社会的历史变化。故选 A。

2. C。词义猜测题。画线单词所在句意为：它们也是文化、社会价值观和社会阶层的_____。服饰和文化、社会价值及社会阶层的关系是服装能够为这些内容提供证据，是一种论证关系，故选 C。

3. D。细节理解题。根据第二段可知，衣服、鞋子、帽子、缝纫工具、陶器和古典绘画在展览中都有展出，故选 D。

4. A。推理判断题。最后一段第一句指出，这些展品最早可追溯到新石器时代，最晚到清朝。由此可知，B 项错误，A 项正确。C 项无法从文中推测出来，故排除。根据 The exhibits come from the collections of various museums across the country（这些展品是全国各地不同博物馆的收藏品）可知 D 项与原文不符。故选 A。

5. A。主旨大意题。本文主要在介绍展出的各种物品，是一篇以介绍展品为主题的说明文，故选 A。

• 【词汇碎片】

culture *n.* 文化
exhibition *n.* 展览；展览会

• 【重难句讲解】

（第三段第一句）

The exhibits come from the collections of various museums across the country, and date as early as the Neolithic period and through the end of Qing Dynasty (1644-1911), China's last empire. 这些展品是全国各地不同博物馆的收藏品，最早可追溯到新石器时代，直到中国最后一个封建帝国——清朝（1644—1911 年）——结束。

本句是一个简单句，为主谓结构。across the country 为介词短语，作 museums 的后置定语。China's last empire 为 Qing Dynasty 的同位语。

Friday [任务型阅读 D]

• 【答案解析】

1. F。根据第一段中的 Taijiquan means "supreme ultimate fist"（太极拳的意思是"至高无上的拳头"）可知，选项中只有 F 项最为符合文意，该项是对空格前一句的解释说明，故选 F。

2. C。根据第二段第一句中的 the origin of Taijiquan（太极拳的起源）及空格后出现的"以柔克刚"可知，此处内容应指出太极拳与道教之间的关系，故选 C。

3. E。根据空格后面的 It is represented by the famous symbol of the Yin and Yang which expresses the continuous flow of Qi（以著名的阴阳符号为代表，表示连续的气息）可知，此处讲的是道教。第 2 题和第 3 题易混淆，不太好选，但可以对比 C 项和 E 项，Taoism 分别出现在句尾和句首。一般情况下，出现在句尾的为新信息，出现在句首的为旧信息，由此可判断，C 项应该出现在 E 项之前。将 E 项代入原文后符合语境，故选 E。

4. D。空格前提到 The most famous forms of Taijiquan practiced today are the Chen, Yang, Wu, Wu and Sun styles（如今最著名的太极拳门派是陈、杨、武、吴、孙），而 D 项也是对这五大太极拳门派的说明，故选 D。

5. B。根据空格后的 it is practiced by millions of people（并有数百万人练习）可知，此处应该填入表示太极拳的影响很广泛的句子，B 项符合此意，故选 B。

• 【词汇碎片】

origin *n.* 起源
balance *v.* （使）保持平衡

• 【重难句讲解】

（第三段第一句）

The most famous forms of Taijiquan practiced today are the Chen, Yang, Wu, Wu and Sun styles. 如今最著名的太极拳门派是陈、杨、武、吴、孙。

本句是一个简单句，为主系表结构。practiced 为过去分词作后置定语，修饰前面的 forms of Taijiquan。

Saturday [短文填空]

●【答案解析】

（1）interviewed。空格前面是 has，再根据句意可知，此处为现在完成时态，所以要用 interview 的过去分词形式，故填 interviewed。

（2）has recorded。空格所在句是由 and 连接的并列句，前面的第一个并列句为现在完成时，故空格所在的第二个并列句也要用现在完成时。故填 has recorded。

（3）known。根据句子结构可知，know 与主语 a history 之间为被动关系，表示"为人所知"，故此处为被动语态，要用 know 的过去分词形式，故填 known。

（4）worked。空格所在句中 and 连接了两个并列谓语，并列部分的语法形式相同，lived 为过去式，work 也要用同样的形式，故填 worked。

（5）writing。空格所在句中 and 连接了两个并列宾语，并列部分的语法形式相同，interviewing 为动名词形式，write 也要用同样的形式，故填 writing。

（6）was。根据语境，此处为过去时态，空格后面是 interviewing，所以这里为过去进行时态，又因为主语是第三人称单数 she，故填 was。

（7）photos。空格后面提到了 229 veterans（229 名老兵）和 published five books and photo albums（出版了 5 本关于他们的书籍和相册），所以此处要填 photo 的复数形式，故填 photos。

（8）collected。空格前面是 has，逗号后有 and 连接的并列谓语动词 published，并列部分的语法形式相同，所以要用 collect 的过去分词形式，故填 collected。

（9）marked。根据 The year 2020 可知，这里时态为一般过去时，故填 marked。

（10）years。空格前面是 two，所以要用 year 的复数形式，故填 years。

●【词汇碎片】

history *n.* 历史
meaningful *adj.* 有意义的

●【重难句讲解】

（第二段第一句）

The idea of tracing the history of people who participated in the war in Korea came to her as she was interviewing Xu Zhenming. 在采访徐振明的时候，她想到了追溯参加抗美援朝战争的人的历史。

本句是一个复合句，包含定语从句和时间状语从句。The idea came to her 是主句的主干，of tracing the history of people 为后置定语，修饰主语 The idea。who 引导定语从句，修饰 people。as she was interviewing Xu Zhenming 是时间状语从句。

Sunday [拓展阅读]

●【词汇碎片】

return *v.* 返回
business *n.* 商业

Week Ten

Monday [完形填空]

【答案解析】

1. A。考查动词辨析。A项意为"提供",B项意为"有",C项意为"种植",D项意为"买"。空格后面为marker,将A项代入后意为"提供一个标志",符合文意,故选A。

2. C。考查上下文语义。空格后面以西伯利亚举例,且由was可知此处主语为第三人称单数,故此处应填One of,意为"……之一",代入后符合上下文语义,故选C。

3. D。考查形容词辨析。A项意为"困难的",B项意为"悲伤的",C项意为"可怕的",D项意为"最近的"。将四个选项代入文中后,只有"最近的"符合句意,故选D。

4. C。考查动词辨析。A项意为"拿;取",B项意为"制作",C项意为"发生",D项意为"丢失"。将四个选项代入文中后,只有"发生"符合句意,故选C。

5. B。考查形容词辨析。A项意为"高的",B项意为"增加的",C项意为"缓慢的",D项意为"开放的"。将四个选项代入文中后,只有"增加的"符合句意,故选B。

6. A。考查上下文语义。空格前面的such提示可从前文找到类似表述,本段开头出现heat records,与A项相同,且将"记录"代入文中后,符合上下文语义,故选A。

7. C。考查介词辨析。A项意为"从",B项意为"用;与……一起",C项意为"在……(两者)之间",D项意为"在……(三者及三者以上)中"。空格后为and,连接的是两个表示年份的名词,表示位于两者之间,故选C。

8. B。考查形容词辨析。A项意为"旧的",B项意为"新的",C项意为"不同的",D项意为"一样的"。空格所在的句子提到在那些年间,最热年份的纪录会有变动,所以变动的就是新的纪录,且"新的"代入文中后,符合句意,故选B。

9. D。考查介词辨析。A项意为"……的",B项意为"在",C项意为"在……里面",D项意为"到;朝"。空格前后为两个数字,且根据句意可知这里表示"每8到11年",故选D。

10. B。考查动词辨析。A项意为"看见",B项意为"预料",C项意为"说",D项意为"采访"。空格所在句的内容是在前文分析之后得出的结论,即2020年的高温纪录是可以预料到的。故选B。

【词汇碎片】

recorded *adj.* 记录的
history *n.* 历史
greenhouse gases 温室气体
be linked to 与……相关

【重难句讲解】

(第一段第二句)

The year provided an important marker of the long-term warming caused by human activities producing greenhouse gases. 这一年为产生温室气体的人类活动导致的长期变暖提供了一个重要标志。

本句是一个简单句。句子主干是The year provided an important marker,为主谓宾结构。caused by human activities producing greenhouse gases作后置定语,修饰warming。

Tuesday [阅读理解 A]

【答案解析】

1. B。语篇理解题。根据题干提供的句子定位至第三个对话内容:即使流行病暴发也无法阻止它的进程,言外之意是全球变暖是不可能避免的,故选B。

2. D。推理判断题。根据Dr. Lizzie中的Dr.可知这个人的身份是医生或者博士,故可排除B项和C项,而对话内容主要围绕全球变暖展开,与医学无关,其他两个人为提问者,对话形式为一问一答,故可推测他们三人为师生关系,故选D。

3. C。主旨大意题。根据对话内容可知他们讨论的是全球变暖的问题。A项和B项只是对话中提及的例子，故排除，D项无中生有，故排除，故选C。

【词汇碎片】

climate change 气候变化
global warming 全球变暖

Wednesday [阅读理解 B]

【答案解析】

1. A。细节理解题。根据第一段第一句和第二句可知，中国对长江经济带未来五年的发展规划，是要实现绿色和可持续的发展，故选A。

2. B。推理判断题。根据第二段内容可知，长江经济带在地理面积和人口方面都占了不少比重，可以说是一个重要的区域，故B项符合文意。A项和C项与第二段所述不符，故排除。D项在文中未被提及，故排除。故选B。

3. A。细节理解题。文章第三段提到了长江经济带的经济发展状况和交通运输情况，所以a和c在文中是有提及的，b和d在文中没有提及，故选A。

4. B。推理判断题。文章前面提到该地区要发展绿色、可持续的经济，从最后一段的经济发展数据来看，长江经济带也一直没有放弃发展经济，所以应该是经济发展与环境保护并重，故选B。

5. C。细节理解题。文章最后一段提到的长江经济带近两年的发展数据都处于上升的状态，所以A项错误，C项正确。根据During the first nine months of 2020, the number rose to 46.6 percent（在2020年的前九个月，这一数值跃升至46.6%）可知，不是在九月升至46.6%，所以B项错误；长江经济带的经济占比到达46.6%，将近50%，即二分之一，所以D项错误。故选C。

【词汇碎片】

development *n.* 发展
make progress in 在……取得进步

【重难句讲解】

（第三段第四句）

In terms of transportation and connectivity, the economic belt's railway network grew to 43,700 kilometers as of last November, and the high-speed rail network reached 15,400 kilometers. 在交通运输和互联互通方面，截至去年11月，经济带的铁路网总里程增至4.37万公里，高速铁路网总里程达到1.54万公里。

本句是一个由and连接的并列句。and前面the economic belt's railway network grew to 43,700 kilometers是句子的主干，and后面the high-speed rail network reached 15,400 kilometers 也是句子的主干。In terms of为固定短语，意为"在……方面"。

Thursday [阅读理解 C]

【答案解析】

1. C。细节理解题。根据题干中的关键词tragedy定位到第一段，可知这场悲剧发生在印度北部的一个邦，故选C。

2. B。细节理解题。根据题干中的关键信息destroyed many villages定位到第二段第二句，可知是一场可怕的洪水摧毁了村庄，故选B。

3. B。细节理解题。根据题干中的关键信息origin of avalanches定位到第三段第一句，可知雪崩起源于喜马拉雅北阿坎德邦地区的一处"悬空"冰川断裂，故选B。

4. D。细节理解题。A项在文中没有提及，故排除；根据scientists say it is possible that global warming played a role（科学家们表示，全球变暖可能有一定的影响）可知科学家们也只是猜测冰川坍塌与全球变暖有关，不能完全肯定，所以B项错误；第四段最后三句提到冰川融化可能形成冰川湖泊，而冰川到了某个崩溃的临界点时会释放出大量的水，可能造成灾难性的事件，所以冰川湖泊并不安全，所以C项错误，D项正确，故选D。

5. C。主旨大意题。文章第一段讲印度北部的一个邦发生了一场悲剧；第二段讲具体的情况；第三段和第四段讲这场悲剧发生的原因及造成灾难的可能原因，故选C。

【词汇碎片】

flood *n.* 洪水
region *n.* 地区
exact *adj.* 准确的；精密的
lead to 导致

【重难句讲解】

（第二段第二句）

It caused a terrible flood that destroyed many villages along the Alaknanda and Dhauliganga Rivers. 它引发了一场极其可怕的洪水，摧毁了阿拉克南达河和道里根加河沿岸的许多村庄。

本句是一个复合句，包含定语从句。主句是 It caused a terrible flood。that 引导的定语从句修饰 flood。

Friday [任务型阅读 D]

【答案解析】

1. F。观察所给选项，能发现 A、B、C、D 四项都是小标题的形式，明显不适合放于段落中间，所以先排除，只剩下 E、F 两个选项。空格后面提到发生了许多变化，所以可推测空格处描述的是一种现象，E、F 两项中只有 F 项是描述一种现象，故选 F。

2. B。短文第一段最后一句提到发生了许多变化，可推测下文会具体介绍发生了哪些变化，又根据空格后的内容 Arctic sea ice hit its lowest extent in September, at the end of the summer melting season（北极海冰的范围在九月份，也就是夏季融化季节结束时达到最低点）可知这一段涉及海冰的融化，故选 B。

3. C。空格后提到 This year was a record-breaking summer for wildfires in the Arctic Circle（今年是北极圈野火破纪录的一个夏天），句中的 wildfires 与 C 项对应，且后文提到了导致野火的原因，故选 C。

4. D。空格后文提到 Climate change is affecting plant and animal life in the Arctic Ocean, from the bottom of the food chain up（气候变化正通过食物链自下而上地影响着北冰洋的动植物的生命），句中的 affecting 意为"影响"，与 D 项中的 Influenced 对应，故选 D。

5. E。空格前提到气候变化正通过食物链自下而上地影响着北冰洋的动植物的生命，而微小的藻类是北极海洋生态系统的基础，由此可知生态情况不容乐观，将剩下的选项代入文中后，E 项符合文意，故选 E。

【词汇碎片】

scientist *n.* 科学家
the Arctic Ocean 北冰洋

【重难句讲解】

（第四段第一句）

Climate change is affecting plant and animal life in the Arctic Ocean, from the bottom of the food chain up. 气候变化正通过食物链自下而上地影响着北冰洋的动植物的生命。

本句是一个简单句，句子的主干为 Climate change is affecting plant and animal life，为主谓宾结构。from the bottom up 为固定搭配，意为"自下而上"。

Saturday [短文填空]

【答案解析】

（1）are。空格前的主语是 their lives，是复数形式，且短文时态为一般现在时，故填 are。

（2）growing。空格后面为名词，所以空格处应填入修饰这个名词的形容词，动词的现在分词形式具有形容词的特性，故填 growing。

（3）make。空格所在句的主语是 women，是复数形式，短文时态为一般现在时，故填 make。

（4）increasing。空格后为名词，所以空格处应填入修饰这个名词的形容词，动词的现在分词形式具有形容词的特性，故填 increasing。

（5）shows。空格前面是 Data，短文时态为一般现在时，所以谓语动词要用第三人称单数形式，故填 shows。

（6）names。空格前面是 their，所以此处的 name 应填其复数形式，故填 names。

（7）working。空格前面的介词 of 后面常跟名词，所以需要将 work 改成其动名词形式 working，意为"有工作的"，故填 working。

（8）means。空格前面是 That，所以谓语动词要用第三人称单数形式，短文的时态为一般现在时，故填 means。

（9）worse。空格后出现的 than 是比较级的标志，故填 worse。

（10）have。空格前面是 women，为名词的复数形式，且短文时态一般现在时，故填 have。

● 【词汇碎片】

climate change 气候变化
natural *adj.* 自然的
be dependent on 依靠；依赖
information *n.* 信息，资料

● 【重难句讲解】

（第一段第一句）

Across the world, poor people are among those worst hit by climate change and natural disasters, resource shortage and poverty resulting from climate. 在世界各地，穷人是受气候变化和气候引起的自然灾害、资源稀缺和贫穷影响最严重的群体之一。

本句是一个简单句。poor people are among those 是句子主干，resulting from climate 作后置定语修饰 natural disasters, resource shortage and poverty。resulting from 意为"起因于；由……造成的"。

Sunday [拓展阅读]

● 【词汇碎片】

express thanks to 向……表示感谢
get through 度过
carry *v.* 携带

Week Eleven

Monday [完形填空]

【答案解析】

1. B。考查名词辨析。A项意为"年"，B项意为"天"，C项意为"小时"，D项意为"分钟"。根据最后一段第二句提到的"历时70天3小时48分钟"可知，B项符合语境。故选B。

2. A。考查名词辨析。A项意为"经验"，B项意为"时间"，C项意为"钱"，D项意为"空间"。下文提到，哈里森女士看到……挑战赛之后才有了划船横渡大洋的想法，由此可知她之前是没有相关经验的，故A项符合语境。故选A。

3. D。考查状语从句。A项意为"为什么"，B项意为"什么"，C项意为"在哪里"，D项意为"当……时"。空格所在句的前半句提到 three years ago（三年前），由此可知此处应填入表示"时间"的连词。故选D。

4. C。考查形容词辨析。A项意为"困难的"，B项意为"高兴的"，C项意为"容易的"，D项意为"悲伤的"。空格后面提到哈里森女士经历的一系列困难，由此可知划船横渡大洋并不是一件容易的事情，C项符合语境。故选C。

5. B。考查名词辨析。A项意为"车"，B项意为"船"，C项意为"自行车"，D项意为"食物"。空格所在句的前一句提到，哈里森女士每天有12个小时左右的时间都在划船，故B项符合语境。故选B。

6. B。考查动词辨析。A项意为"玩"，B项意为"说话"，C项意为"跳舞"，D项意为"唱歌"。空格所在句意为：哈里森女士有一个电话，所以她可以每天和家人、朋友_____。四个选项中只有B项符合语境。故选B。

7. C。考查上下文语义。空格所在句意为：但是，她还是有_____时间不得不独处。上文提到哈里森女士可以和家人、朋友通话，But表转折，故此处填入C项 much（许多）符合语境。故选C。

8. B。考查连词辨析。A项意为"但是"，B项意为"而且；然后"，C项意为"或者；否则"，D项意为"因为"。空格所在句意为：在旅行的过程中，她的扬声器掉到了水中，_____她再也不能听音乐了。故此处应填入B项 and，表示动作的先后。故选B。

9. B。考查上下文语义。下文提到了哈里森女士遇到的两次危险，故B项 Twice（两次）代入后符合文意。故选B。

10. A。考查动词辨析。A项意为"到达"，B项意为"离开"，C项意为"经过"，D项意为"停留"。根据空格后提到的 the end of the journey（旅行的终点）可知A项符合语境。故选A。

【词汇碎片】

push v. 推动（人或物）

journey n.（尤指长途）旅行，行程

【重难句讲解】

（第二段第二句）

She got the idea three years ago when she saw the end of the 2017 Talisker Whisky Atlantic Challenge. 三年前，当她碰巧看到2017泰斯卡威士忌跨大西洋划艇挑战赛结束时，她才有了这个想法。

本句是一个复合句，主句是 She got the idea three years ago，when引导时间状语从句 when she saw the end of the 2017 Talisker Whisky Atlantic Challenge，对主句中动作的发生的时间进行说明。

Tuesday [阅读理解 A]

【答案解析】

1. B。细节理解题。根据第一段第二句中的 They bought all the things that were used for building their house（他们买了所有用来建房子的材料）可知，莫斯·苏伯尔和其他几个村民买材料是为了建房子。故选B。

2. D。细节理解题。根据第二段第一句 The "cliff village" is in Southwest China's Sichuan Province（"悬崖村"位

于中国西南部的四川省）可知,"悬崖村"位于中国的西南部。故选 D。

3. A。词义猜测题。根据最后一段画线单词所在句后面的 started a partnership in a plan to build a homestay in November last year（在去年11月开始了合作，计划建一个家庭旅馆）可以推断出 A 项"发现"符合语境。故选 A。

4. D。推理判断题。第二段最后一句提到攀登"悬崖村"钢梯的短视频在网络上走红，但这并不能推断出攀登钢梯在中国很流行，故 A 项错误。B、C 两项属于无中生有，故均排除。根据第二段第三句中的 the travel conditions became better（旅游条件变得更好了）和第二段第四句 The introduction of the Internet also changed the village（互联网的引进也改变了这个村庄），以及第三段中的 the living conditions of these families have become much better（这些家庭的生活条件得到了很大的改善）可知,"悬崖村"村民们的生活条件越来越好了。故选 D。

5. A。细节理解题。根据第二段中的 with the construction of the steel ladders... became better（钢梯的修建……变得更好了）可知，钢梯是游客进入"悬崖村"的道路，A 项符合文意；文中提到，村民们在政府的帮助下搬往新家，村民们的生活得到了很大的改善，B、C 两项与文意不符，故均排除；D 项在文中并未被提及。故选 A。

【词汇碎片】

build v. 建造
condition n. 状况；条件

【重难句讲解】

（第二段第五句）

In 2017, a short video of women climbing the steel ladder in the "cliff village" became popular on the Internet. 2017年，一段女子攀登"悬崖村"钢梯的短视频在互联网上走红。

本句是一个简单句，句子主干为 a short video became popular。介词短语 of women climbing the steel ladder in the "cliff village" 作后置定语，修饰 a short video。on the Internet 作地点状语。

Wednesday [阅读理解 B]

【答案解析】

1. A。细节理解题。根据第二段中的 the Garze Tibetan Autonomous Prefecture has become a popular place for travelers（甘孜藏族自治州成了受游客欢迎的地方）可知，A 项正确。故选 A。

2. C。细节理解题。根据第三段中的 Tamdrin, whose name in Mandarin is Ding Zhen, a 20-year-old from the Tibetan ethnic group in Sichuan（Tamdrin 的汉语名字是丁真，20岁，四川藏族人）和 his good looks（帅气的长相）可知，A、B、D 三项均正确。丁真是四川藏族人，而不是来自西藏，故 C 项表述有误。故选 C。

3. B。细节理解题。根据第三段最后一句中的 helped the tourism in Sichuan to develop by posting short videos（通过发布短视频来促进四川旅游业的发展）可知，B 项"通过制作短视频"符合文意。其他三项在文中均未被提及。故选 B。

4. D。细节理解题。根据第四段第二句 These places are located about a 12-hour drive from Chengdu Shuangliu International Airport, so travel there has driven car rentals（这些地方距离成都双流国际机场约12小时车程，因此当地的旅游业也推动了汽车租赁行业的发展）可知，D 项"因为这些景点距离机场远"正确。故选 D。

5. B。主旨大意题。文章第二段提到了甘孜成为旅行热门目的地；第三段提到了其人气提升的推动因素；第四段和第五段提到了其游客量的增多。全文围绕着甘孜成为旅游热门目的地展开。故选 B。

【词汇碎片】

abroad adv. 到国外
ticket n. 票

【重难句讲解】

（第三段第一句）

Garze's popularity was boosted by Tamdrin, whose name in Mandarin is Ding Zhen, a 20-year-old from the Tibetan ethnic group in Sichuan. 甘孜的人气受到了 Tamdrin 的推动，Tamdrin 的汉语名字是丁真，20岁，四川藏族人。

本句是一个复合句，主句是 Garze's popularity was boosted by Tamdrin，whose 引导的定语从句 whose name in Mandarin is Ding Zhen 修饰 Tamdrin。a 20-year-old from the Tibetan ethnic group in Sichuan 是 Tamdrin 的同位语，对其进行解释说明。

Thursday [阅读理解 C]

【答案解析】

1. B。根据第二段第一句中的 the West Lake, a popular scenic spot in the city of Hangzhou, capital of East China's Zhejiang province（中国东部浙江省省会杭州市的热门景点——西湖）可知，西湖位于中国东部，而不是西部。故选 B。

2. A。根据第二段第二句中的 Cameras were used to control tourist flow on Broken Bridge（使用摄像头来控制断桥的客流量）可知，工作人员可以使用摄像头来控制断桥的客流量。故选 A。

3. A。根据第三段中的 the West Lake used an LED screen showing some information, including the route map of bus travel（西湖使用了 LED 屏幕来显示一些信息，包括公交车旅行路线图）可知，旅客可以在 LED 屏幕上获取公交车旅行路线图。故选 A。

4. B。根据第二段第一句 During the holiday, the West Lake... saw more than 1.66 million visitors（在假期期间……西湖，接待了超过 166 万名游客）和第四段第一句 Qiandao Lake... received 78,500 tourists during the Spring Festival holiday this year（千岛湖……在今年春节假期期间接待了 78 500 名游客）可知，西湖比千岛湖接待的游客要多。故选 B。

5. A。根据第四段第二句中的 Tourists can book on the Internet（游客可以在网上预约）可知，该表述正确。故选 A。

【词汇碎片】

capital *n.* 首都；省会
control *v.* 管理；控制

【重难句讲解】

（第二段第二句）

Cameras were used to control tourist flow on Broken Bridge, an important scenic spot of the West Lake, during the peak holiday period. 在假期的高峰时段，（景区工作人员）使用摄像头来控制断桥（西湖的一个重要景点）的客流量。

本句是一个简单句，句子主干为 Cameras were used to control tourist flow on Broken Bridge。an important scenic spot of the West Lake 是 Broken Bridge 的同位语，对其进行解释说明。during the peak holiday period 是时间状语。

Friday [任务型阅读 D]

【答案解析】

1. B。上文提到广东省决定建造磁悬浮铁路线，下文提到和时速有关的信息，所以此处应该是介绍磁悬浮列车的具体时速。B 项中的 600 kilometers per hour（六百公里每小时）和下文中的 several hundred km/h（几百公里每小时）相呼应。故选 B。

2. D。根据下文中的 the province's capital（该省的省会）可知，此处提到了广东省的省会广州市，故将答案定位在 A、D、E 三项。D 项中的 The two lines（这两条线路）和上文 The two maglev lines（这两条磁悬浮铁路线）相呼应，且句尾的 Guangzhou 正好和下文 the province's capital（该省的省会）衔接。故选 D。

3. A。上文提到，要建造两条将广东省分别与北京和上海连接起来的磁悬浮铁路线，下文提到了北京和广州之间的旅行时间，因此可以推断此处提到的是上海和广州之间的旅行时间，A 项符合语境。故选 A。

4. C。根据上文中的 a line connecting Shanghai, Shenzhen and Guangzhou（一条连接上海、深圳和广州的线路）和下文中的 However... probably will be the first to be built（然而……可能会是最先修建的）可知，此处提到的是一条计划修建的线路，因此 C 项"但那条线路还没有建成"符合语境。故选 C。

5. E。根据下文中的 the Shenzhen Development and Reform Commission（深圳发展和改革委员会）可知，此处提到了深圳的相关信息，只有 E 项符合语境。故选 E。

● 【词汇碎片】

decide *v.* 决定
train *n.* 火车；列车

● 【重难句讲解】

（第四段第一句）

The plan also mentioned a line connecting Shanghai, Shenzhen and Guangzhou. 该计划还提到一条连接上海、深圳和广州的线路。

本句是一个简单句，句子主干是 The plan also mentioned a line，现在分词短语 connecting Shanghai, Shenzhen and Guangzhou 作后置定语，修饰 a line。

Saturday [短文填空]

● 【答案解析】

（1）was。根据空格前面的 reported 可知，此处时态为一般过去时，主语 Wednesday 是第三人称单数，故填 was。

（2）began。根据空格后面的时间状语 in mid-March 可知，COVID-19 是已经发生的事情，所以时态为一般过去时，故填 began。

（3）flew。本句讲述美国运输安全管理局统计民众乘飞机出行的数据，是已经发生的事情，所以时态为一般过去时，故填 flew。

（4）wear。please 后面跟动词原形，意为"请某人做某事"，please wear a mask 意为"请戴口罩"，故填 wear。

（5）getting。空格前的 and 表示并列，因此 get 的形式应与 spreading 一致，故填 getting。

（6）protect。空格处为 to + 动词原形构成的不定式，故填 protect。

（7）didn't stop。前面提到疾病控制与预防中心建议居民在疫情期间待在家中，紧接着 But 表示转折，说明建议的成效不大，即并未成功阻止居民出行。此处描述的是已经出现的结果，时态为一般过去时，故填 didn't stop。

（8）needs。主语 My mom 是第三人称单数，且由后文中 Brownlee 说的话可知，时态应为一般现在时，故填 needs。

（9）told。根据空格后面的时间状语 earlier this week 可知，时态为一般过去时，故填 told。

（10）going。此处考查固定搭配 be going to do sth.，意为"打算做某事"。故填 going。

● 【词汇碎片】

spread *v.* 传播
holiday *n.* 假期

● 【重难句讲解】

（第五段第二句）

CDC continues to recommend staying home because this is the best way to protect yourself and others this year. 疾病控制与预防中心继续建议大家待在家里，因为这是今年保护自己和家人的最好的办法。

本句是一个复合句，包含原因状语从句。CDC continues to recommend staying home 是主句，because 引导的原因状语从句对主句进行补充说明。

Sunday [拓展阅读]

● 【词汇碎片】

traditional *adj.* 传统的
calender *n.* 日历

Week Twelve

Monday [完形填空]

【答案解析】

（1）cartoons。根据前文提到的 The art festival of Chinese opera cartoons（中国戏曲动漫艺术节）可知此处指的是将戏曲制作成动漫，故填 cartoons。

（2）public。本句句意为：中国经典曲目……向_____展出。public 意为"公众"，符合语境，故填 public。

（3）like。like 在此处作介词，表示"例如"，符合语境，故填 like。

（4）Because。后半句提到人们可以通过观看在线短视频平台上的视频来参加活动，故"该艺术节主要在网上举行"是原因。另外，这里要注意首字母大写，故填 Because。

（5）watching。空格所在句的句意为：人们可以通过_____在线短视频平台（如抖音和火山视频）上的视频来参加活动。watch 和 look 都表示"看"，都符合语境。但 look 是不及物动词，后面接宾语时要和 at 连用。而表示观看电视、表演、比赛等一般用 watch，故填 watching。

（6）enjoy。空格所在句的句意为：人们还可以在网上_____360度的活动全景。enjoy 表示"享受"，符合语境，故填 enjoy。

（7）choose。空格所在句的句意为：通过点击鼠标或使用手机，人们可以_____他们喜欢的任何角度在家里观看活动。choose 意为"选择"，符合语境，故填 choose。

【词汇碎片】

festival *n.* 节日
choose *v.* 选择
activity *n.* 活动
online *adv.* 在线地

【重难句讲解】

（第二段第一句）

Classical Chinese operas chosen from 360 types of opera in China, are made into cartoons, and will be exhibited to the public. 从中国360种戏曲中选出的中国经典曲目被制作成动漫，并将向公众展出。

本句是一个简单句，主干为 Classical Chinese operas are made into cartoons and will be exhibited to the public，两个谓语动词由连词 and 连接，chosen from 360 types of opera in China 为后置定语，修饰主语 Classical Chinese operas。

Tuesday [阅读理解 A]

【答案解析】

1. B。细节理解题。由第一段中的 a bus driver in Beijing（一名北京的公交车司机）可知，孟大鹏的工作地是北京。故选 B。

2. C。词义猜测题。画线单词位于第一段第二句，本句描述了孟大鹏一天中的工作内容：完成对车辆的全面_____，对事物保持谨慎的观察，并把他的乘客从一个站送到另一个站。由此可知，孟大鹏做的第一件事应该是对车辆进行全面检查，故选 C。

3. D。细节理解题。根据第一段第二句中的 finishing a full inspection of the vehicle, keeping a cautious eye on things and taking his passengers from stop to stop（完成对车辆的全面检查，对事物保持谨慎的观察，并把他的乘客从一个站送到另一个站）可知，A、B、C 三项内容均是公交车司机需要做的工作，故选 D。

4. C。细节理解题。第二段提到 Meng has a special, deeper, emotional connection with being a bus driver: His father was one as well（孟大鹏与公交车司机这个职业之间有着一种特殊的、更深层次的情感联系：他的父亲也曾是一名公交车司机）。由此可知，孟大鹏成为公交车司机是因为他的父亲也曾是公交车司机，从而他内心对于这个职位有种特别的情感，故选 C。

5. B。推理判断题。A 项"孟大鹏在除夕夜吃了一顿丰盛的团圆饭"与第一段所述内容相悖，故排除。文中提到了孟大鹏认真细致的工作态度，对自身职业的特殊情感，以及在业余时间所做的与职业相关的事情，B 项"孟大鹏热爱他的工作"符合文意。C 项"孟大鹏从事公交车司机这份工作 9 年了"与第一段末尾提到的 10 years（10 年）不符，故排除。D 项"孟大鹏小时候没有吃过团圆饭"与第三段所述内容相悖，故排除。故选 B。

● 【词汇碎片】

passenger *n*. 乘客；旅客
deep *adj*. 深的；深切的

● 【重难句讲解】

（第一段第二句）

The day consists of finishing a full inspection of the vehicle, keeping a cautious eye on things and taking his passengers from stop to stop, a routine Meng has stuck to for 10 years. 这一天（的工作）包括完成对车辆的全面检查，对事物保持谨慎的观察，并把他的乘客从一个站送到另一个站，这是孟大鹏坚持了 10 年的例行工作。

本句是一个复合句，其中含有三个 consists of 的宾语，皆为动名词形式，分别是 finishing a full inspection of the vehicle、keeping a cautious eye on things、taking his passengers from stop to stop。routine 后面跟的 Meng has stuck to for 10 years 是定语从句，修饰先行词 routine。

Wednesday [阅读理解 B]

● 【答案解析】

1. B。推理判断题。根据 Judy Woodruff 提到的 Tens of millions have decided to stay at home（数千万人决定待在家里）可知，只有 B 项符合文意，故选 B。
2. A。细节理解题。根据 Jacqui Falluca 第一次发言中的 at my aunt's house（在我阿姨家）可知 A 项正确，故选 A。

3. C。细节理解题。根据 Selena 第二次发言中的 because I have a new baby（因为我有个刚出生的孩子）可知 C 项正确，故选 C。
4. B。细节理解题。最后一句提到 So we didn't think it would be safe to be around all of the big family（因此我们觉得和一大家人待在一起并不安全）。由此可知，Jacqui Falluca 认为生活在一个大家庭里不安全，故排除 A 项和 C 项，题干疑问句为一般现在时，故选 B。
5. B。细节理解题。Phil Wright 提到 We're going to reach out to everybody that couldn't be with us（我们会联系所有不能和我们待在一起的人）。由此可知，A 项与文意相悖。根据 Jacqui Falluca 提到的 I work as a nurse and he has to travel for work（我是一名护士，他则经常出差）可知 B 项正确。根据 Judy Woodruff 提到的 public health officials are concerned that too many people will travel this holiday（公共卫生官员担心太多人在这个假期外出）可知 C 项与文意相悖。Selena 在第一次发言中提到她在感恩节时候会做火鸡，而 D 项将文中的 turkey（火鸡）改为 chicken（鸡），不符合文意。故选 B。

● 【词汇碎片】

decide *v*. 决定
special *adj*. 特别的
important *adj*. 重要的

● 【重难句讲解】

We're going to reach out to everybody that couldn't be with us. 我们会联系所有不能和我们待在一起的人。

本句是一个复合句，主句是 We're going to reach out to everybody，that 引导的定语从句修饰 everybody，且 that 指代 everybody，在定语从句中充当主语。

Thursday [阅读理解 C]

● 【答案解析】

1. A。细节理解题。由第一段末尾的 from January 23（从 1

月23日起）可知展览会开始的时间，故选A。

2. C。细节理解题。根据第二段中的 The sculptures...will be on display through the website as well as the official WeChat account of the exhibition（这些雕塑……将通过网站和展览的微信官方账号进行展示）可知C项正确，故选C。

3. C。细节理解题。根据第三段中的 held by the Chinese Folk Artists Association（由中国民间文艺家协会主办）可知答案为C项。根据第三段中的 organized by the Painted Sculpture Professional Committee and the China Intangible Cultural Heritage Art Design and Research Institute（由彩塑专业委员会、中国非遗艺术设计研究院组织）可知后面两者只是组织方，故排除A项和B项。D项与原文不符，故排除。故选C。

4. B。词义猜测题。画线单词所在句的句意为：十二生肖是一种特殊的文化和民族记忆，已经_____了中国人民数千年。D项含贬义，故直接排除。根据常识，此处应填"陪伴"。故选B。

5. A。主旨大意题。文章第一段提到以中国十二生肖为主题的彩塑将在网上展出；第二段和第四段分别提到展览会和其研讨会将在网上进行；第三段提到此次展览会的主办方和组织方。由此可知，文章内容主要与展览会相关，故A项"中国生肖彩塑在网上展出"符合文意。B项"中国特殊的文化和民族记忆"在文章尾段有出现，但不能概括全文，故排除。C项"2021牛年"出现于文章第三段，只是与活动名相关，也无法概括全文，故排除。D项"中华民族的智慧"指的就是十二生肖，不能概括全文，故排除。故选A。

• 【词汇碎片】

art *n.* 艺术；美术
national *n.* 国家的；民族的

• 【重难句讲解】

（第五段第一句）

The Chinese zodiac is a special culture and national memory that has accompanied the Chinese people for thousands of years. 十二生肖是一种特殊的文化和民族记忆，已经陪伴了中国人民数千年。

本句是一个复合句，主句是 The Chinese zodiac is a special culture and national memory，属于主系表结构。that 引导的定语从句修饰 a special culture and national memory。

Friday [任务型阅读 D]

• 【答案解析】

1. More than 360. 根据第二段第一句中的 the administration of the Yuanmingyuan ruins shared more than 360 old photos（圆明园遗址管理部门分享了360多张老照片）可直接得出答案。

2. Few. 根据第三段前半句 Most of the photos had never been publicly displayed（大多数照片从未被公开展示过）可知，只有少数的照片被公开展示过，根据题目要求，我们需要填入一个含有否定意义，且可以修饰可数名词复数的数量词，few 意为"很少"，符合语境，且可以用在可数名词前。另外，单词位于句首，需注意首字母大写，故填 Few。

3. Next month. 根据第三段中的 around 100 of them will be exhibited over the next month（其中大约100张照片将于下个月展出）可直接得出答案。

4. Yes, they will. 根据最后一段中的 These findings will help people get a better understanding of how Yuanmingyuan has changed throughout history（这些发现将有助于人们更好地了解圆明园在历史上的变迁）可知，本题为肯定回答。

5. 但他们现在或许能够对它过去的辉煌有更清晰的认识。

• 【词汇碎片】

ancient *adj.* 古代的；古老的
imagination *n.* 想象力；想象

● 【重难句讲解】

（第二段第一句）

On Tuesday, the administration of the Yuanmingyuan ruins shared more than 360 old photos, which were collected from all over the world in recent years. 周二，圆明园遗址管理部门分享了360多张老照片，这些照片是近年来从世界各地收集的。

本句是一个复合句，逗号后which引导的定语从句修饰photos，其中引导词which在从句中作主语。

Saturday [短文填空]

● 【答案解析】

（1）quickly。根据句子结构可知，空格处所填词修饰前面的形容词popular，故用副词，quick的副词形式为quickly，故填quickly。

（2）starts。根据句子结构可知，空格处需要填入一个谓语动词，且主语为单数名词dance，根据空格后面的are可知时态为一般现在时，故其谓语动词用第三人称单数形式，故填starts。

（3）to。on one's way to... 表示"在某人去……的路上"，为固定搭配，故填to。

（4）playing。根据空格前的be动词are可知此处时态为现在进行时，其结构是"am/is/are+ 现在分词"，故填playing。

（5）a。此处表示泛指，且garden的发音以辅音音素开头，故填不定冠词a。

（6）is。根据句子结构可知，空格处需要填入一个be动词，主语是It，为第三人称单数形式，且此处时态为一般现在时，故填is。

（7）brings。根据句子结构可知，空格处需要填入一个谓语动词，主语是performance，为第三人称单数形式，且此处时态为一般现在时，故填brings。

（8）well。根据句子结构可知，空格处所填词修饰谓语动词play，修饰动词应该用副词，形容词good的副词形式是well，故填well。

（9）writes。根据句子结构可知，空格处需要填入一个谓语动词，主语是one viewer，为第三人称单数形式，且此处时态为一般现在时，故填writes。

（10）highest。空格后的in China（在中国）限定了范围，可知此处应填形容词high的最高级，故填highest。

● 【词汇碎片】

amazing *adj*. 令人惊诧的
perform *v*. 表演

● 【重难句讲解】

（第二段第一句）

The dance starts with a scene where a group of young women are on their way to a banquet. 舞剧以一群年轻女子去参加宴会的场景开始。

本句是一个复合句，where引导的定语从句修饰先行词scene。其中on their way to 表示"在她们去……的路上"，为固定搭配。

Sunday [拓展阅读]

● 【词汇碎片】

history *n*. 历史
opera *n*. 歌剧

● 【重难句讲解】

（第二段）

Kunqu, a Chinese opera form with a history of hundreds of years, is listed by UNESCO as an intangible cultural heritage. 昆曲——一种有着数百年历史的中国戏曲形式——被联合国教科文组织列为非物质文化遗产。

本句是一个简单句，主干是Kunqu is listed，为被动句。a Chinese opera form with a history of hundreds of years 是同位语，补充说明Kunqu。by UNESCO as an intangible cultural heritage 是状语。

Week Thirteen

Monday [完形填空]

【答案解析】

1. D。考查形容词辨析和上下文语义。A 项意为"更多的"，B 项意为"更远的；进一步的"，C 项意为"更少的（常修饰不可数名词）"，D 项意为"更少的（常修饰可数名词）"。第一段第一句提到现在越来越多的人喜欢在手机或电脑上读电子书，因此读纸质书的人更少了，又因空格处修饰的名词 people 是可数名词，故选 D。

2. C。考查动词辨析和上下文语义。A 项意为"开始"，B 项意为"感觉"，C 项意为"变得；变成"，D 项意为"覆盖"。由上文可知，现在读电子书的人越来越多，读纸质书的人越来越少了。又根据后面的 because of the COVID-19 pandemic（由于新冠肺炎疫情）及常识可知，病毒的流行会让这种趋势"变得"更加严峻，故选 C。

3. B。考查动词辨析。A 项意为"上升"，B 项意为"下降"，C 项意为"进入"，D 项意为"关闭"。由空格后的 by 5.08% 可知，空格处应填表示"上升"或"下降"等变化的词，故排除 C 和 D，又由第一段最后一句 It's the first fall in twenty years（这是 20 年来的首次下降）可知，纸质书的零售销售额下降了，故选 B。

4. A。考查代词辨析。A 项意为"这样一个"，其后若跟可数名词单数，一般要加 a；B 项意为"任一"，C 项意为"那个"，D 项意为"这个"。B、C 和 D 三项后面跟名词时一般不加冠词，故选 A。

5. A。考查形容词辨析。A 项意为"有希望的"，B 项意为"与众不同的"，C 项意为"危险的"，D 项意为"重要的"。以第一段描述为背景，可知小鸟 Aves app 的推出是既及时又充满希望的，故选 A。

6. A。考查动词辨析。A 项意为"支付"，B 项意为"花费；成本为……"，C 项意为"花费"，D 项意为"耗费"。A、B、C 三项在表达"付钱"的语境中经常遇到。pay 的主语一般是人；cost 的主语一般是物；spend 一般用于短语 spend (money) on sth. 中；take 一般用于 it takes sb. (money) to do sth. 句型中，此处的主语是 One，指的是人，故选 A。

7. B。考查名词辨析。A 项意为"书"，B 项意为"篇"，C 项意为"段落"，D 项意为"行"。由该空所在句的前半句可知，付费前只能读一篇文章中的一部分，付 12 元就可以读三篇文章，the first three pieces 意为"前三篇文章"，故选 B。

8. C。考查上下文语义。将四个选项代入文中，只有 a whole 符合上下文语义，a whole year's articles 意为"一整年的文章"，故选 C。

9. B。考查形容词辨析。A 项意为"便宜的，廉价的"，B 项意为"昂贵的"，C 项意为"极好的"，D 项意为"特殊的"。根据上下文语义及常识可知，一年花费 588 元在 app 上读文章是昂贵的，故选 B。

10. C。考查介词辨析。A 项意为"在……之前"，B 项意为"在……之后"，C 项意为"在……期间"，D 项意为"在……之上"。during the first month 意为"在第一个月期间"，符合语义，故选 C。

11. B。考查动词辨析。A 项意为"想要"，B 项意为"预期，期望"，C 项意为"解释"，D 项意为"担心"。将四个选项代入文中可知"预期，期望"符合语义，故选 B。

12. D。考查宾语从句。文章此处表达的意思是"我不知道我们是否会有一个美好的未来"，四个选项中只有 D 项 if 可表达"是否"之意，故选 D。

13. A。考查名词辨析。A 项意为"读者"，B 项意为"作家"，C 项意为"文章"，D 项意为"语言"。由句子结构和句意可知，下文的 of them 指代的就是空格处的内容，又由下文的 would like to pay 可知，此空格处应填表示"人"的一类词，而且是需要支付费用的一方，故选 A。

14. B。考查固定短语。one out of 10,000 意为"万分之一"，为固定搭配，故选 B。

15. C。考查形容词辨析。A 项意为"令人愉快的"，B 项意为"外国的"，C 项意为"严肃的"，D 项意为"流行的，通俗的"。由第二段第三句可知，此 app 上的文章大多是好作家写的文章，属于严肃文学，故选 C。

【词汇碎片】

sale *n.* 销售；销售额
timely *adj.* 及时的，适时的
editor-in-chief *n.* 总编辑
expect *v.* 期待

【重难句讲解】

（第二段第七句）

However, Yang Ying, the editor-in-chief, says that subscription levels during the first month are better than expected. 然而，主编杨樱表示，第一个月的订阅量比预期的要好。

本句是一个复合句，句子主干是 Yang Ying says...，后面跟了一个 that 引导的宾语从句。the editor-in-chief 作 Yang Ying 的同位语，补充说明杨樱的身份。

Tuesday [阅读理解 A]

【答案解析】

1. B。细节理解题。根据 This exhibition was very important because it marked the 600th anniversary of the Forbidden City（这次展览非常重要，因为它标志着紫禁城建成 600 周年）可知，紫禁城已有 600 年的历史，故选 B。

2. D。细节理解题。根据 These objects help people today understand the social ranks, ceremonies and customs of the Hongshan culture（这些玉器帮助现在的人们了解红山文化的社会排名、仪式和风俗）可知 A、B、C 三个选项均可在 "玉出红山" 展览中学习到，故选 D。

3. B。细节理解题。根据表格中 Time 一栏的信息可知，12 月 10 日只能参加 "玉出红山" 艺术展，故选 B。

4. C。细节理解题。根据 More than 160 jade objects were showed at the exhibition（该展览展出了 160 多件玉器）可知，"玉出红山" 艺术展展出了 160 多件玉器，所以 C 项

正确。从 Six Centuries at the Forbidden City（紫禁城建成六百年）这个展览的具体信息可知，明清年间，24 位皇帝曾在紫禁城居住，且清朝的历史是从 1644 年至 1911 年，故 A 项和 B 项均错误。根据表格中 Rank 一栏的信息可知，"玉出红山" 艺术展排名第二，比 "紫禁城建成六百年" 艺术展的排名低，故 D 项错误。故选 C。

【词汇碎片】

cultural *adj.* 文化的
area *n.* 面积
social *adj.* 社会的

【重难句讲解】

This exhibition was very important because it marked the 600th anniversary of the Forbidden City. 这次展览非常重要，因为它标志着紫禁城建成 600 周年。

本句是一个复合句，句子主干是 This exhibition was very important，为主系表结构，后面跟了一个 because 引导的原因状语从句。

Wednesday [阅读理解 B]

【答案解析】

1. C。词义猜测题。live 一词多义，四个选项均是 live 的词义。根据句子结构可知，live 修饰后面的 music，因此 A、B 两项均不合适。D 项 "生动的" 往往用于表达 "形象的、具有活力的、能使人感动的"。根据上下文可知，C 项 "现场的" 符合文意，故选 C。

2. B。细节理解题。根据第一段倒数第二句中的 Wuhan was locked down on Jan 23, 2020（武汉在 2020 年 1 月 23 日被封锁）可知 B 项正确，故选 B。

3. D。细节理解题。根据最后一段前两句中的 Audience members are offered face masks（我们会给观众提供口罩）、All tickets are sold online（所有的门票都是网上销售的）和 the number of audience is limited（观众数量被限制）可知，A、B、C 三项均是 VOX 重新开放后

采取的措施。根据第三段第二句中的 cut the number of shows（削减演出数量）可知，VOX 重新开放后减少了演出的数量，因此 D 项错误，故选 D。

4. B。细节理解题。根据第二段第二句 For the first time in 15 years, VOX closed for several months（15 年来，VOX 首次关闭了好几个月）可知，VOX 之前从未关闭过如此长的时间，B 项错误，故选 B。

● 【词汇碎片】

founder *n.* 创立者
celebrate *v.* 庆祝
return *v.* 返回
reopen *v.* 重新开放，重新营业

● 【重难句讲解】

（第二段第三句）

We didn't know if it would open again. 我们不知道它是否会重新开放。

本句是一个复合句，主句是 We didn't know...，后面跟了一个 if 引导的宾语从句，该从句作 know 的宾语。

（第四段第一句）

Audience members are offered face masks before they enter the venue. 在进入场地前，我们会给观众提供口罩。

本句是一个复合句，主句是 Audience members are offered face masks，后面跟了一个 before 引导的时间状语从句。

Thursday [阅读理解 C]

● 【答案解析】

1. A。语篇理解题。首先我们可以采用排除法，人一般不用 it 指代，故排除 C 项和 D 项。由第一段第二句 Because that is the color of the teapots which are produced in the city of Yixing, Jiangsu Province（因为那是江苏省宜兴市生产的茶壶的颜色）可知，江苏省宜兴市是生产紫砂壶的胜地。江苏省的范围太广，不具体，故排除 B 项，故选 A。

2. B。细节理解题。根据最后一段第一句中的 there are 30 master craftspeople in Yixing who are known as national masters of Zisha art（宜兴有 30 名工匠大师，他们被称为"国家级紫砂艺术大师"）可知，"国家级紫砂艺术大师"指的就是宜兴的 30 位紫砂手工艺大师，故选 B。

3. C。细节理解题。文章第一段和第二段分别提到宜兴市生产的紫砂壶是最好的，并且它们的价格很高，故 A 项和 B 项与原文相符；根据第二段第一句 Thousands of craftspeople make those teapots in that city（那座城市里有数千名工匠制作那些茶壶）可知 D 项正确。C 项所述在文中未提及相关信息，无法推断，故选 C。

4. A。主旨大意题。由文章标题 Masters of the Zisha Pots 可知，本文主要介绍了宜兴市生产的紫砂茶壶和宜兴市的紫砂工匠，所以 A 项概括得比较准确，故选 A。

● 【词汇碎片】

a 10-piece Zisha tea set 紫砂茶具十件套
reach *v.* 达到
million *num.* 百万

● 【重难句讲解】

（第一段第二句）

Because that is the color of the teapots which are produced in the city of Yixing, Jiangsu Province. 因为那是江苏省宜兴市生产的茶壶的颜色。

本句是一个复合句，句子主干是 Because that is the color of the teapots，后面跟了一个 which 引导的定语从句修饰 teapots。

（第二段第三句）

But everybody knows that the price of those teapots and cups are very high. 但是所有人都知道那些茶壶和杯子的价格很高。

本句是一个复合句，句子的主干是 But everybody knows...，that 引导的宾语从句作 knows 的宾语，说明 knows 的内容。

Friday [任务型阅读 D]

●【答案解析】

1. Nv Shu was popular in Jiangyong county, Hunan Province many years ago. 根据第一段第二句 A thousand years ago, it was a popular language in Jiangyong county, Hunan Province（一千年前，它是湖南省江永县的一种流行语言）可知，多年前女书曾在湖南省江永县流行。

2. Nv Shu is based on a local language in Jiangyong county. 根据第二段第二句 It is based on a local language in Jiangyong county（它基于江永县的一种当地语言）可知，女书基于江永县的一种当地方言发展而来。

3. No, she didn't. 根据第三段第三句 However, she didn't know the mystery of the language in her childhood（但是，她小时候并不知道这种语言的奥秘）可知，周娜小时候并不知道女书这种语言的特别之处。

4. Because the books on Nv Shu are difficult to find in the market and she wants the readers to have those books soon. 根据最后一段最后一句 Because the books on Nv Shu are difficult to find in the market, I hope that the publications hit the market in the first half of the year（由于有关女书的书籍很难在市场上找到，所以我希望能在今年上半年将这些出版物投放到市场）可知，周娜想要在今年上半年将她的书推向市场是因为有关女书的书籍很难在市场上找到，她希望读者们能够尽早阅读到这方面的书。

5. Yes, I would like to learn how to write in Nv Shu, because I think Nv Shu is a special language and it's interesting, too. 根据自己的真实想法合理作答即可。

●【词汇碎片】

written *adj.* 书面的
be based on 以……为基础
carry *v.* 传送

●【重难句讲解】

（第三段第二句）

The first character that she learned to write was in Nv Shu. 她学会写的第一个字就是用女书写的。

本句是一个复合句，主句是 The first character was in Nv Shu。中间嵌套了一个 that 引导的定语从句，修饰 character。

（第三段第五句）

Because the books on Nv Shu are difficult to find in the market, I hope that the publications hit the market in the first half of the year. 由于有关女书的书籍很难在市场上找到，所以我希望能在今年上半年将这些出版物投放到市场。

本句是一个复合句，主句是 I hope that the publications hit the market in the first half of the year，其中 that 引导宾语从句，介词短语 in the first half of the year 作时间状语。句首是 Because 引导的原因状语从句。

Saturday [短文填空]

●【答案解析】

（1）in。"在某村/镇/县/市/……"这类范围比较大的地点前面的介词一般用 in。故填 in。

（2）its。此处表达的意思是"用竹子制成龙的'骨头'"，这里的 it 指代前面的 The dragon，后面是名词 bones，故填入 it 的形容词性物主代词 its。

（3）or。根据语境可知空格前后是龙抬头节日的两种不同的表述方式，因此应使用表示选择含义的并列连词。故填 or。

（4）the most。空格后的 in Chinese culture（中华文化中）限定了范围，可知这里是想表达"龙是中华文化中最为传奇的生物"。故填 the most。

（5）believe。根据句子结构可知，believe 前面的 people 是主语，为复数名词，且根据空格前后的时态可知这里应用一般现在时，故填 believe。

（6）go。make sb. do sth. 为固定用法，其中 do sth. 其实是省略了 to 的不定式。故填 go。

（7）became。由空格前面的 At the age of 15（15岁那年）可知，此处应用一般过去时。故填 became。

（8）skills。skill 作"技巧"讲时为可数名词，此处指"用稻草制作草把龙和表演舞龙的技巧"，应用复数，故填 skills。

（9）that。根据句子结构可知，谓语动词 remembers 后面是宾语，且空格后是一个完整的句子，故此处应填入宾语从句引导词 that。

（10）because。空格前提到人们以前通过舞龙来驱赶疾病，空格后提到过去的医疗服务有限，空格前后构成因果关系，所以此处应填表示原因的连词，故填 because。

• 【词汇碎片】

rice *n.* 稻（米）
cloth *n.* 布
drive away 赶走

• 【重难句讲解】

（第二段第四句）

So, people believe that performing dragon dance on Longtaitou Festival can make bad things go away and bring good luck. 因此，人们认为在龙抬头节表演舞龙可以使坏事消失并带来好运。

本句是一个复合句，主句是 people believe...，that 引导宾语从句作 believe 的宾语。该宾语从句中，performing dragon dance on Longtaitou Festival 是动名词短语，作从句的主语。

（第三段第四句）

He remembers that people would perform dragon dance to drive away illness, because medical care was limited in the past. 他记得，因为过去的医疗服务有限，所以人们通过舞龙来驱赶疾病。

本句是一个复合句，主句是 He remembers...，其中，宾语是 that 引导的从句。不定式短语 to drive away illness 是目的状语。后半句是 because 引导的原因状语从句。

Sunday［拓展阅读］

• 【词汇碎片】

kitchen *n.* 厨房
delicious *adj.* 美味的

• 【重难句讲解】

（第一段第三句）

Here are five things you should know about the Little New Year. 关于小年，你应该了解以下五点。

本句是一个复合句，主句是 Here are five things，后面的 you should know about the Little New Year 是省略了引导词 that 的定语从句，修饰 five things。

Week Fourteen

Monday [完形填空]

【答案解析】

1. A。考查固定搭配。put... in the first place 意为"将……放在首位",为固定搭配,故选A。

2. B。考查名词辨析。A项意为"数字",B项意为"费用;成本;代价",C项意为"美元",D项意为"钱包"。the cost of medical treatment 意为"医疗费用",符合此处语义,故选B。

3. C。考查连词辨析和上下文语义。空格所在句指出人们可以得到资金;下文指出,地方政府将不会受到医疗和疫情控制费用的阻碍,由此可以看出上下文属于前因后果的逻辑关系。A项意为"和;并且",B项意为"所以",C项意为"因为",D项意为"但是"。代入原文后,C项符合语义及上下文逻辑,故选C。

4. D。考查形容词辨析。A项意为"健康的",B项意为"当地的",C项意为"私人的",D项意为"医疗的"。代入原文后D项符合语义,且上文出现过 the cost of medical treatment,故选D。

5. B。考查名词辨析。A项意为"希望",B项意为"影响",C项意为"速度",D项意为"注意力"。空格所在句意为:财政体系已经找到了降低疫情对经济_____的方法。第一段提到我国为抗击新冠肺炎疫情投入的财政资金超过4 000亿元,这显然是疫情造成的不良影响,所以此处填入 influence 最符合上下文语义。故选B。

6. A。考查名词辨析。A项意为"困难",B项意为"惊喜",C项意为"发展",D项意为"运动;练习"。由文意可知,疫情带来的影响是负面的,只有A项 difficulty 符合文意。故选A。

7. D。考查名词辨析。A项意为"点",B项意为"价格",C项意为"元(中国货币单元)",D项意为"百分比"。空格所在句意为:中国设定的2020年财政赤字至少占国内生产总值的3.6_____,_____去年的2.8%。由此断定,本句是拿2020年和2019年的数据进行比较,所以3.6后面跟的应该也是百分比。故选D。

8. B。考查形容词辨析。A项意为"更低的",B项意为"更高的",C项意为"低的",D项意为"高的"。上文提到,中国设定的2020年财政赤字至少占国内生产总值的3.6%,而2019年的数值为2.8%,前者比后者高,故选B。

9. A。考查动词短语辨析。give out 意为"分发;发出",give away 意为"捐赠",give in 意为"屈服;让步",give back 意为"归还"。空格后为名词短组 1 trillion yuan of government bonds,B、C、D三个选项均无法与 1 trillion yuan of government bonds 构成合理的动宾搭配,因此均可排除。give out 1 trillion yuan of government bonds 表示"发放1万亿元国债",符合语义,故选A。

10. C。考查名词辨析。A项意为"指示牌;迹象",B项意为"礼物",C项意为"钱;货币",D项意为"食物"。空格所在句意为:中国已累计发放新冠肺炎疫情防控国债1万亿元,以加大对企业和个人的_____投入。上文提到我国为抗击新冠肺炎疫情投入了大量资金,所以联系上文可知,此处指的应该是"资金投入",故选C。

【词汇碎片】

fight v. 与……作斗争
difficulty n. 困难;难题

【重难句讲解】

(第二段第一句)

The fiscal system has put funds in the first place for fighting COVID-19 so that people will not be scared by the cost of medical treatment, said Finance Minister Liu Kun in an online speech. 财政部部长刘昆在一次线上讲话中表示,财政体系已将资金放在抗击新冠肺炎疫情的首位,让人们不会被医疗费用吓到。

本句是一个复合句,包含一个主句、一个宾语从句和一个由 so that 引导的结果状语从句。said Finance Minister

Liu Kun in an online speech 是主句，逗号前面的内容是间接引语，相当于省略了 that 的宾语从句，作 said 的宾语，so that 引导结果状语从句。

Tuesday [阅读理解 A]

【答案解析】

1. C。细节理解题。根据题干中的 as of mid-December 定位到文章第二段，本段提到截至 2020 年 12 月中旬，中国已建成 71.8 万多个 5G 基站，故选 C。
2. A。词义猜测题。画线单词前面提到中国已建成 71.8 万多个 5G 基站，可推测出 5G 信号应该是"可用的"，故选 A。
3. A。细节理解题。根据题干中的 industrial application scenarios 定位到文章第四段，本段提到形成 20 个典型的工业应用场景，故选 A。
4. A。细节理解题。文章最后一段中的 lay a good basis for 意为"给……打下好的基础"，与 A 项中的 is helpful to 属于同义替换，由此可知 A 项正确，故选 A。B 项与第三段中的"加快 5G 在主要城市的覆盖"不符，故排除；C 项由文章第四段中的"没有提供更多细节"臆测而来，故排除；D 项则与第三段第一句中的"国家将有序推进 5G 网络的建设和应用"相悖，故排除。
5. B。主旨大意题。文章主要谈及中国 5G 基站的建设，且首句提到"2021 年，中国将建设 60 多万个 5G 基站"，B 项可以概括文章主旨大意，故选 B；A 项、C 项和 D 项只是文中提到的细节，并不能概括文章主旨大意，故均排除。

【词汇碎片】

speed up（使）加速
technology *n.* 技术；工艺

【重难句讲解】

（第五段）
The 5G rollout plan for next year will lay a good basis for deeper integration of the digital and real economies, help stabilize investment and speed up industrial upgrades, experts said. 专家表示，明年的 5G 部署计划将为数字经济和实体经济的深入融合奠定良好的基础，有助于稳定投资，加快产业升级。

本句是一个复合句，主句的主干是 experts said...，宾语是前面的间接引语，相当于省略了 that 的宾语从句，从句的主语为 The 5G rollout plan，后面跟着三个并列的动宾短语：will lay a good basis、help stabilize investment 和 speed up industrial upgrades。

Wednesday [阅读理解 B]

【答案解析】

1. C。细节理解题。根据题干中的关键词 engine、work 和 fired 定位到第二段，由该段可知探测器的引擎工作时间为 15 分钟左右，故选 C。
2. B。词义猜测题。画线单词后面提到 28 km/s（每秒 28 千米），这是超级快的速度，故可推测画线的单词意为"极快的"，故选 B。
3. D。细节理解题。根据题干中的关键词 the Wenchang Space Launch Center 定位到第四段第一句，由该句可知"天问一号"是在 7 月 23 日发射的，故选 D。
4. B。细节理解题。根据题干中的关键词 missions 和 succeed 定位到文章最后一句，由该句可知在这些火星探测任务中，只有 18 次成功了，故选 B。
5. B。细节理解题。文章第三段第一句提到探测器进入近地点约 400 千米的轨道，而不是 40 千米，故排除 A；第四段第一句提到"天问一号"是我国首次独立的火星探测任务，B 项与文意相符，故为正确选项；第四段第二句中提到这是自 1960 年 10 月以来，世界上第 46 次火星探测任务，而不是第 56 次，故排除 C；第四段第二句提到苏联发射了第一个火星探测器，但 D 项未指明是火星探测器，故排除。故选 B。

【词汇碎片】

spacecraft *n.* 航天器；宇宙飞船
planet *n.* 行星
launch *v.* 发射

【重难句讲解】

（第三段第二句）

The move was difficult because it required the probe to slow down within 10 minutes from the ultrafast speed of 28 km/s to about 1 km/s. 这一行动很困难，因为它要求探测器在 10 分钟内从每秒 28 千米的超高速减速到每秒 1 千米左右。

本句是一个复合句，由一个主句和一个 because 引导的状语从句组成，主句为 The move was difficult，为主系表结构，because 引导的状语从句表示原因，短语 from... to... 意为"从……到……"。

Thursday [阅读理解 C]

【答案解析】

1. A。细节理解题。根据题干中的关键信息 China called for 定位到第一段第一句，由该句可知中国呼吁其他国家加强气候适应行动，故选 A。
2. B。词义猜测题。画线单词所在句意为：他说，应对气候变化是人类面临的共同_____，需要兼顾减缓和适应（气候变化）。此处填入"挑战"最符合上下文语义，故选 B。
3. C。细节理解题。根据题干中的关键词 Han Zheng 和 technology 定位到第三段，由该段可知韩正认为发达国家在技术方面应该给发展中国家提供帮助，第一个空格应填 developed，第二个空格应填 developing，故选 C。
4. A。细节理解题。文章第四段第一句提到"他还呼吁各国根据本国实际，制定和实施国家气候适应计划"，A 项符合原文，故选 A；B 项扭曲了第四段第二句"这将使它们的适应措施更加有效"的意思，以此作为干扰，故排除；C 项意为"他不关心全球气候和环境治理"，与文意不符，故排除；D 项在文中并未提及，无法得知是韩正主持了"一个星球"峰会，故排除。
5. A。主旨大意题。本文提到中国呼吁各国加强合作，加强气候适应行动，又提到韩正呼吁各国根据本国实际，制定和实施国家气候适应计划，所以 A 项符合本文大意，故选 A；B 项只是韩正的观点，在文中是细节信息，并不能概括全文，故排除；C 项刚好与文义相悖，故排除；D 项也只是文中提及的细节，故排除。

【词汇碎片】

climate *n.* 气候
change *n.* 变化

【重难句讲解】

（第三段）

In order to actively carry out the Paris Agreement, Han said that developed countries should offer more financial and technical support to developing countries. 为积极落实《巴黎协定》，韩正提到发达国家应向发展中国家提供更多的资金和技术支持。

本句是一个复合句，In order to actively carry out the Paris Agreement 为目的状语，逗号后面是主句部分，主句为主谓宾结构，that 引导宾语从句作 said 的宾语，developed countries 意为"发达国家"，developing countries 意为"发展中国家"。

Friday [任务型阅读 D]

【答案解析】

1. At the Shanghai Museum. 根据题干中的关键词 Chinese zodiac show 定位到第一段，由 at the Shanghai Museum 可知展览的地点是在上海博物馆。
2. Four objects. 根据题干中的关键信息 glass cases in the hall 定位到第二段开头，由 Four objects stood in glass cases in the hall（有四件产品陈列在展厅的玻璃柜里）可知是四件展品。
3. They could understand the wide representation of oxen in ancient Chinese culture. 根据题干中的关键词 Chu Xin 和 visitors 定位到第三段第一句，由 visitors could take a journey of discovery through the showrooms, to understand the wide representation of oxen in ancient Chinese culture（参观者可以通过展厅进行一次

探索之旅，了解古代文化中"牛"的广泛代表意义）可知游客可以了解中国古代文化中"牛"的广泛代表意义。

4. Because it is closely related to two important issues in traditional Chinese society: farming and rituals. 根据题干中的关键词 ox 和 important 定位到第三段第二句，由 The ox is important in Chinese art because... farming and rituals（牛在中国艺术中很重要，因为……农耕和仪式）可知，牛在中国艺术很重要的原因是牛与中国传统社会的农耕和仪式密切相关。

5. No, they weren't. 根据文章最后一段的 two objects from Republic of Korea were borrowed from the National Museum of Korea（还有两件是从韩国国立中央博物馆借来的）可知，展品有来自上海博物馆的，还有向韩国国立中央博物馆借来的，所以展品不都是来自中国。

【词汇碎片】

museum *n.* 博物馆
show *n.* 展览
object *n.* 物品；东西

Saturday [短文填空]

【答案解析】

（1）different。空格后面为名词 dynasties，故空格处应该是缺少修饰 dynasties 的形容词，将方框中所给的形容词一一代入文中，只有 different 符合句意，ancient tombs of different dynasties 意为"不同朝代的古墓"，故填 different。

（2）team。空格前面的有不定冠词 an，故空格处应该填入一个名词，将方框中所给的名词一一代入文中，只有 team 符合句意，an excavation team 意为"一支挖掘队伍"，故填 team。

（3）locally。空格前面谓语和宾语完整，可知空格处应该是缺少修饰动词 celebrated 的副词，方框中只有一个副词 locally，且代入文中后符合语义，celebrated the Spring Festival locally 意为"在当地庆祝春节"，故填 locally。

（4）holiday。空格前面是动词词组，故空格处缺少名词作宾语，将方框中的名词一一代入文中，只有 holiday 符合语义，gave up the holiday 意为"放弃了假期"，故填 holiday。

（5）discovered。根据句子结构可知，空格所在句的主语是前面的 4,600 cultural relics（4 600 件文物），空格前是 were，因此空格处要么填入一个形容词作表语，修饰主语，要么填入一个动词的过去分词构成被动语态。discovered 意为"发现"，符合语境，故填 discovered。

（6）number。空格前面有不定冠词 a 和形容词 large，可知空格处应该填入一个名词，由上文的 4,600 和 3,500 可知这是很大的"数字"，所以 number 符合句意，故填 number。

（7）difficult。空格前面有 be 动词，quite 为副词，意为"十分；相当"，故空格处缺少形容词作表语，将方框中的形容词一一代入文中，只有 difficult 符合句意，quite difficult 意为"非常困难"，故填 difficult。

（8）times。空格前面为数词，后面应接名词，方框中只有 times 符合此处文意，times 在这里表示"次数"，为可数名词。

（9）capital。根据历史常识可知，西安在中国历史上是十三朝古都，将 capital 代入文中后符合句意，故填 capital。

（10）hit。hit the headlines 为常用搭配，意为"登上新闻头条"，故填 hit。

【词汇碎片】

discover *v.* 发现
hit *v.* 击；打

【重难句讲解】

（第二段第一句）

From Feb 4 to 17, more than 60 members of an excavation team lived near the airport, and together with 900 workers, celebrated the Spring Festival locally.

从 2 月 4 日到 17 日，一支挖掘队伍的 60 多名成员住在机场附近，与 900 名工人一起在当地庆祝春节。

　　本句是一个 and 连接的并列句，主语是 more than 60 members of an excavation team，谓语分别是 lived 和 celebrated，From Feb 4 to 17 是时间状语，near the airport 是地点状语，together with 900 workers 为插入语。

Sunday [拓展阅读]

【词汇碎片】

surprise *v.* 使惊讶；使惊奇
folk songs 民歌
perform *v.* 表演